LIBERAL LEARNING

AND RELIGION

Contributors

EDWIN E. AUBREY, Professor of Religious Thought, University of Pennsylvania

VICTOR L. BUTTERFIELD, President, Wesleyan University

VIRGINIA CORWIN, Associate Professor of Religion and Biblical Literature, Smith College

MILDRED McAFEE HORTON, Former President of Wellesley College

DOUGLAS M. KNIGHT, English Department, Yale University

BERNARD M. LOOMER, Dean of the Divinity School, University of Chicago

PATRICK MURPHY MALIN, Executive Director, American Civil Liberties Union

ROLLO MAY, Consulting Psychologist, New York City

HOWARD Y. McCLUSKY, Professor of Educational Psychology and Consultant in Adult Education, University of Michigan

THORNTON W. MERRIAM, Dean, Springfield College

WALTER G. MUELDER, Dean and Professor of Social Ethics, Boston University School of Theology

ROGER L. SHINN, Head of the Departments of Philosophy and Religion, Heidelberg College

WILLARD L. SPERRY, Dean, The Harvard Divinity School

GREGORY VLASTOS, Professor of Philosophy, Sage School of Philosophy, Cornell University

AMOS N. WILDER, Professor of New Testament Interpretation, The Chicago Theological Seminary and Federated Theological Faculty of the University of Chicago

LIBERAL LEARNING
AND RELIGION

Edited by

AMOS N. WILDER

KENNIKAT PRESS/PORT WASHINGTON, N. Y.

CONTENTS

FOREWORD

It is in higher education that the deeper issues of our time should and often do come most clearly into the light for recognition and scrutiny. Not only our cultural but our moral predicaments emerge here as matters for deliberate assessment in terms both of historical and of scientific study. Moreover, our dilemmas remain dilemmas at this level. For though the college and the university may be free from some confusions that hold sway in the general community, yet differences in basic values and perspectives here take on a conscious and sophisticated form which all too often confirms their stubborn character. Yet it is in higher education that resources should be available for understanding and synthesis.

The campus has to a notable degree been the scene of ferment and change during the last quarter century. The widespread reexamination of general and higher education has been occasioned in part by the practical problems incident to rapid growth in the number of students and by the acute needs of a great democracy in a critical period. But, what is more significant, basic presuppositions with regard to education and learning have been under revision, in all that concerns science and its methods, tradition and its transmission, and values as they come to expression whether on the campus or in the common life.

But such issues are fundamentally religious, and at no point have the discussions especially of general education been more noncommittal and inconclusive than at this point: the place of religion in higher education. Yet there has been a widespread feeling in the general public that this factor in our tradition and in the training of citizens should be assigned its rights—and at

all levels of education. Here a basic dilemma of our society
forces itself into the open and calls for recognition in that continual discourse which is a chief feature of higher education and
the university. The problem of religion in higher education is,
indeed, many-sided. In tax-supported schools it is a problem of
the relations of Church and State. We are presented with a
variety of problems at the level of subject matter, curriculum and
administration in different types of institutions. Another set of
problems arise with regard to confessional agencies, ministries to
students and counseling. But the most fundamental problem and
the one with which this volume is largely concerned is that of
presuppositions, criteria and values. Indeed so far as these ultimate issues are involved in the ferment and re-examination that
characterize the college and the university today we may well
say that not only education but religion itself, particularly the
Christian religion, is in course of reassessment and restatement.

The present volume is concerned with religion in higher education at this level and in these bearings. We believe that the
perspectives and values of our religious tradition have an indispensable role to play in liberal learning, in the academic disciplines and in the academic community. We also recognize that
this interaction involves a continuing criticism and transforma-
tion of the religious tradition itself.

The contributors to the volume are all Fellows or officers of
the National Council on Religion in Higher Education, founded
in 1922 by Charles Foster Kent, then Woolsey Professor of
Biblical Literature in Yale University. The primary purpose of
the National Council has been to stimulate more adequate instruction in religion in colleges and universities, but also to bring
to bear the insights and motivations of religion and the religious
traditions upon all aspects of higher education. For more than a
quarter of a century it has appointed Fellows dedicated to this
task. It has not only enabled them by the grant of stipends to
pursue their graduate studies in religion and other fields, but it

has helped to place them in responsible positions and has brought them together in annual meetings for fellowship and discussion of their common problems. It now has more than three hundred Fellows in teaching and administrative positions in 125 institutions of higher learning throughout the United States and Canada, as well as in college pastorates and other professions. The first chapter includes references to past activities of the Council and the concluding chapter is devoted to its present task and opportunity.

The work here offered had its inception in the decision of the Council to signalize the twenty-fifth anniversary of its first annual conference by a survey and stock-taking of the situation that confronts us today in the areas of its responsibility. In view of changing factors in higher education the time appeared opportune to identify and clarify the most pressing challenges to those concerned with religious and moral values in the college and the university. We have wished to evaluate trends, to identify the changing features in the total picture, the subtle shifts in the deeper assumptions with regard to education and its methods, to recognize allies and obstacles in the new circumstances, and to offer a normative lead in debated areas.

Papers dealing with selected topics were presented and discussed at two of the annual meetings of the Council. An anniversary publication committee was chosen made up of John A. Hutchison (Williams College), Albert C. Outler (The Yale Divinity School), Gregory Vlastos (Cornell University), and the editor, together with the then Chairman of the Central Committee of Fellows, Roger Hazelton (Andover-Newton Theological School), and the Executive Director of the Council, Seymour A. Smith. A plan for the volume was adopted and particular members of the Council were invited to write the various chapters. These chapters have had the benefit of criticism by readers from among the Fellows. Though the book does not propose to speak for the National Council officially, one of the distinctive resources of the writers has been their past participation in its fellowship and discussion.

Obviously in a work of this kind some selection imposed itself with respect to the topics treated. As the Table of Contents indicates, the bulk of the book is given to discussion of issues and criteria, first in connection with the chief disciplines of instruction, and second in connection with the life of the academic community. From the beginning of our undertaking our attention has been drawn to the antipositivist turn in the sciences and the humanities. What this means or can mean in terms of presuppositions and educational philosophy we have sought to clarify. Our aim has been to further the discussion at a level worthy of attention on the part of those who recognize the issues here at stake whether as regards scientific method or philosophical and religious implications. In what concerns the educational community more generally we have sought to test various areas and procedures in terms of the personal values at stake. What has perforce been omitted is any adequate treatment of that whole concern of religion with higher education which comes to expression in religious agencies serving the campus, whether from without or within the institution, whether college chaplaincies, Christian Associations, denominational centers or other ministries to students, the growing significance of which is so well indicated in the first chapter. To this subject another volume could well be devoted.

The common perspective of the contributors appears rather in the concerns they share and the spiritual resources they assume than in any proposed definition of religion. The reader will find particular formulations of the religious criterion especially in chapters 2, 12 and 14. It is to be borne in mind that the special aspects or levels of religion brought forward are commonly determined by the immediate context of discussion. Moreover, it is often felt by our contributors that religious claims on either curriculum or community are not to be viewed as something to be added or superimposed. When the subject matter and implications of science, social science, historical study, the humanities, etc. are richly and relatedly grasped, these fields of study themselves require and pass over into a religious dimension. In the religious perspective the subject matter in question can be better grasped and taught. A context of religious conviction and vision offers a more adequate, a more complex and sensitive understanding of and operation with the data. Correspondingly, the religious perspective in what concerns the person represents in a very true sense the fulfillment and release of those personal values often thwarted on the campus. What further terms and levels of religious affirmation and celebration may also be invoked will vary with the particular religious tradition of the individual in question, but need not be viewed as in disagreement with religion as we have characterized it.

The editor wishes to express his great appreciation in the name of the National Council to all those who have had a part in the volume, and to The Edward W. Hazen Foundation for a grant toward expenses involved in its preparation. Special thanks are due to Mr. Iver F. Yeager, graduate student in the University of Chicago, for his invaluable assistance in connection with the proof reading and the Index.

THE EDITOR

PART I

Retrospectively!

I

Religion in Higher Education Through the Past Twenty-five Years

Thornton W. Merriam

NEAR the close of the quarter-century (1925-1950) Albert C. Outler stated the fundamental task of religion in higher education in these arresting words:

> We . . . dedicate ourselves to the task of building a human community in a world shattered by violence and scarred by the malignant wounds of war; and this calls for the truth and power of Christian faith. If our schools and colleges can be made into communities of common concern for truth and goodness, they will be the seedbeds for men and women of real quality, fit for the challenges of the era upon whose threshold we stand. It is this context . . . which, as I profoundly believe, holds our best hope to find the way through the complicated labyrinth of the years ahead.[1]

This interpretation of what the religious worker or teacher or administrator in colleges and universities thinks he is about would, I believe, have wide acceptance. Its challenge and poignancy lie in its suggestion of the inescapably reconstructive thrust of Christianity in modern education and in contemporary society. The essence of the relationship of religion to education is partnership in the presence of staggering forces now threaten-

[1] Albert C. Outler: A Christian Context for Counseling, p. 18. Hazen Pamphlets No. 18.

ing our civilization. Its method consists in creating and energizing communities of devoted learners.

In thus exposing the motif of religion in higher education today, Mr. Outler helps identify certain landmarks in the development of the religionist's concept of his job within what used to be called the "walls" of the American campus.

The unfolding of events during the past twenty-five years must be seen against a background of social conflict and disruption. It is not easy to keep one's eyes on the foreground. The struggles, victories, and defeats of religion and education often seem not too important except possibly for those professionally engaged in them. The student who wonders what difference it makes whether he studies hard today when tomorrow he will be the target of an atom bomb is only asking, with perhaps a greater sense of urgency, what his teachers and counselors are themselves asking.

It is this acute awareness of all-enveloping and uncontrolled social forces and bafflement as to how religion and education ought to be related to them which mark a major difference between the attitude of the sensitive religious educator today and his predecessor of a quarter-century ago. What then looked like a land of promise, to be laid under cultivation by hard work and good will, now seems like a land of doom. The sense of impending chaos demanding critical review of mission and method characterizes the times in which we are now living.

It is illuminating to reflect on some of the changes in thinking about the task of religion in higher education which have taken place in the past twenty-five years.

Dr. Charles Foster Kent, long-time professor of Biblical literature at Yale University, was a pioneer thinker in this field during the first quarter of this century. His concerns provide a springboard for assaying developments of recent years. Dr. Kent died in 1925, but not before he had given cogent and persuasive interpretation of the essential task and strategy of religion in higher education in his day. This scholar of vision and practical wisdom saw beneath events and identified some of the long-run necessities if religion were "once again," as he used to say, to regain a significant place in college and university life.

The task of religion in higher education, as he saw it, was to establish the intellectual and educational respectability of religious studies. He viewed with deep concern the low estate to which religion as a subject in the college curriculum had fallen. Men who had not succeeded or who had worn themselves out in the parish ministry were all too frequently presented a sinecure in the form of a chair of religion in a college. Dr. Kent saw that little of importance and much of disvalue to the cause of religion resulted.

He moved swiftly to project a program designed to meet the situation, and carried his message far and wide, particularly into state universities where in the opinion of many people the difficulties were almost insurmountable. He proposed a forward step in the form of schools of religion, to be financed from funds outside the university budget wherever it was necessary. More significantly he proclaimed the problem of leadership as the essential challenge. He insisted that if religion were to become a respected and vital subject it must be represented by persons who had paid the price of intellectual and scholarly discipline. High motive, human interest, deep and personal commitment to religion he considered of great importance but not enough. His major strategy pointed toward the development of men and women of tested scholarship who believed in the cause and who gave promise of distinguished leadership. This, rather than particular institutional forms, was the essence of Dr. Kent's vision.

In the passing of years, it can be said with some confidence, Dr. Kent's analysis of need and his effectiveness as an interpreter of the importance of the cause were landmarks in the development of religion in higher education in the United States.

If Patrick Murphy Malin is right in stating that "the cause of religion in higher education seems to be in much better shape in recent years than it was in the early twenties," the reason lies primarily in the improvement of leadership and specifically in the quality of religious teaching. In this respect progress has been made. The status of religion is well up to that of most other subjects in the college curriculum.

It is not so clear that comparable progress has been made respecting another facet of Dr. Kent's concern: The bringing of students in college under the influence of scholarly and inspiring teachers of religion *in order that* American medicine, law, politics, business and industry, and finance might in the years to come have ethically enlightened leadership.

Restraint is surely of the essence when considering how effective his successors have been with respect to this important ideal. There are evidences of achievement, but on the whole the impression remains that the program has been ineffective. Religion is characteristically weak whenever it seeks embodiment and expression in the processes through which men make a living. Beyond that, faced with the larger and destiny-determining movements of economic and international political life, Christian people have often manifested a tendency to draw back and to take refuge in groups devoted to enhancing "spiritual" security. This will be the interpretation placed, unjustifiably, by some on Mr. Outler's emphasis on "community." What teachers trained in religious studies conceivably might do about this responsibility is a good question, not to be solved by revisions of "message," but requiring a fundamental reorientation in approach and an enlargement of one's relations as religious teacher to scholars and workers in adjacent fields.

It may not be assumed that religion or ethics or any other subject well presented and well taught will have any specific effect on current and future actions of students. The point here to be made is that Dr. Kent's interest in socially applied religion has not been carried through with anything like the success which during twenty-five years has crowned efforts to get religion well taught as judged by prevailing standards in colleges and universities.

There were many assumptions underlying the effort "to make religion intellectually respectable on the campus" which first had to be identified and then subjected to critical examination. This important consideration will have to be passed over here because the sociology of the development is possibly more illuminating than its ideology. And this takes us into the optimistic and invigorating atmosphere of the twenties.

The proclamation of an intellectually respectable, modernist and liberal, scholarly and scientific approach to religion on the campus, which would take all that science had to offer and come back for more, and which would move on a level beneath but respectful to all faiths inevitably drew to the banner a wide variety of folk. In the twenties there were large numbers of thoughtful people who while recognizing something vital in Christianity and Judaism were offended by the propaganda of many religious groups. They felt the need for a reconstruction in their thinking that would do justice to the claims of religious faith and the insistent claims of science, new knowledge, the facts of present-day living, and plain honesty.

Despite later aspersions cast on the sanity of the twenties in the United States, it was a period of great energy output. Doubt as to the sanity of these years in a later perspective was based on the apparent unawareness of the oncoming deluge of depression, war, and revolution. There was, however, a tremendous outburst of power, and in many respects it was a creative period of imaginative vision and imperial design.

There were some great gatherings in those memorable days. "Seekers" after a new basis for religious faith came to many a market place of ideas. There was great hospitality to views and backgrounds of all kinds. These people came to talk mostly, but not lacking was a determination to seek out the implications of faith for life. The impetus for many of these gatherings was the hope that religion at long last might become the vital center of an inclusive action program to make life better. So came everybody, it seemed, except perhaps the ultraconservative, and so departed many with disappointment in their hearts. Never had they been exposed to such a babel of discordant voices. They found little that provided that inner satisfaction and security, which, "when the chips were down," they had really been seeking.

This outburst of energy, the result of long smoldering resentments or conflicts within the individual growing up in the twentieth century, was perhaps on the whole a disappointment, but it did dramatize possibilities of relationships which a religious movement might establish, and brought out clearly a basic issue for all times: Can religious faith be the center around which may be arrayed all the truth-seeking disciplines of man and the whole directed toward the improvement of human living?

College and university religious strategy was deeply influenced by these events. It was an experience to hear a theologian, then only "promising," today distinguished, declare in a group of sociologists and psychologists, that psychology had freed religion from all supernaturalistic connotations and that "henceforth, if theology is to be included at all, it belongs at the circumference and not at the center. . . . No very specific adherence to traditional theological beliefs is necessary to support religion."

A friendly critic has summed up his own conclusion in this way: "In the 'twenties Christianity continued its efforts to conquer the world; in the 'thirties it pulled in its horns, and since then its energies have gone into tidying up its own house."

One can accept this statement as a rough approximation of what was happening—despite the mixture of metaphors—but it may be questioned that "tidying up" does full justice to the reconstruction of theologies, the new ventures in Protestant church relations, and other moves to meet human need which developed in this period of history.

It cannot, however, be gainsaid that social calamity and internal conflict combined to produce fear and insecurity in persons and institutions, and that in many respects the Christian has been willing to settle for much less than he was willing to agree to under the majestic influence of religious aspiration in the twenties. His ambitions were then more bold as to the possibility of his religion doing something about the so-called secular aspects of the campus and the community, such as intercollegiate athletics, fraternities and sororities, campus politics, local and international politics, and social and economic order, and, in the vernacular of the times, other "hot-spots."

While there is still discussion of some of these matters, it may be said that on the whole religion seems to have decided to let some of these problems severely alone, to give only passing attention to others, and believes that in so doing it has more important concerns. It is quite possible that this reduction of the agenda has been based on some shrewdness in analyzing the possibilities and limitations of religion's influence. A tear, nonetheless, is perhaps not out of place.

Sir Walter Moberly, surveying the English scene, states what I regard as equally true in the United States:

Today many university teachers and administrators are Christians. But few, if any, of us are *Christian teachers* or *Christian administrators*. That is, we have failed so far to bring any distinctive Christian insight to the problems of university training and governance with which, in our professional capacity, we are constantly concerned.[2]

Many will say that there is no problem here, or will ask with some smugness: What is the solution which Christianity proposes? The issue is missed. The question is: Is there any widespread, incisive effort to grapple with such problems? One would

[2] Sir Walter Moberly, *The Crisis in the University* (London: S.C.M. Press Ltd., 1949), p. 26.

certainly do grave injustice if he were to say that there is none, thus overlooking a few administrators of rare perception and an unknown number of college and university teachers who are undergoing considerable soul-searching regarding the meaning of their faith and ethic for teaching method and curriculum, public relations, financial programs, selection, retention, and training of staff, academic freedom and related matters.

The impression remains, however, that religion in higher education or religiously motivated persons in higher education have made few if any notable advances in these areas in the past quarter-century. Why? Lack of energy after wrestling with problems of survival? Shrewd insight into the radical nature of such undertakings and the risks involved? The possibility must not be overlooked that the general insecurity of the times has turned attention inward toward personal matters of belief and faith with accompanying abandonment of courageous and persistent search for ways of thinking about and controlling our institutions for religious and ethical ends.

Nels Ferré gives more than a suggestion of this kind of thinking in an unpublished paper entitled, "Contemporary Civilization and Christianity in Higher Education":

> I should not do my duty . . . unless I suggested that we prepare to go underground. What if communism does come and sweeps away the . . . Church. How shall we then sing the Lord's song?

Concern for group survival and personal witness, rather than thinking about ways of shaping social forces and institutions toward Christian ends, is the consequence of such basic fears.

The issue may be proposed like this: Granted that religion in higher education is in better shape and enjoys greater respect now than it did in the twenties, what is it going to use this improved status for? Further enjoyment which such recognition brings or as the vantage point for an attack on the problems which Sir Walter poses?

It is easy to give an irresponsible answer to such questions, to change the words which are used in talking about religion's task in higher education, but without counting the cost involved in implementing our affirmations. Risk is involved. One runs counter to some deeply entrenched customs and prejudices. In meeting them will the hard-won academic respectability, the source of security for many a worker, emerge unsullied?

Colleges appear to like a certain amount of innovation, enough to give them a mark of distinction in the minds of educators and in their public relations. They are seldom willing to risk their reputations for being places of "sound scholarship and learning." The mores defining sound scholarship and academic respectability are potent and quite resistant to change. That much President Victor L. Butterfield seems to me to be suggesting in discussing the wide ferment of reformism in higher education today when he says in a later chapter:

One cannot deny genuine gains in educational reform since the war, and even before, on some campuses. In general, however, one questions whether the reforms have been as significant or meaningful as first impressions would indicate, since the general attitude towards knowledge and its function in life has not significantly changed. It cannot change dramatically until there is much more awareness among our intellectuals of the social and psychological need for a more profound moral orientation.

Occasionally interpreters of religion in higher education leave a bad impression. They seemingly take pains to prove that Christianity is compatible with any philosophy of education proposed in the ferment of competing reform and reaction. It is as if they said to the college administrator: Try a little religion; it can't do you any harm.

There is such a thing as overeagerness to make religion or anything else respectable. In academic circles the notion that religion in the twenties needed to make itself over to improve its status and give it a place of influence was certainly a powerful concept which, as we have seen, brought changes of a very valuable kind. The point needs making, however, that such an ambition has limitations and may actually impede progress if not balanced by an emphasis, valid in the Christian tradition, on religious activity as an intellectual and moral "seedbed."

Here, then, is a challenge, implied in the energetic aspirations of the twenties, with which religion in these days has not yet quite come to terms, and which invites action.

What development in religion in higher education in the past quarter-century is likely to have the most permanent effect?

I have asked this question many times—of others and of myself—and have come to this conclusion: The most significant gain has been *the identification of religion in higher education as a distinctive area of professional activity.*

While it is true that for generations men and women had devoted their lives or parts of their lives to teaching and guiding the religious education of college students, only recently has this activity shown the marks of a profession. It was once somewhat common in the earlier part of the careers of many religious leaders to spend a few years after college or seminary in college religious work, then to move out into their "life-work." During the past twenty-five years significant advances have been made in establishing the variety of religious ministries to the college campus as a clearly definable, lifelong profession. The process began with a more trenchant and thoroughgoing analysis of the field itself and of the demands which effectiveness in that field placed on the worker.

In Clarence Prouty Shedd this development has found its prophet, its promoter, and its educational statesman. The emergence of religion in higher education as a profession is worthy of extended examination. Only a few high points can here be mentioned.

The breadth of the task envisioned by Charles Foster Kent and his contemporaries had a tonic effect on students. The prospect of teaching religion in colleges on a broad base of liberal scholarship, of undertaking administrative responsibility for religion on the campus, and of becoming a counselor made a strong appeal. Young people with vocational leanings toward the Christian ministry, college teaching, or Christian Association work or programs sponsored by church boards and foundations saw here an area of significant and stimulating service.

Mr. Shedd had worked long enough in this field to recognize that effective leadership would in the long run depend on a type of professional training not then given in any seminary or graduate school. He proposed that a program was needed that would be related to, but in many important items distinctive from, the professional preparation of the parish minister, the college teacher, or the community Christian Association secretary, at least as these careers were usually understood. There was common ground in many of the varied approaches to campus religious life, but that ground was different from, and not adequately represented in, any existing program of study. There was required a blending of studies and experience not embraced in the curriculum of the graduate school, the school of education, or the theological seminary.

The identification of this need and the projection of curricula of professional significance to meet it came and went in many institutions, but found sharp and continuous focus in the Yale Divinity School. The program was based on a realistic analysis of the religious needs of students, the administrative and social environment of higher education, and the potentialities implicit in the growing participation of churches in religious work with students. A sound program developed. Its development required a creative co-ordination of resources available only in a large university and in a seminary which was willing to move ahead in a statesmanlike way.

The yield from this pioneering effort has been great. A steady stream of graduates has gone into the field. They are today giving outstanding leadership as teachers, administrators, chaplains, Christian Association secretaries and church foundation directors. The day is happily past when it was thought that one might qualify for these positions if he had a college education, a sound motive, and was willing to attend an occasional conference.

Underlying the program of professional studies and fortunately an integral part of it has been the acceptance of research in religion in higher education. The identification of problems in the field and bringing them under the scrutiny of persons trained in the best available techniques of research are surely an indication of a maturing profession. Studies in the history of religion in higher education, philosophical examination of goals and presuppositions, critical appraisal of programs and administrative policies have contributed to right thinking about this broad field. Such studies have enriched the professional curriculum and have brought the institution sponsoring them and the individuals participating in them into living contact with the realities of campus life. No ivory tower this!

The results have been profound. I believe that in the perspective of the years nothing that has happened in religion in higher education during the past quarter-century will be viewed as more permanently creative and more stabilizing to this great concern than this development which has identified the field as a profession and established a program of studies and research supporting it.

Accompanying the emergence of religion in higher education as a profession and in some respects an outcome of it has been a clearer definition of the qualifications required of persons who are successfully to teach, or administer, or guide in this field. Dean Willard L. Sperry used to speak of the "inevitable man" who ought to be found for this kind of work. He thus emphasized qualities of the person beneath and beyond trainability. There is no place like a professional school rightly conducted for sifting out the unfit and for revealing to the individual his own inadequacies while providing opportunity for self-improvement as far as that is possible. The integrity of the profession requires such a process. While the basic and essential qualities are insight and felicity in human relations and in the difficult art of "colleagueship," it has become clear that breadth of intellectual interests and capacity to learn from and contribute to fields and interests adjacent to religion in the give-and-take of academic life are of great importance. One may admit that religion gets "left out" in many movements to reform the college curriculum because of prejudices on the part of educators which circumscribe religion's activity and meaning. But it requires to be added that religion is sometimes neglected because its representatives have been without competence or even interest outside their field.

To relate religious faith to the pressing problems of educational change, or changes in any field, must remain the perpetual challenge to religious leaders. There is more here than meets the eye. While professional training that sees this as a fundamental requirement and makes provision for it is of great importance, something more is demanded. I refer to moves that establish lines of communication between experienced persons in religion and persons in other fields. It is here that some real gains have been made in recent years.

The consultations on religion sponsored by The Edward W. Hazen Foundation and the National Council on Religion in Higher Education are good examples. College and university presidents have been brought together in small groups in various parts of the country to discuss the problems of their institutions with respect to religion in the company of a few religious philosophers and theologians of competence. These consultations have been a creative force. They represent a type of fruitful communication on a "high level" which is capable of wide application and experimentation. Despite the absence of formal "conclusions and recommendations," so dear to the heart of the professional organizer, the untabulated results of such gatherings are probably great.

Here and there during these twenty-five years have appeared religious fellowships or societies which have persistently kept open the doors to scholars and teachers in other fields whose religious interests, in the traditional sense, might be described as peripheral or at least undefined. They have met because of common concern for spiritual values in education, for integration of knowledge, or for welfare of students. One of the notable examples of such societies is the National Council on Religion in Higher Education. The remarkable thing about this society has been its continued existence and the vigor of its activity. Other groups have come and gone, but this society, united by ties of friendship and interest in a broadly based search for intellectual clarity, spiritual reality, and social effectiveness, after nearly thirty years is still vigorous.

Mention should also be made of a slightly different type of communicative effort. Recently The Edward W. Hazen Foundation has brought together scholars in various fields to write about the bearing of religion on the teaching of philosophy, social sciences, English, and other subjects of the college curriculum. The brochures emerging from this activity have been enthusiastically received. The project suggests both the liveliness of the interest in relating religion to other fields and the willingness of scholars and teachers who are not specialists in religion to share with those who are in a common quest for better approaches to students. Perhaps a ferment more potent than curricular reformism is at work in the hearts and minds of teachers.

The status and function of the so-called "voluntary" religious agencies have undergone considerable change and adaptation during the past quarter-century. While the forms and relationships of these organizations are a subject of great importance, I cannot discuss them here. These movements now seem to me more firmly rooted than was true in the twenties. Superficially it might appear that the reverse is the case. Some would say that under the hammer blows of the taking of more and more responsibility by college and university administrations, voluntary agencies had waned. I would interpret the facts otherwise. Changes in the setting in which these agencies do their work, as well as broader cultural changes, have required of them adaptation in purpose and method. No unified pattern has emerged but generally the result has been a clearer understanding of the nature of the task to which they are committed and a sharper focus on those parts of the task which, given the present trends in higher education, a voluntary agency outside the administrative control of the college or university is peculiarly fitted to perform. The role is perhaps more akin to Mr. Outler's "communities" energized by a common concern for truth and goodness than is that of any other groups within the campus that readily come to mind not excluding well-taught classes.

This creative adaptation to change came about because the same influences previously described which improved and strengthened the teaching of religion in colleges and universities also produced higher leadership standards among Christian Association and church foundation workers. Increasingly their leaders have viewed the ministry to student religion as a totality, and have seen the division of labor between the classroom teacher, the college chaplain, the church foundation, and the Christian Associations as of secondary importance. Two results have followed. Professional preparation has been increasingly emphasized, and advantage taken of the greatly improved training programs which have become available. A second result is the development of increasingly co-operative relations between all religious and educational agencies within the college or university community. A sense of partnership is emerging which is characterized by mutual respect. This is undoubtedly based in part on a common and overwhelming sense that opportunity and need exceed the capacity of all even when united.

If it has not been clear from what has already been said it should now be stated that the atmosphere of higher education, including the attitudes of faculties, administrative officers, and students is more favorable to religion today than was true in the twenties. However puzzled responsible administrators may be as to methods of organizing this interest, increasing numbers seem ready to acknowledge that it has or should have a place in an institution of higher education. While many of the developments referred to in this chapter have had something to do with the change of atmosphere, by far the most important influence has been a change in the temper of the times. This change reflects an increasing sense of need for something to tie to amid the turbulence of the age. Few institutions dealing with youth or with education have failed to feel the effect.

The limitations of this chapter permit only very brief reference to the important subject of methodology. Important changes have taken place, and it would be a serious mistake to fail to mention them.

The energies of the twenties did not exhaust themselves in laying the foundations of a new profession. In this same period two important methods or approaches to experience were identified for subsequent experiment and development. These were counseling and group work. It is a temptation to say that they were invented, but it would be more accurate to say that they were adapted from previously existing approaches.

For our purposes it is not important to trace the genealogy of counseling and group work. Religious workers have been active in their development in company with specialists in psychology, personnel work, social work, and elsewhere. Both counseling and group work have opened up approaches to student life which have affected the development of religion in higher education. Particularly is this true of counseling. Group work, as the term is used here, has not been as ingeniously exploited.

Isolating counseling as a distinctive approach and tool was

important partly because in the somewhat chaotic period of the thirties it offered a way of serving the needs of students even when budgets were being reduced and drastic organizational changes were taking place. While it is true that some workers have shown a tendency to regard counseling as the whole and universally valid answer to the religious leader's problems, their wholeheartedness has been useful in that it has compelled a definition of the possibilities and limitations of the method.

Religious workers in colleges and universities were among those who first distinguished counseling as *process* from the activity of working with individuals. "Personal work" has had a long and honorable history in Christianity. As far as education is concerned the vocational guidance movement of the early years of the twentieth century was the beginning of counseling.

By the twenties the old "annual evangelistic campaign" had waned, although it had not been entirely abandoned. Religious workers were seeking a more effective method. The tremendous growth in size of student bodies following World War I, accompanied by mass-production methods in education, revealed glaringly the need for a more individualized approach. It was natural and traditional for the religious worker in his personal relations with students to "pick up the pieces" of frustrated, fractured, and puzzled lives. What was not traditional and required some touch of genius was to isolate the *process* of helping individuals under these conditions and to reach out to the developing movements within psychology, mental hygiene, and education for significant insights and pertinent methodology. This process became the focus of study and research.

As the new field bloomed there began a process of critical comparison, evaluation, invention, and rejection. Here again was a vital center around which the religious worker could draw collaborators from psychology, sociology, psychiatry, and other fields of interest. For a time it seemed that religious differences did not matter very much provided only one could contribute to a better understanding of how to help perplexed or upset individuals. "Student counseling" thus got placed on the agenda of most religious conferences.

The Hazen Conferences on Student Counseling were in some respects a precedent-setting influence in stimulating and guiding this whole development. One must say "guiding" reservedly; the genius of these conferences was that they gave to planning committees of experienced and interested teachers and leaders the responsibility of guiding themselves in their exploration of religious counseling in higher education. Experts were brought in to contribute what they could to an understanding of the counseling process, the needs and dynamics of student life, the educational environment. The emphasis was on counseling as an approach to students for use by the teacher or leader and not primarily on counseling as a specialized profession.

Further emphasis on the importance of personal relations with students was given by The Hazen Foundation's plan of agency grants. Through small allocations of money, hundreds of teachers, pastors, administrative officers, and Christian Association secretaries, often on inadequate salaries, have been able to multiply and enrich their personal contacts with students. The encouragement of entertaining students in homes of leaders has been an aspect of the program.

Beyond saying that he wanted to help individuals, the religious counselor was not immediately propelled into defining his objectives and into thinking through the relation of counseling methods to Christian theology. The question, however, has soon to be faced: In what sense and with what limitations is this a technique for the achievement of Christian objectives? What is its relation to the Christian faith? Is the individual being helped to become more effective in achieving his own objectives merely, or do counselors have—and have a right to have—some responsibility for reshaping them? If so, in what context of values? Further, what is the responsibility of the counselor, if he has any, for the social and economic setting and the educational policies and environment which sometimes produce the disharmonies and frustration of the individual?

The emergence of such issues was a healthy sign, and indicative of maturing on the part of those interested in counseling. The issues are by nature comprehensive, and demand a wider context—philosophical, administrative, social, and educational—if they are to be discussed intelligently. Let it be said that the impulse to follow through has not been wanting. *A Christian Context for Counseling,* previously quoted, is one indication of this outreach, and it is significant that this pamphlet contains a lecture given at a conference on student counseling.

There are today administrators and teachers who view counseling with misgivings, and in some cases disdain. A manifestation of paternalism, a sentimental intrusion into the personal life of the student, an impractical expectation for most teachers who are necessarily preoccupied with their own studies and their teaching responsibilities, a way of meeting abnormalities and exceptions with which the teacher-counselor usually ought not to meddle—these and other objections surround counseling today. There are answers which seem decisive to those who offer them, but much remains to be done not only in interpretation but in adjusting the concepts and methods to the realities of the educational situation.

When this has been said, however, it requires also to be stated as historical fact that in counseling, religious action on the American campus has found a useful and enriching concept and approach to religious communication and experience.

In group work, it must be admitted, one is dealing with a concept and an approach which on the whole have not been as much explored and exploited in college religious methodology as has counseling. Campus religious work, however, was the scene of some of the early developments when working-with-groups began to be distinguished from a group process.

Harrison Sackett Elliott of Union Theological Seminary forcefully directed attention to the "process of group thinking" in the twenties, and much of his work was done in college student conferences and institutes. Later the concept broadened from discussion or idea-exchange to what was called group experience in which consideration was given to the psychosocial forces involved in interpersonal relations in organized groups. An understanding of the play of these forces and to some extent their manipulation in the interest of individual growth are involved in any concept of leadership. Group work thus draws on sociology, philosophy, and cultural anthropology for light on the group process. Group work helps us understand how "community" may develop and operate. It would seem to have important implications for Mr. Outler's "communities of common concern for truth and goodness."

Why this important development, so rich in possibilities for religious leadership in colleges and universities, has seen no marked development there, where to some extent it got its start, is not easy to explain. Traditional concepts, limiting teaching to instruction by one who knows of others who do not and (hopefully) want to know, probably offer one part of the answer. It must also be recognized that some resistance comes from views concerning the cultivation and transmission of religious experience. In some of these views, leadership and discipleship are less a matter of mutuality and sharing than of authoritative communication of truth, or alleged truth which might better be called conviction.

Be that as it may, group work offers possibilities for the teacher and religious worker. I am the more certain of this because I have seen its effectiveness amply demonstrated in Christian Association groups under specially competent leaders on a few campuses.

In closing this impressionistic report of a quarter-century one is keenly aware of the fact that memories and impressions are inevitably influenced by the prejudices of the reporter. His estimates of what is relevant, prophetic, commendable, or sad inevitably reflect a not too easily analyzed frame of reference, which in turn is not so much personal as the deposit of group and cultural and institutional relationships which he has sustained.

Underlying, however, is a thought and a question which can best be expressed by a paraphrase of some words of George Albert Coe written in the twenties:

> Did we not assume that by and by when we have set things right in our thinking and in our organization of things, then God will be able to get at the student in our colleges?
>
> Might we not ask whether we permitted God to work through us in our teaching, our revisions of curricula, our administrative processes, our financing, our counseling, our guiding of campus life?

To manifest the qualities of honesty, courage, intellectual integrity, and humility so that perchance God might work through us is fitting dedication for years that lie ahead.

PART II

The Academic Curriculum

2

Scientia, Scientific Method, and Religion

Edwin E. Aubrey

SCIENCE has certainly won its place in the sun of the academic world today. This achievement was not easily accomplished. Even in the seventeenth century science was largely pursued in the scientific academies rather than in the universities.[1] The term then used was "natural philosophy" rather than "science," as the name of the American organization that called itself The Philosophical Society indicates. The term "science," in its Latin form *scientia*, stood for knowledge in general, and it was only gradually that science differentiated itself from philosophy and asserted its independence. That its declaration of independence gave it a freedom to develop its own methods, and that careful delimitation of its area of inquiry saved it from much interference in its work, is very clear in the record. Without this it is doubtful whether modern science as we know it could have reached its present stature.

I. THE PLACE OF SCIENCE IN EDUCATION TODAY

Indeed the outstanding feature of recent educational history is the extent to which science has risen to dominance in the

[1] See Martha Ornstein, *The Role of the Scientific Societies in the Seventeenth Century* (Chicago, 1928); W. C. D. Dampier-Whetham, *The History of Science* (Cambridge, 1930), p. 311.

universities and colleges. The present emphasis on the natural sciences in the curriculum has in fact aroused many educators to protest that something valuable in the earlier *scientia* has been lost.[2]

At the same time there has been keen controversy among the scientists themselves about their relation to other disciplines. Some among them feel that the rigorous pursuit of scientific studies requires extreme caution in regard to other methods of acquiring knowledge, if its purity is to be maintained. A few feel that there is no other valid knowledge than that gained in scientific inquiry. Still others acknowledge that science is only one avenue of search for truth, and seek to keep it in its special place among the forms of knowledge, admitting special limitations in the type of knowledge that scientific method yields. Very often these last have made their own study of the nature of the knowledge that science gives, from the standpoint of philosophical theory of knowledge.

In the opposite camp are the professors who resent the ubiquity of science and the consequent thrusting of the humanities into the background, and who are driven at times to defend their own disciplines by making them seem "scientific" by the application of a rigorous method of treatment ill-suited to the subject matter.[3] Still other opponents of the dominance of science disparage it in various ways: by showing its newness in the ancient academic scene, by taking their cue from philosophical critiques of the scientific method, by warning against the impoverishment of the life of appreciation that overtakes the scientist, or by showing the frightening results of applied science in war and the terrors of the atomic age.

[2] Thus Dampier-Whetham points to the value in German education of the term *Wissenschaft*, which has a broader meaning of critical and systematic knowledge, and which served to maintain relations between the various disciplines (*op. cit.*, p. 310).
[3] A. Flexner, *Universities, American, English and German* (New York, 1930), pp. 20 ff.

But the major issue in education today is whether science, knowledge, and wisdom are identical terms. Here lies a fundamental problem in the relation between vocational and general education. Granting that science yields knowledge, is the knowledge it yields adequate to the needs of human life? Can that soundness of judgment that we call wisdom be developed by scientific training alone, or does it contain an ingredient derived from forms of sensitivity which are best developed by aesthetic, moral, and religious experience? Are all aspects of human experience susceptible of analysis by methods developed by the natural sciences without loss of significant meanings; i.e., is all knowledge worthy of the name at bottom scientific? Shall we grant that science yields adequate knowledge even of the physical objects and events that it describes? If we step outside its limits how shall we distinguish between wisdom and superstition? These are by no means merely rhetorical questions today. Equally competent and thoughtful people give opposite answers to each of the questions just stated. Nor are these people just like the blind men examining the elephant, for they are aware of each other's methods of investigation; and so we cannot settle the questions by a simple addition of the knowledges gained, nor presuppose an easy harmonization of the methods of physical sciences, social studies, and philosophy.

The spectacular successes of the natural sciences in the seventeenth century led many to think that all problems could be solved by recourse to natural science methods. Mechanism was to furnish the clue to explanation of all phenomena.[4] But gradually, as men recognized that time is a crucial factor in biological processes and that those processes are irreversible (you cannot push the hen back into the egg), the concept of organic growth was given its place in the scheme of scientific explanation. The presence of physical or chemical mechanisms within the or-

---

[4] See, for instance, Laplace, *Mécanique céleste* (1799-1805) for astronomy, and de la Mettrie, *L'homme machine* (1748) for biology.

ganism was not denied. (On the contrary, the effective use of synthetic drugs suggests that there are chemical processes reacting in the body at a mechanistic level; and the measurability of brain activity by electronic devices points to the physical processes as a constituent part of this organic behavior.) But these mechanistic processes were brought within the framework of organic, integrated behavior in such a way as to change their meanings in important respects.[5] This change is in the nature of a concentration so that the organism as a whole reflects back upon the subordinate processes and in this context their activity has a different significance.[6] Accordingly, the organic level required new categories of explanation: the terms developed for the "lower" levels were not adequate for the new biotic processes. The controversy between biologists who are "vitalists" and those who are "mechanists" has been confusing because the peculiar quality of organic relations has been obscurely referred to a vague "vital impulse," as though this were some entity. Had the term "mechanistic" been set over against the term "organismic" the debate might have been more fruitful. The problem was really a question of the continuity between inorganic and organic, as one sample of the general issue of continuity between the various levels of natural process.

We stand at the present time at a point where the hypothesis of a real continuity between levels of nature has demonstrated its fruitfulness in scientific research, but where we lack satisfactory categories to describe the transitions from one level to another.[7] Hence science has been busy at the points where these

[5] The organismic view was developed by R. W. Sellars, *Evolutionary Naturalism* (Chicago, 1922); C. L. Morgan, *Emergent Evolution* (London, 1923); J. Smuts, *Holism and Evolution* (New York, 1926); and A. N. Whitehead, *Process and Reality* (Cambridge, 1929).

[6] G. P. Conger has worked it out in detail in his *A World of Epitomizations* (Princeton, 1931).

[7] See the divergences among the naturalistic authors in Y. H. Krikorian (ed.) *Naturalism and the Human Spirit* (New York, 1944). I have dealt with these in an article in the *Journal of Philosophy*, XLVIII (1950-51), 57-66.

transitions appear: from physics to chemistry, from neurology to psychology, from chemistry to biology, from the "social" behavior of subhuman forms to that of men. The philosopher or religionist who seizes on these discontinuities to support belief in some "supernatural" force at work is on very precarious ground. But as long as the naturalistic philosopher is unable to give a self-contained and complete account of the continuities which he feels to be present he can state his confidence in continuity of analysis only as an unverified faith, though perhaps supported by probability.

It is not surprising that, in view of the complexity attending the problems, some have turned from scientific canons of investigation to other modes of research. They have spoken of history as an art rather than a science, or they have sought to deal with social phenomena at the level of social process without commitment to any particular theories regarding scientific foundations, preferring to call their disciplines "social studies," or they have treated religious behavior as having its own laws at a level where scientific categories are useless if not irrelevant.

Nor is it surprising that some scientists have tended to neglect some important data that could not be accommodated within the categories with which they were working. The result has been a serious loss of communication between scholars in the different fields, and this in turn has had bad effects in the educational system, since it has led to disintegration of that unity on which wisdom depends. Science has divorced itself from scientia. Specialization has been the keynote; and this specialization has led in turn to some mutual recrimination within the faculties. In the face of such attitudes all talk of education as a process of developing integrated personality has been all but futile, and the student has been victimized by a process that leads to more confusion than wisdom, to a separated array of knowledges never brought into fruitful relation to each other. I am not decrying the value of specialized research in which distinct problems are accepted for intensive treatment. Little is to be gained by having a faculty made up entirely of comprehensive scholars ranging over all the field of knowledge. I am asking only that the lines of communication between the researchers be maintained so that students may have some conception of the interrelatedness of the problems and achievements of human knowledge.[8] Without this the acquisition of several bodies of facts in different fields of study does not make an educated man.

Another problem arises from the present vogue of logical positivism. The critical thinker, starting with a proper concern with precision of methods of thinking—the age-old discipline of logic —seems to become so preoccupied with the clarification of logical method that he deliberately ignores the world of things and people with which this method is to deal. Logic without ontology is the slogan of the movement:[9] the task of philosophy is defined as that of developing a critically exact terminology in order to avoid the ambiguities which confuse any and all discussion of metaphysical problems and render such discussion otiose. This looks like a type of perfectionism which will not undertake the metaphysical task until all the media of discourse about it are completely refined. Or else it is a flat refusal to acknowledge that any

[8] Karl Jaspers concludes his book on *The Perennial Scope of Philosophy* (Eng. tr., New York, 1949) with a similar plea.

[9] See the essay by Ernst Nagel in Y. H. Krikorian (ed.), *op. cit.*, chap. X. He says:

"The study of scientific inquiry requires us to admit that structures cannot be known independently of activities of symbolization; that structures considered for investigation are selected on the basis of special problems; that the various structures discovered are not, according to the best evidence, all parts of one coherent pattern; and that the precise manner in which our theories are formulated are controlled by specifically human postulates no less than by experimental findings. The attempt to justify logical principles in terms of their supposed conformity to an absolute structure of facts thus completely overlooks their actual function of formulating and regulating the pursuit of human ideals" (p. 233). And again, his "sole objective is to make plausible the view that the role of the logico-mathematical disciplines in inquiry can be clarified without requiring the invention of a hypostatic subject matter for them . . ." (p. 212).

correspondence can be established between laws of thought and objective laws of behavior in an independently existent world. Here logic becomes a function of human discourse and its referents are restricted to human discourse: all attempts to ascribe to "nature" the consistency discovered in a system of logical relations are rejected; and equally all attempts to assert the knowability of the subject himself are regarded as vain,[10] not only because in so far as he is knowable he is object not subject, but also because the subject is again a term in discourse rather than a metaphysical reality. The only reality to which philosophy can point is, on this basis, its own system of discourse, and within this system terms and propositions are studied in their mutual relations rather than in their correspondence to any "reality." Indeed, the very term "reality" now becomes a matter for multiple definition in different semantic contexts.[11]

One is reminded here of the strictures placed upon science by A. S. Eddington,[12] and the problems raised are fundamental for both science and philosophy. For most scientists take for granted the reality of the objects with which they deal, as well as the reliability of their own empirical modes of verifying their conclusions. To the devotee of applied science, the logical questions are remote theoretical quibbles, and even to most pure scientists they represent a skepticism which is not troublesome. But the reliance of the general populace on science is so great, and the claims of some popularizers of science so pretentious, that logical analysis of this sort may well prove to be revolutionary. Much of the theoretical foundation of modern life would disintegrate if the "scientific world-view" were to be undermined.

[10] So L. Chwistek in *The Limitations of Science* (London, 1948), p. 42.

[11] This is very clearly discussed in C. A. Benjamin, *Introduction to the Philosophy of Science* (New York, 1937), where the views of Rudolf Carnap are examined at some length. See esp. pp. 164-67; and also chap. XX which deals with the nature of reality.

[12] *The Nature of the Physical World* (New York, 1929), esp. chap. XII; and *Science and the Unseen World* (New York, 1929), esp. chaps. V and VI.

II. Science and Culture

For science has acquired such a central place as the pre-eminent intellectual force in contemporary culture that if it were to be discredited, the effects would be devastating. Ours is a technologically dominated civilization. We live in a gadgeteer's paradise, but we also plan vast programs of human betterment premised on highly organized technical schemes of control. Effects of climatic conditions are modified by great irrigation projects. Industries that required a certain degree of humidity in the atmosphere now control that by air conditioning. Hydroelectric power is created by enormous dams with far-reaching results in the life of whole agricultural populations. The uncertainty of the catch for fishing fleets is greatly reduced by developments in radar detection of schools of fish.

How far is the scientist to be held responsible for the technological uses of his findings? This question was answered quite simply fifty years ago by a declaration that the scientist seeks the truth and that what men do with it when they have it is not his responsibility. But this disclaimer plagues thoughtful men today. Certainly the educated man in his capacity as citizen must reckon with the challenge;[13] for it affects not only the physical welfare of his fellow men but also the moral structure of society. Technological unemployment is an old problem, but it may be rapidly accelerated in our time. The results of vast aggregations of people in industrial cities, the concentrations of commerce in areas apart from the productive industries themselves, the increasing anonymity of the worker and the apartment dweller, all produce more acute problems in the area of personal responsibility in the community. It is often a question not so much of doing our duty as of defining it where we cannot see the remote effects of our

[13] This has been, perhaps, John Dewey's greatest contribution to American education. The more specific implications for scientific education have been discussed by Sidney Hook in *Reason, Social Myths and Democracy* (New York, 1940), chaps. IX-XII.

labor in an intricate and highly co-ordinated industrial enterprise. If, as the old saying goes, nine tailors make a man, the modern factory or office worker is often the hundredth part of a man.

At the same time, the acceleration of the rate of production and the emancipation of many industries from exclusive reliance on natural raw materials by the scientific development of synthetic stuffs has shifted the economy of most industrial countries from one of scarcity to one of abundance. This requires not only a great expansion of the markets on an international scale and the development of new markets in "backward" areas, but also a higher rate of consumption at home. At this point the problem of the level of consumption becomes an important one. Many things that were formerly regarded as luxuries are now considered necessities, so that a new form of scarcity appears. A shifting of standards is taking place and with it there arises the whole question as to what is essential to human happiness. The question is one of values, and the repercussions of value judgments back upon scientific technology demand that more attention be given to appraisal of the nature and ends of human life.

This is happening at the very time when preoccupation with scientific means has tended to preclude thought about ends. It is here that the deeper question of the place of science in culture appears. The general tendency of scientific education is toward positivism, i.e., toward thought about immediate, sensorily perceptible relations or those which are visibly present in social life, to the exclusion (intentionally or else by inertia) of more remote implications. Philosophical speculation is suspect as too remote to be relevant. But the measure of intelligence is after all the capacity to keep the remote relevant in one's thinking. Its key is imagination of the invisible.[14] Men of faith are those who "endure as seeing the invisible."

[14] For an interesting review of this problem see C. A. Benjamin, *op. cit.*, chap. XX.

The "ages of faith" were, to be sure, often characterized by superstitition; but they were ages when men kept their thinking in perspective. They kept their awareness of realms that transcended their organized knowledge. Pride in achievement was tempered by recognition of the activity of forces that transcended their understanding.[15] Men might then misinterpret the nature of these forces and land in superstition, but at least they kept the problem before themselves. The workers in pure science are more aware than applied scientists of the element of mystery in existence and keep their humility. The danger of the technologist is that, dealing in the practical application of established knowledge, he loses his awareness of his own ignorance. Just as the Lisbon Earthquake of 1755 was a blow to eighteenth-century rationalistic self-confidence by the rude reminder of forces beyond human rational control, so in our own day the terrifying explosion at Hiroshima has been a blow to our assurance that scientific knowledge is intrinsically good. Man visited destruction on his fellows and then tried to find out what he had actually done—and still he does not fully know. To advocate a moratorium on science is hysterical nonsense. What we need is a recovery of perspective. And this is the meaning of wisdom.

A culture is the complex of perspectives, values, and judgments that undergirds a civilization. The cultured person is one who has a deep and critical knowledge of his culture: not a conventional acceptance of the current opinions, but a grasp of the history of his tradition with its possibilities and limitations, an ability to see his own culture in the broader perspective of the general human scene, and a philosophy of life that looks

[15] This note of pious acknowledgment is seen very clearly in the seventeenth-century scientists like Galileo, Kepler, and Newton. The problem of a critical agnosticism which accepted science but perceived its limitations was discussed by the brothers du Bois-Reymond: Emil du Bois-Reymond, *Ueber die Grenzen des Naturerkennens* (Leipzig, 1876) and Paul du Bois-Reymond, *Ueber die Grundlagen der Erkenntnis in den exacten Wissenschaften* (Tuebingen, 1890), and has frequently been treated since.

beyond the present historical situation to the meanings of human existence. To develop such persons is the proper aim of liberal education. In the life of such a person science has an important place. It gives him tested and dependable knowledge of the world in which he lives so that he can make independent judgments of popular opinions, becoming thereby both free and realistic. It trains him in disciplined thinking so that he seeks to verify claims by recourse to facts, examines events in their relations, discriminates between prejudice and objective thought, and humbly submits his own views to criticism. Mere knowledge of the findings of science without these attitudes may lead to a dogmatism that contradicts the spirit of science itself.

But to say this is also to say that there are areas of experience like art, morality, and religion which must be accorded their place in his life and thought. For culture transcends science and includes these other aspects of human experience as well, so that aesthetic, moral, and religious values are part of cultured living. They have all had their share in the development of the cultural tradition in which a man stands and which he must appreciate; but they also have their own disciplines of understanding. To be conscious of the distinctive qualities of these disciplines is part of the flexibility of the cultured mind. To reduce any one of these disciplines to terms of another is to be bigoted, whether this be a religious, scientific, or moralistic bigotry. In a word, each must be seen in the perspective of the whole complex of experience. This is the secret of the balance of the cultured man.

III. Science as a Way of Knowing

In this perspective he will examine science itself. If this examination is carried out he will find himself dealing with the philosophy of science. By this I mean not the philosophical world view based on scientific findings, but the critical study of the presuppositions and methods of scientific inquiry.

In science the reality of the world is taken for granted. But "reality" is a perplexing term, for it is used in many ways. Early in the history of philosophical thought, men felt that the realities they saw about them were derived from some primeval stuff—be it earth or air or fire or water—from which they had become differentiated: in a word, that all observable objects could be traced back to some one original form of matter. But two truths forced themselves upon human attention. One was that all the stuff they observed had some structure, and that in some cases this structure was very complex. The other truth was that things move, that there is activity abroad in the world, that it is a world in process, that there is always something going on.[16]

This realization posed the question whether, on the analogy of the human mind, the form of something might be determined before the thing was brought into being. So strong was the conviction that this was the case that some thinkers declared that there was an antecedent form required for each class of objects, and that this prior form was in some sense more "real" than the physical objects themselves. Reality had become something different from observable things, a hidden realm of which the things seen and handled were imperfect representations. Reality had passed from the empirical world to a world accessible only to pure thought and not to sense. Others doggedly insisted that whatever reality there was must somehow be found within the observable world, perhaps as the secret process within it shaping its special forms, and directing them toward their proper completion in their development. But still this was itself an invisible process, the hidden kernel of which we see only the shell, the soul which we see only bodied forth. Speculations as to the

[16] This recognition of a sort of dualism of substance and process, or form and vitality, has constituted a central issue in philosophy from the Greeks to our own day.

nature of this hidden reality have continued to the present day, and are reflected in such terms as atoms, electrons, protons, genes, lightwaves, point-particles and mind-stuff—none of them directly observable.

From this it would appear that our knowledge of things is a variable combination of sensory awareness, discrimination, symbolization, organization, and inference. "The real world out there" is now not so obvious as one might think. It has been somewhat "sicklied o'er with the pale cast of thought." No wonder, then, that many have been led to eschew philosophy, and to concentrate on what they regard as the concrete. Unfortunately the problem cannot be escaped so simply. Let us then look a little more closely at the knowledge that we possess.

I have just said that our knowledge of things is a medley of sensation, discrimination, symbolization, organization, and inference. The development from the vague reactivity of the babe to the precise hypothesis of a trained scientist is a gradual process. Slowly the babe discriminates within its "big, blooming, buzzing confusion" of a world some highlights here, some hardness there, some warmth elsewhere. By a process of very elementary correlation its world shapes up for it until it "recognizes" objects or persons. Things happening in sequence—if that is not too tenuously connected—are identified as related to each other, and the environment takes on organized meanings. A part of this meaning is that if the mother hovers over the crib one may expect to be lifted up and fed. The expectation is an inference, and it is sometimes disappointed and thus the inference becomes precarious. More discrimination is called for, and details of the hovering are distinguished till a surer prediction can be made. As this process of noting, connecting, discriminating, correcting, predicting, and organizing continues, knowledge grows and is refined, till eventually it becomes a sophisticated understanding. The sophisticating process is painful but rewarding, for with it the area of our security grows.

Science is no exception to this process of acquiring understanding. It is shot through with inferences that go beyond direct sensory perception, even when these inferences are subjected to careful verification by further observation. But there is also present another phase of knowing which appears when the educative process is begun: conclusions reached by others who have anticipated our experience are transmitted to us. In teaching us our mother tongue they give us accepted definitions of things and happenings around us. Many, if not most, of these we shall accept to our dying day. Others we shall be subjecting to examination: they will be criticized, brought to the bar of judgment of other definitions furnished by our own experience and testing or by the authoritative conclusions of people we trust. Our ability to make critical judgments will be the criterion of our maturity.

Indeed, we shall even examine our very method of securing information about our world and other people. We shall discover that there are different sorts of judgment which are not apparently commensurable. A chemist will see in a test tube of copper sulphate solution a number of chemical possibilities; an artist will see in it a gorgeous blue. Both judgments will be true, yet they are made in different contexts of meaning. The medical technician will recognize in a microscopic piece of human tissue a definite stage of the onset of cancer; the family doctor will see in that the tragic frustration of his patient's life. These two judgments are not inconsistent, they simply move in different dimensions. The inferences are carried in different directions. Thus the same event may symbolize different things.[17]

Accordingly the scientist exercises a certain asceticism, disciplining himself to exclude the sorts of meaning that would confuse the main objective of his search. Other meanings become irrelevant for him so far as his scientific activity is concerned. He has indulged in a valuable form of abstraction or simplification in order to make his specialized contribution to knowledge.

[17] C. A. Benjamin, *op. cit.*, chap. IV.

Being aware of the abstraction he accepts the fact that his knowledge is tentative in character, for some all-important factors may have been ignored in the process which will turn out to have been more immediately relevant than he had supposed. The history of science is full of such instances, so that the careful scientist is always on his guard against conventionalized experiments which may be persistently overlooking a key datum. But there are other self-limitations of the scientist that need to be recognized. One of these is that he proposes to deal only with measurable data, with spatial dimensions and temporal intervals. His ideal formulation of a relation is a mathematical equation. Based as it is upon statistical computations the relation is stated with reference to some one or few characteristics of the phenomena agreed on in advance as "restricting the area of inquiry." Thus Jones counts in the economic study only as a representative of a given salary level. His marital relations, his taste in music, his ideas about Europe are excluded from consideration. The total meaning of Jones as a unit is not included in the investigation, so that it is a somewhat abstract Jones who appears in the scientific study. This does not necessarily invalidate the study, though it may be discovered later that Jones's tastes in music have something to do with his salary level and that this is a variable that needs to be brought into the investigation.

The main point is that a process of abstraction has taken place, and that therefore the particular bit of knowledge gained about Jones and his class is only part of the truth about him. Other facts about him will be equally important for other concerns about him. Even if all these bits of scientific knowledge about him were added together, they would not give us the real Jones. He must be known in the *interrelation* of these knowledges in some integrated picture of the man. Indeed it is possible that the most important thing about him may not be known apart from some elusive fact about him called his attitude toward the situation; and the wise investigator may find himself called upon to seek a sufficiently confidential rapport with Jones to ascertain Jones's attitude in an interview in which subtle contact of personalities plays a very important role in gaining the information desired. This is not *un*scientific. It is an adjunct of scientific method, if by the latter we mean accurate, discriminating, systematized organization of knowledge. But here an important variable of social science appears.

In the knowledge of persons we are forced to interpret the meanings of their acts in terms of "attitudes" or "motives" which we cannot directly observe but only infer from those acts. Is Jones deceiving us so that his testimony in the interview is unreliable as to his intent? This can be partly checked by comparison with other phases of his behavior, but the most reliable man may on occasion resort to deception. How do we know that in this particular instance Jones is not choosing to act out of character and deciding deliberately to upset our inquiry? Here we encounter the puzzle of human freedom. We may seek to circumvent it in one of two ways: we may resort to inference and ask ourselves whether in his place we would be likely to resort to some subterfuge to conceal our real intentions, or we may seek by recourse to his unconscious reactions to get behind his façade. The former method is open to the familiar "psychological fallacy," the latter leaves us the task of converting physiological reactions (e.g., those secured in a lie detector test) into ideational complexes. In either case a large degree of empathy on the part of the investigator is involved. Does this invalidate the inquiry from the standpoint of scientific method? Psychologists will disagree on this important point; and it is a point of prime importance for the student of human behavior, and therefore for the social sciences. But this problem is part of another chapter in this volume.[18]

Meanwhile the wise man will probably refuse to be restricted to too rigid canons of method in dealing with the behavior of

[18] Chap. 5.

persons. He will recognize that science gives him the most coherent picture available of his world, but that it is incomplete and cannot therefore be dogmatically insisted on. He will acknowledge that it offers a disciplined method of securing knowledge, and valuable protection against premature or prejudiced conclusions. But he will insist that its knowledge and its method need supplementation from less precisely tested understanding of the world and of men. This understanding will be gained often from insights acquired in the study of such subjects as history, biography, and literature. In this way science will be only part of a broader education which will also include the humanities.

But there is another aspect of wisdom which has not here been included, for it goes beyond the normal intent of science. It is the highest expression of human intelligence. It consists of the purposeful behavior in which men construct ends in harmony with what they understand the universe to be like, examine the possible means at their disposal and then develop programs of action for the most effective realization of those ends. After all, this is the meaning of wisdom; and apart from it learning finds little justification. Even to seek knowledge for its own sake implies that knowledge is better than ignorance, and what does this imply in turn about the world in which we live and about our relations with our fellow men?

It is in this area of defining proper ends harmonious with the basic realities of our world that philosophy finds its constructive task. The experience of the race in dealing with this central problem of human life yields the body of judgments that constitute a culture, with its presuppositions. Every civilization rests upon such a culture, and the meaning of science itself is defined in terms of that culture. The fact that today we think in terms of a cosmopolitan culture does not alter this fact: we are now rethinking the body of judgments of our western culture in the light of our contacts with oriental cultural thinking. Men have always sought to find some universally valid assumptions on which to rest their case or to promote their culture, and at the same time they have always been dogged by the suspicion that what they considered to be universal truths might be provincial after all. Yet we have to act on the widest basis we can command.

Without taking up the problem of relativism in ethics and religion, we may still pause here to note that we are in an area where science makes no claims except to help us discover means when the ends have once been determined, and to help us to check the ends against what we know about the nature of our universe. But since we have at each moment to act once for all (i.e., the act, once committed, cannot be retrieved), yet without the complete knowledge that would be an infallible guide for action, we are forced to act in faith. Man's consciousness of this dilemma of absolute decision based on relative and limited knowledge is the heart of religion. In it, as Paul Tillich has pointed out, man's fatality and his freedom are brought together. Faced by his need to act once for all, he rebels against the limitation of his knowledge. Recognizing the limitations of his knowledge he rebels against the responsibility of acting once for all. Forced to bow before powers that transcend his understanding he grovels or defies, or else he humbly accepts his responsibility with faith and trust that outrun his intellectual grasp of the situation.[19] This is the core of the religious experience.

Our study of the place of science in higher education would seem to point to the following conclusions:

(1) Science can no longer carry on in isolation from the broad educational context in which it finds itself, nor from the social scene over which its own findings exercise so great an influence.

(2) The scientific enterprise has its own presuppositions regarding what is "real" and how reliable knowledge is gained.

[19] On this see Reinhold Niebuhr, *The Nature and Destiny of Man*, I, 251 ff.

(3) The scientist who is self-critical concerning his methods of gaining knowledge realizes that there are other dimensions of meaning (aesthetic, moral, metaphysical, religious) than those with which he is properly preoccupied in his experiments and observations.

(4) He is therefore called upon to exercise in his research a sort of ascetic discipline in order to concentrate on his proper data, and scientific method is thus a process of abstraction.

(5) This in turn limits the scope of the validity of scientific method.

(6) In consequence a tension is set up between this limited, specialized function of science and the demands of integrated social and educational experience.

IV. Science and Religion in Higher Education

Here a more comprehensive perspective is required, and this is something that religion is able to offer. The fundamental problem of the relation of science to religion in higher education is not, therefore, one of "harmonizing" two bodies of opinion.[20] It is rather that of bringing science into relation to the depth of human experience, the fullest conceivable breadth of view of the world with which both deal, and the most remote relevant implications for the destiny of the human race. When scientists refuse to recognize these relations they have no protection against sinister forces in society which, as in Nazi Germany, prostitute science to the cause of oppression, deception, and false propaganda. The uneasy conscience of nuclear physicists about the atom bomb is a hopeful sign, for it betokens a sensitive recognition of the larger perspectives mentioned above. But beneath such uneasy awareness lies the deeper question as to the nature and destiny of the human race. Man now finds himself in a position

[20] The problem of harmonizing scientific and theological views of the origin of man, or of the age of the world, still occupies many minds; but as I try to show below, the issues have been deepened by recent discussion and analysis.

to bring human history to an end, and he is not only frightened by the prospect but confused about its meaning. Another step has been taken in his control of his environment, an enormous step, and he feels that he has assumed some of the divine power without knowing the divine purpose, or—what is worse—without knowing whether there is any ultimate purpose or meaning in it all.[21]

The term "religion" carries a variety of meanings. To some it means assent to a theologically formulated system of beliefs. To others it denotes a body of customary practices consisting of rites, mores, and private acts of devotion. To still others it is an intimate personal experience of communion with God, or of acute decision in which eternal values are at stake, or of standing under the judgment of the Ultimate. All of these are legitimate definitions, and these various aspects in religious life do not always appear in any one sequence.

Eventually all of them are involved, so that the religious man acts in any given moment with a consciousness of its infinite outreach, and the significance of this infinite outreach is defined in some fashion. But he also acts as a member of some fellowship which has established for itself certain practices and attitudes expressive of its faith and hope. Every thoughtful man finds himself caught at some time or other in what Sartre, the French existentialist, has called "total engagement." The meaning of his life as a whole is called in question. He cannot evade action, since even to refrain from action is itself an act of restraint. Yet he knows that the consequences of his act go far beyond his ken. This responsibility outruns his knowledge, and this leads him either to pretend to knowledge that he does not possess, or to try to escape the responsibility by some evasion, or to accept the necessity of faith. The criticism has often been brought against

[21] Note the disillusioned sense of frustration reflected in the presidential address of Sir Alfred Ewing before the British Association in 1932, quoted in W. Moberly, *The Crisis in the University* (London, 1949). In chap. IV Sir Walter Moberly discusses this dilemma in penetrating fashion.

education that it is too frequently an elaborate process of evading responsibility either by retreat into the "ivory tower" or by a type of skepticism that defers action in view of the complexity of the problem faced. Since the operation of analytic intelligence can always discover new complexities in any situation, the educated man thinks he can defer responsible action indefinitely. The sad truth is that, while he waits, others determine the situation in which he must live. Thereby he sacrifices his freedom, which is perhaps the most cherished value of educated minds. The alternative is to act in terms of a future not known but accepted in faith.[22] It may be said, then, that religion serves to maintain the integrity of science itself.

It is in this way that we must see the role of religion in higher education. We cannot preserve that role by merely instituting courses in religion, valuable as these are in clarifying the nature of the religious moment we have discussed. The religious perspective must be brought to bear on the determination of the function, the methods and the content of education.

For too long we have assumed that the task of the educator was accomplished when he had provided means whereby knowledge might be increased. This implied that knowledge and more knowledge would solve the human problem. But today we are seeing that factual knowledge must be reinforced by strong motivation to act wisely. Motivation, however, means the engagement of the emotions in some integrated plan of action. Higher education is therefore required to deal with the student as a total person, with his motivations as well as his "mind." It is here that we encounter the subtle problems of his emotional life, hidden, much of it, in deep recesses which we cannot penetrate. Here too we run up against the fact of inner freedom in the student. Every teacher knows that the student may in an examination regurgitate the opinions of his instructor without

[22] There is a sympathetic treatment of this problem in the essay by John Macmurray in B. H. Streeter (ed.), *Adventure* (London, 1909), p. 151.

sincere subscription to them. In the interests of academic success, in terms of marks and graduation, the student may sacrifice his own integrity. There is a moral factor here that is far more important for his future than his command of the facts or opinions he has heard in the classroom. The issue is whether the function of education is to enable one to achieve superficial success by social conformity or to develop personal integrity in judgment.

Furthermore, much of this hypocrisy of which we have been speaking is due to a desire for security: the individual does not want to risk his future by asserting too much independence. Thus the search for security may end in slavish social conformity. But the secret of both security and freedom lies in preserving personal integrity.

This integrity requires also that we reckon with the widest range of our experience and the highest reaches of our imagination. If life is to have a solid core relevant to the whole sweep of personal life, obviously it must include in its integrated system of meanings these breadths and heights.

It is not the primary purpose of this chapter to delineate the place of religion in higher education, but I have sought to indicate how religion is related to thinking about the function of science in education. In a word, religion makes its contribution at the point where inner integrity and inclusive organization of experience are involved in education; and education cannot satisfy the religious man until it provides for these.

Again, religion is concerned with the methods of education. The integrity of the person is a primary religious concern, and this has clear implications for the educative process. Intellectual bludgeoning of the student by a dogmatic teacher, fallacious treatment of the pupil as merely a "brain," professorial sneering at the attempts of the immature student to formulate a thoughtful opinion that may seem naïve, unwillingness on the teacher's part to step outside the immediate subject matter to discuss its relation to an allied subject or a remoter implication —these belie the aims of religion and are therefore cause for religious criticism of educational method.

As to the *content* of the program of higher education, this is in large part a matter for the special disciplines to decide in so far as competent grasp of their special subject matters is concerned. Yet even here there are opportunities for the cultivation of wisdom that are often ignored. I can do no better than refer the reader to the valuable series of monographs published by The Hazen Foundation on "Religious Perspectives of College Teaching" where the neglected opportunities in such subjects as economics, history, English literature, and philosophy are discussed.

But there is also the problem of the over-all distribution of subjects in the curriculum. Here the planning must be guided by some view of the chief ends of human life. The purely vocational aim must be modified and supplemented by the effort to enrich the life of the student as a person and to set the vocational task in the broader context of social life and human destiny. Yet it is precisely here that the narrowly specialized interests of the members of a faculty curriculum committee tend to assert themselves in a competitive struggle for precedence and vested interest. The significant trend in the last twenty-five years is toward a more balanced diet in the college program, and toward increasing provision in technical schools for studies in the humanities and the social sciences. This is a source of encouragement. Whatever can be done to get the student to see his own special vocation in the larger perspective is to be welcomed.

But this does not suffice. If religion is a significant part of human culture, clearly it should be studied as carefully as other factors. If we are to talk of religion as an integrating force in human life, we must know what religion is. There is need, therefore, for systematic courses in the field of religion: its history, its basic concepts, its psychological processes, its great literary products and expressions, its role in social change, its demands on conduct. Such studies must be carried on with exacting scholarship, with appreciative understanding, and with a sense of its crucial importance comparable to the best in scientific and humanistic study. Only against such a background can any useful appraisal be made of the so-called "spiritual aspects" of our experience. And there is now a sufficient body of scholarly material available for such studies.

At the same time such courses give opportunity for studied consideration of other aspects of our common life in the light of religion. They deal with convictions about the nature of man in relation to his responsibilities, about the extent of his knowledge of his world, about the meaning of history seen in reference to the universe of which it is a part, about the evasions to which men resort to escape the pressures of the infinite upon them; and thus reach out into other disciplines. In this way courses in religion can themselves be centers of integrative education in the university or the college. But it must be reiterated that this comprehensive evaluation can be carried out only from the firm center of a thoroughly competent grasp of the essential facts about religion itself. The careless student of religion is no qualified judge of social and educational programs and practices, but the careful and competent student of religion can offer a more profound critical estimate of human life than those who have not faced the searching questions which religious thought raises.

The question of the relation of scientific education to religion may be dealt with at three levels. The first and most superficial of these is found in the discussions where the compatibility of the interpretations of the world and of man offered respectively by science and by theology is the main issue. Except for the dogmatic rigorist who denies the truth of a scientific theory simply because it contradicts Scripture or an ecclesiastical creed, we find few trained theologians who seem to oppose science. Where they do so, it is on the ground that the scientific theories are established by reference to "facts" secured on the basis of certain presuppositions lying behind the scientific hypothesis—presuppositions which have not themselves been empirically established but which reflect some bias antithetical to the fair examination of the claims of the theology in question. Such objections stem from a deeper consideration: that into scientific inquiry there may enter postulates which, while not perhaps affecting the actual observations directly, do influence the explanations of the data collected. Thus Ernst Haeckel[23] hailed the materialistic monism of Darwin. This was a judgment not about Darwin's facts but about the philosophic character of the Darwinian explanation. A theologian objecting to the Darwinian theory on the basis of this judgment might then reject the theory not because he refused to accept the *data* on which it rested but because he objected to a *materialistic interpretation* of the data. Clearly the answer of the scientist at this point must not be a mere asseveration of the Darwinian theory (or some modified form of the evolutionary hypothesis) as what all "sensible men" today believe. He must rather show that the way in which the data for that hypothesis were collected and interpreted was free from predetermination by any such presupposition. This has moved the discussion to the second level.

The problem then centers in the metaphysical context of the scientific inquiry;[24] and in order to meet it the scientist must move into the area of philosophy. Either he must show in terms of philosophical positivism that empirical science is a self-sufficient procedure which requires no metaphysics; or he must make explicit his metaphysical position. If the latter option is taken, the issue is no longer that of science versus religion, but rather of the relative merits of two metaphysical systems. It is also possible in the latter case that the opponents find themselves sharing a common metaphysics, whether it be naturalism or some form of supernaturalism (of which there are several). Much of the

[23] *Darwin and Modern Science* (London, 1909), p. 151.
[24] For a delineation of this phase of the problem see C. J. Wright, *Miracle in History and in Modern Thought* (New York, 1930), chap. III and pp. 178 ff.

difficulty arises here from limitations in the philosophical training of the scientist who is not prepared to enter this terrain, and who covers up his inadequacy with what is often a naïve dogmatism.

But today the metaphysical problem is dogged by the nagging questions of the epistemologist who asks the positivist and the metaphysical philosopher alike by what means of knowing each has arrived at his conclusions. We are here thrown back to the problems raised earlier in this essay: what is a fact and how is it perceived? This is the third level of the discussion, and since both scientist and philosopher are concerned with knowledge there is a better chance of finding common ground for the discussion. This is the point at which theologians are today taking up the problem.[25] Some of them will insist on the independent validity of religious intuition, others will accept the empirical method but will still want a clearer definition of what is a "fact." The nature of intuition remains a difficult philosophical problem and is recognized as an important one for science as well as for religion, since studies of the biography and psychology of scientific discovery have led their authors to insist that many of the great insights have come to leading scientists as intuitive leaps of insight.

In general religious intuition has been treated primarily as mystical insight; but there is today a growing body of religious writing which relates the intuition to the "existential moment" in which the individual feels himself confronted by God at the point of his own moral extremity.[26] This shift in theological

[25] The recent literature on this topic is reviewed up to 1940 in D. C. Macintosh, *The Problem of Religious Knowledge* (New York, 1940). See also E. W. Lyman, *The Meaning and Truth of Religion* (New York, 1933), chaps. VII-IX, and Richard Niebuhr, *The Meaning of Revelation* (New York, 1941).

[26] The movement known as existentialism in theology has grown rapidly in recent years. Resting back largely on the writings of the Danish philosopher of the nineteenth century, Sören Kierkegaard, it is expounded today in the works of Karl Barth and Emil Brunner in Switzerland, Gabriel Marcel in France, and Paul Tillich and Reinhold Niebuhr in the United States.

thinking reflects a revulsion against the monism of earlier idealistic philosophies, and stresses a dualistic distinction between man and God. Here man is thought of as being *in* nature but not wholly enclosed by nature, since his human character is defined by his awareness of being confronted by Something beyond nature which makes demands upon him. These demands create in him an acute unrest (what the German existentialists call *Angst*) which drives him beyond nature, either in a desperate leap of imaginative transcendence in which he vigorously asserts his freedom, or in a humble submission to the grace of God. Knowledge here comes in the act of commitment rather than in the detached contemplation.

While there is a significant affinity between this view of the dependence of knowledge on commitment and the scientific insistence that knowledge comes from actual experimental activity, it is a commonplace to say that on the whole the scientific temper favors detachment.

At this point we confront one of the most difficult problems which attends the study of religion as it is compared with the studies in science. The aim of science is detached objectivity. The scientist seeks to stand outside the situation which he investigates.[27] He demands freedom from direct emotional involvement in the data which he studies. The study of religion, on the other hand, demands personal involvement if the situation is to be understood. To put it another way, the man who has never made a personal commitment in the area of religion cannot know what religious experience is. In this respect religion is closer to art than to science. Is it possible, then, for the study of religion to be objective?

[27] It is true that recent theoretical considerations in physical science have stressed the relative position of the investigator as an all-important factor in the elemental process of measurement; but even here Einstein has been seeking an absolute independent of man in the speed of light. See, for instance, C. A. Benjamin, *op. cit.*, p. 305, and A. S. Eddington, *The Nature of the Physical World*, chap. II, and p. 46 n.

Some would say that this is the crucial question which determines whether religion is a proper subject for inclusion in the college curriculum. To this extreme statement I cannot agree. It would lead to the exclusion of artistic and literary appreciation from college study. To be sure, there are some professors in the scientific fields who actually take this position, but they are narrow in their view of education as I have tried to argue above. This by no means impugns their ability as scientific researchers, but it does question their competence as educators; and it is interesting to note that outstanding scientists who have become educational administrators have seen clearly the error of this limited view.

Can study of religion be objective? I believe that it is possible to answer in the affirmative. It cannot be objective in the sense of being completely detached. But is this the only form of objectivity? What is sought in objectivity is really freedom from personal bias in the reporting of experience and in the forming of conclusions based on experience. This may be achieved by refusing steadfastly to allow one's feelings to be engaged in the investigation—the asceticism of the scientist which we have mentioned above, or what is sometimes called "the professional attitude." But it may also be secured by trying to enter into the experience of others so as to feel as they feel, and then comparing their feelings with those of others or with one's own. In this way an effort is made to transcend one's own subjectivity. A variety of professed views, including one's own, are then compared, and organized into a comprehensive view which may then serve as a basis for critical evaluation of one's own personal bias. This is admittedly a counsel of perfection, since men are prone to self-centeredness and pride which prevent them from entering fully into another's experience, and are also incapable of dispossessing themselves in imagination sufficiently to become identified with the other. As the theologians would say, there are limitations of both sin and finitude which restrict us in the endeavor. It is to the credit of religion that it freely recognizes these limitations. This is in itself a corrective. This corrective is part of the discipline of religious studies. It is a condition of that humility which we admire when we see it in the trained and disciplined scientist.

To this extent the religious man and the scientist (I am not denying that the scientist may be a religious man!) are on common ground when at their best. Furthermore, both are keenly aware of the relative and limited character of their knowledge; and both are disposed to be realists in the sense that they recognize that there are realities to which their own interpretations must in the end conform. This too is a corrective for subjectivity.

The striking thing to the scientist is that these realities with which he deals are knowable, which implies that they have some structured character which lends itself to orderly knowledge. In Judeo-Christian thought it is claimed that this structured character is derived from God whose ordered and consistent activity expresses in the observed world a creative purpose. And since this purpose moves through human history as well as through the nonhuman world, there is a unity of meaning which is the basis of that integrated wisdom which education seeks. It all "hangs together," and this is the source of any hope that men may have for the unification of knowledge and for the integration of meanings which are the obverse and reverse of the human quest in education.

3

Religious Faith and the Task of the Historian

Roger L. Shinn

AMONG the many things that have a history is men's attitude toward history. A generation ago it was a common enough opinion that, as Henry Ford is supposed to have said, "History is bunk." Now the quotation is as dated as Ford's Model-T. If we would match it with a statement from our time, we might choose General Marshall's advice that to understand our own world we need to know the history of the Peloponnesian Wars.

Neither Ford nor Marshall is formally a spokesman for higher education. But each has spoken with the voice of his time. The unlearned but highly efficient industrialist, supercilious toward the past but confident of his ability to shape the future, was undeniably one of the powerful and typical leaders of his generation. And the able soldier-statesman, aware of the deep-flowing tides of history and of his historical responsibility, is one of the most respected leaders of ours. In the few years between the two ages events of history had their cataclysmic impact. And history, as an academic discipline with an urgent significance for all who would think or live, came into its own as perhaps never before on the American scene.

Simultaneously religious thought—and particularly Christian theology—was making a similarly striking shift. It too responded to the momentous historical crisis. Its rethinking of its basic ideas in the light of new realities was helped by advances in historical scholarship, which rediscovered certain biblical and traditional conceptions long encrusted in patterns typical of the Renaissance, the Enlightenment, and evolutionary progressivism. With increasing conviction Christian thinkers proclaimed that neglected strains in the Judeo-Christian tradition offered a more realistic basis for understanding history than did the modern secular conceptions which had so often replaced them.

These two movements—the one in the general appreciation of history, the other in religious thought—have produced a recent surge of writings on the understanding of history. Historians,[1] philosophers,[2] and theologians[3] have published volume upon volume of writings dealing with interpretation of history. Not only university libraries but even best-seller lists have shown the trend.

I. Faith and Historical Investigation

This recent tendency raises a question which neither historian nor philosopher nor theologian can avoid. Does religious faith make any difference for the understanding of history? More specifically, does faith affect the place of history in higher education and the techniques of the historian? Or does honest research demand that the historian, however compelling his personal faith, set aside all religious beliefs when he takes up the specific tasks of his profession?

One aspect of the answer is clear. Certainly one of the achieve-

[1] E.g., Carl Becker, Herbert Butterfield, Gordon Childe, Christopher Dawson, Arnold Toynbee.

[2] E.g., Morris Cohen, R. G. Collingwood, B. Croce, Karl Löwith, John Macmurray, Karl Popper, H. N. Wieman.

[3] E.g., Paul Althaus, John Baillie, Karl Barth, Nicolas Berdyaev, Emil Brunner, Oscar Cullmann, C. H. Dodd, Walter Horton, Reinhold Niebuhr, Otto Piper, E. C. Rust, Paul Tillich, H. G. Wood.

ments of modern history has been the skillful development of
painstaking means of research for discovering evidence about
the past. It is part of the historian's discipline and integrity that
he can set aside his personal inclinations and desires in the interests of an honest reading of the records. The achievements of
modern historians have shown many a failure of earlier (and
sometimes recent) historians who, because of provincial or
patriotic or ecclesiastical or economic prejudices, distorted the
facts.

The dangers of reading one's assumptions into history are all
too obvious. The miserable squabbles which sometimes center
around school boards and choice of textbooks to please pressure
groups illustrate the point. The cheap "slanting" of history to
meet prejudices gives point to Napoleon's cynical view that "history is a fable agreed on," or Voltaire's statement that "history
is after all only a pack of tricks we play on the dead."

Furthermore, there is a brute factuality about history which
is likely to upset any scheme which is laid down in advance of
the evidence. The physical scientist tests the accuracy of his
science by its ability to make detailed predictions. The historian
who had to meet such a test would make a sorry record. History
repeatedly discloses the unexpected. The historian dare not pin
his research to prior assumptions which will blind him to any
evidence which may appear.

Religious beliefs, along with many other sorts of belief, have
repeatedly betrayed the historian in his responsibility. There is
obvious persuasiveness in J. B. Bury's statement: "A historian
may be a theist but so far as his work is concerned this particular
belief is otiose."[4] When history is studied and written for the
sake of illustrating certain beliefs, curious results appear: certain
evidences of the past are quietly forgotten; others are exaggerated;
and sooner or later events may be recorded quite contrary to the
evidence. As one historian has written: "The prophetic interpre-

[4] "Darwin and History," in *Selected Essays* (Cambridge: University Press,
1930), p. 33.

tation of history is more convincing in the prophets, who never stopped to write actual history, than in the chroniclers who did."[5] Modern religious thinkers have recognized this problem in their acceptance of the methods of literary criticism in analyzing biblical documents. When Christians have done this, it has meant exactly the recognition that certain traditions of their faith have been untrue to the evidence and that the techniques of historical research must be used to correct history which was distorted by false assumptions.

The lesson is clear: honest history demands that assumptions not take the place of evidence. The historian, whatever his convictions or prejudices, is not permitted to hide, overlook, or distort any historical evidence; and he is not permitted to assert, on grounds of faith, historical claims which can actually be verified only by evidence. He may not, on the basis of a dogma of Marx and Engels, for instance, assert that primitive man lived in an idyllic state of communism. He may not, out of fervid American patriotism, write that "other" countries provoked all the wars in which the United States has engaged. He may not, because of authoritative religious teaching, record that Moses wrote the Pentateuch, that his bishop stands in an unbroken, formal succession, or that "righteous" nations prosper and "unrighteous" nations are destroyed. The truth or falsity of any of these statements must be determined by historical criteria, not by religious faith.

Beside this clear aspect of the problem is a second aspect which cannot be stated so simply. It starts from the realization that there is no historical knowledge which does not involve interpretation. It is probably fair to say that this principle, neglected by positivistic historians of the past, is getting vastly increased recognition from historians today.

There was a time when David Hume could state the "spectator

[5] E. Harris Harbison, "The Problem of the Christian Historian," *Theology Today*, V (1948), 388-405.

view" of history in its baldest form: ". . . 'to see all [the] human race, from the beginning of time, pass, as it were, in review before us; appearing in their true colors, without any of those disguises, which, during their lifetime, so much perplexed the judgment of the beholders—what spectacle can be imagined, so magnificent, so various, so interesting?" Historians, in Hume's description, have a godlike wisdom: They "are sufficiently interested in the characters and events, to have a lively sentiment of blame or praise; and, at the same time have no particular interest or concern to pervert their judgment."[6]

More positivistic historians than Hume have omitted the sentiments of blame and praise and, considering history a science on the pattern of the natural sciences, have set out simply to determine the facts. But far more common today is the recognition that the historian must take some viewpoint in order to deal with history at all. Thus Morris Cohen, firm historical realist though he is, asserts: "The historian must have a point of view in selecting his material, a point of view that determines what is important and what is unimportant in the confusing maze of human events."[7] The unwillingness to admit a viewpoint leads the historian, not to greater objectivity, but to greater naïveté and greater stubbornness in defending prejudices against which he cannot guard since he cannot admit that he has them.

In this situation some historians turn to an utter relativism and skepticism, asserting that there are as many points of view and therefore as many histories as there are historians. One may pick his viewpoint, however partial and specialized; and if he admits his limitations, who can deny him the right to produce histories? Yet few would be content with so complete a historical relativism. A recent writer has produced successively histories

---

[6] "Of the Study of History." (Punctuation slightly modified.) In *Essays, Moral, Political and Literary*, II, 388-91. (Ed. by T. H. Greene and T. H. Grosse, London: Longmans, Green, 1875.)

[7] Morris Cohen, *The Meaning of Human History* (LaSalle: Open Court, 1947), p. 80. Cf. pp. 4-5, 24-31, 46-49, 65-66, 114-15.

of plumbing and of beards; and however informative these histories may be, one would hardly regard them as the most significant of human histories. Thus we must admit that the enterprise of writing or studying history requires a viewpoint and that some viewpoints are more adequate than others.

To state the same problem differently, history is a matter of interpreting evidence. The historian has no right to tinker with evidence in order to suit himself, but he must make use of presuppositions or principles of interpretation which are not established (though they may sometimes be suggested) by the evidence itself.

Since the time of Immanuel Kant most philosophies—whether the idealisms stemming from Kant or the more naturalistic pragmatisms so popular in America—have recognized that the principles of interpretation profoundly influence all our understanding. Thus in the natural sciences certain presuppositions concerning the harmony of the universe (as avowedly in the case of Einstein) or at least of methodology (in the case of more pragmatic scientists) underlie the tremendously successful advances of modern times. These presuppositions are not themselves proved scientifically; they are rather the assumptions and conditions of scientific "proof."

Even more are certain indemonstrable presuppositions the requirement of historical investigation. For history is the example par excellence of an intellectual discipline depending upon selection and interpretation. It offers what Schopenhauer called an "infinite subject matter." The data cannot be abstracted and reduced, by the methods of the physical sciences, to a relatively few uniformities; for history is necessarily concerned with the unique. Any historical work must leave out far more information than it includes. For every death of a Lincoln, Caesar, or Jesus of Nazareth which it records, millions of deaths must go unrecorded. So Burckhardt could describe history as "the record of facts which one age finds remarkable in another." But even in the same age men will differ in their judgment of remarkable and significant facts. On the one hand the process of selection is necessary for any historical thought. On the other hand the same process always carries the danger of misunderstanding and distortion of the past and makes it important that the most adequate available principles of selection and interpretation be used.

A result of the conditions of historical methodology is, then, that not all of the classical arguments among historians may be settled by discovery of new evidence. Gibbon's magnificent intellectual endeavor traces the decline and fall of the Roman Empire from the golden age of the Antonines to death at the hands of religion and barbarism. Toynbee, with many another historian, finds the seeds of decay centuries earlier than did Gibbon. How can the difference be resolved? Possibly discoveries of new evidence will help. But already there is more evidence than can be comprehended. Basically the problem is one of valid appraisal; it depends largely upon presuppositions and principles of interpretation.

Nor is it enough to say that the historian's work depends upon the assumptions which he brings to a *given* body of evidence. For his assumptions will determine the questions he asks, the investigations he makes, and therefore the very evidence available for his (and his generation's) attempt to understand history. Throughout the historian's work it is certain nonevidential factors which determine the distinction between *chronicle* and *history*, between historical *knowledge* and *understanding*.[8]

[8] It is not necessary, for the purpose of this discussion, to go into the controversial question of whether there exists such a thing as historical fact apart from interpretation. Dozens of volumes have dealt with the subject from various points of view; and the final answer depends upon a solution to the whole problem of epistemology and metaphysics. Idealists (especially those influenced by Croce) and pragmatists stress the importance of interpretation; realists stress fact. But only a narrow fringe of writers on either side of the question would deny the importance of both evidence and interpretation. As far as this specific issue is concerned, this essay aims to work on the common ground shared by a realist like Morris Cohen and an idealist like R. G. Collingwood.

The assumptions from which men approach the problems of history often have the nature of a religious faith. Such was certainly the case with the confidence in *progress* which characterized so much of modern thought about history. Bury, the historian of the idea of progress, was wise enough to regard belief in progress as an "act of faith" which "bears on the mystery of life."[9] Many a modern writer has not been so clear on this issue. The early Dewey, for example, although denying certain theories of inevitable progress, insisted that scientific method was the guarantee of progress if men wanted it, and made the amazing claim: "We have now a sure method. Wholesale permanent decays of civilization are impossible." A later, more chastened Dewey, asking whether there are grounds for his own faith in "the potentialities of human nature," says: "I do not attempt to give any answer, but the word *faith* is intentionally used. For in the long run democracy will stand or fall with the possibility of maintaining the faith and justifying it by works."[10]

In analyzing the various assumptions from which men start their thinking about history, we are therefore looking not so much at historical evidence as at the presuppositions, often the faiths, by which men try to understand history. The adequacy of the assumptions depends upon whether they do, in fact, give historical insight. Whether the assumptions be Marxist or capitalist; Christian, Buddhist, or secular; progressive, cyclical, or eschatological, they must first be formulated so that they do not contradict or take the place of evidence; they must, second, be examined for their adequacy in helping the historian with his task.

[9] See *The Idea of Progress*, Introduction (New York: Macmillan, 1932). Carl Becker shows well the religious character of this faith. See "Progress," *Encyclopedia of the Social Sciences;* also, *The Heavenly City of the Eighteenth Century Philosophers* (New Haven: Yale, 1932). Cf. R. G. Collingwood, *The Idea of History* (London: Oxford, 1946), p. 144. Condorcet's *Outlines of an Historical View of the Progress of the Human Mind* is perhaps the most ardent of the many religious expressions inspired by the faith in progress.

[10] See "Progress," *International Journal of Ethics*, XXVI (1916), 314 ff.; *Freedom and Culture* (New York: Putnam, 1939), p. 126.

II. Biblical Faith and the Meaning of History

The relevance of faith to history becomes most decisive when one asks the historian the final question: Has history a meaning, and, if so, what is it?

Many a professional historian earnestly wishes to duck the question. He can hardly be blamed, in view of the immensity of the problem and the sheer fudge that has been perpetrated by propagandists trying to force their own purposes and meanings upon the whole of history. Here men have disagreed utterly. Here has been the greatest diversity of viewpoints. Evidence seems to support many possible answers, but guarantees none. So the historian who is sensitive about the "scientific" respectability of his discipline, hastily and condescendingly turns the question aside as one for metaphysicians and theologians to beat their brains about while he goes on being a historian.

Yet it is precisely this quest for the meaning of history that has turned men again and again to historical studies. It has given much of the impetus to the renewed concern for history in this decade. A professor of history at Princeton writes:

> The question which haunts any historian today who is at all sensitive to the deeper currents of the age in which he lives, the question his students constantly ask of him by implication even when they do not put it into words, is the question of the meaning of history. A great many of the veterans who flocked into courses in history and the social studies in such swollen numbers after the war made it clear to advisers and teachers that they were looking for answers they thought neither the arts nor the letters nor the natural sciences could give. Somewhere in history, many of them thought, the answer to how it all came about was to be found.[11]

It goes almost without saying that if students bring such a question to their courses in history, they will usually get some sort of an answer, even though the historians might prefer not

[11] E. Harris Harbison, *Religious Perspectives of College Teaching: In History* (The Edward W. Hazen Foundation, 1950), pp. 8-9.

to give one. Some kind of confidence (true or false) or some kind of despair will answer the question. And the historian who teaches or writes for the student will, through his own confidence or despair, often impart or provoke the answer.

On this most fundamental of issues the Judeo-Christian tradition offers a principle which differs markedly from most prevalent ones. It protests against all philosophies which find the evidence of history falling into evident patterns and purposes or which seek to formulate the meaning of history in readily comprehensible terms. But it asserts against all philosophies of final skepticism or despair that history has a divinely-given meaning, however indiscernible that meaning may be.

Biblical and Christian history illustrate the idea repeatedly. No one was ever more confident of the sovereignty of God over history than the Second Isaiah, but no one was more ready to acknowledge his inability to trace all the workings of that sovereignty: "Verily thou art a God that hidest thyself" (Isaiah 45:15). Similarly St. Augustine acknowledged the mystery of history, but regarded that mystery as divine and not merely chaotic. He could be confident that "the Almighty does nothing without reason, though the frail mind of man cannot explain the reason." God's judgments in history "are fully comprehensible, justly reprehensible, by none."[12] Again, our contemporary theologians acutely analyze and reject the various schematisms of the modern world for comprehending history; but in a defiance of final skepticism, they assert that eyes of faith can become aware of divine purpose in history.

At first glance the nonbeliever may regard this biblical principle as merely a rationalization to save a faith in defiance of the facts. But the concrete meaning of the principle becomes clearer when it is compared with its alternatives.

On the one hand the biblical presupposition rejects the many philosophies which try to find in history an immanent rationale,

[12] *City of God*, XXI, 5; II, 23.

a simple coherence or unity, an inherent and autonomous meaning. All popular schematisms are rejected. Polybius' cycles,
Vico's spiral, Joachim's three ages and their secularization in
Comte, Hegel's dialectical movement of the *Weltgeist*, Marx's
materialistic dialectic, Spencer's inevitable progress, the revised
cyclicism of Spengler, Sorokin, or Toynbee's magnificent drama
—none is adequate. The very term "philosophy of history," in
the sense of a rational comprehension of history's conflict and
variety, is dubious.

The point is illustrated in Kierkegaard's scathing rejection of
Hegel's philosophy of history, surely one of the most comprehensive and astute attempts at a philosophy of history. Hegel was
determined to sweep all the multiplicity of history into a single
rationale, though he had to revise the principles of logic to do so.
More successfully than most philosophers of history he saw the
diversity of facts, the cruelty of a history which is a "slaughter-
bench" of happiness and ideals, and the impossibility of showing
any smooth path which history takes. Even so he became the
butt of Kierkegaard's ridicule:

> There were philosophers even before Hegel who took it upon them-
> selves to explain existence, history. And it is true of all such attempts
> that providence can only smile at them.
> But Hegel . . . how the gods must have laughed! A miserable don
> like that who had seen through the necessity of everything and got the
> whole thing off by heart: ye Gods![13]

There is thus in historical thought under Judeo-Christian influences a tough-mindedness that scorns the superficial confidence of most of our modern assumptions about history, and
that has earned the respect of astute professional historians. For
example, Arthur Schlesinger, Jr., has said of Reinhold Niebuhr's
analysis of history that it succeeds "in restating Christian insights with such irresistible relevance to contemporary experience that even those who have no decisive faith in the

[13] *The Journals of Sören Kierkegaard*, tr. by Alexander Dru (New York:
Oxford, 1938), Entry 1323 (July, 1854).

supernatural find their own reading of experience and of history given new and significant dimensions."[14] Such a judgment is prompted in large part by the theologian's blasting of illusions and refusal to acquiesce in many a common wistful hope concerning man's historical destiny.

On the other hand the biblical presupposition of a hidden meaning in history opposes those which assume only a final meaninglessness. Illustrations of this latter viewpoint are harder to find, because the human spirit has usually been quicker to reach for premature solutions to its problems than to resort to despair. But one may find a real sense of the meaninglessness of history in some current existential writings. It was evident in the ancient words, which Herodotus attributes to Solon and which echo recurrently through Greek literature, to the effect that man is accident, that happiness depends on fortune, and that death is better than life.[15] It is evident again in the Eastern *maya* doctrine and in those strains of Platonism which find history less than real.

Against all historical despair biblical thought asserts, not that things are not so bad as they seem, but that in the midst of dungeon, fire, and sword men may find the God who is Lord of history and whose purposes are realized even as men oppose them.

Clearly it is not the primary job of the historian in higher education to work out a doctrine along the lines here suggested, or to intrude it into his historical research at every turn. But the historian with Jewish or Christian faith might well bring to his investigation some such implicit idea. If the thought seems strange to scholars trained in modern historical practice, it is probably because of its unfamiliarity. For a random sampling of modern history books will make evident many other presuppositional ideas with nothing more, except familiarity in the modern ethos, to commend them.

[14] *Christianity and Society,* XIV (1949), No. 3, p. 27.
[15] Herodotus, I, 31, 32.

III. Some Specific Historical Insights

Against this background of the general Judeo-Christian understanding of history, several specific principles affecting historical practice may be sketched.

It may be taken for granted, of course, that many closely-defined historical problems will be attacked solely with philological, archaeological, and other historical methods which are usually independent of the historian's faith or general view of life. But as soon as larger questions of historical causation are asked—e.g., the reasons for modern nationalism or for the threats to democracy today—the historian's religious understanding will affect his investigation and methodology. Some of the principles here considered have so entered the texture of western thought as to be taken for granted by historians who are unaware of any debt to religious traditions. Others are less familiar. But all have their roots in biblical faith.

1. Historical method with Judeo-Christian presuppositions assumes historical universalism. It will usually, for various reasons, concentrate upon some particular strand of history. But it will recognize that it is dealing with part of a universal history.[16]

Not all Jewish or Christian historians have successfully practiced the principle of universalism. From biblical times until today some have written as though the history of the Jews or of the church or of so-called "Christian civilization" made the rest of history insignificant. But the protest was also present from early times.[17] Its significance comes out in a comparison of cer-

---

[16] Modern ethical universalism stems from both stoic and biblical thought. Stoic universalism, however, was usually abstract rather than concrete and historical; it stressed the likeness of men and the monotony of history rather than the distinctive vocations under God of various peoples. It was biblical thought which was both historical and universal.

[17] Thus the prophet Amos spoke against false particularism: "Are ye not as children of the Ethiopians unto me, O children of Israel? saith the Lord. Have not I brought up Israel out of the land of Egypt? and the Philistines from Caphtor, and the Syrians from Kir?" Amos 9:7.

tain ancient writers: Second Isaiah and Herodotus (sixth and fifth centuries B.C., respectively), and Virgil and St. Paul (first century B.C. and first century A.D., respectively). Herodotus, of course, contributed far more to the techniques of the historian than did Second Isaiah; but although the records based on his travels and conversations may have broadened the historical horizon of many a Greek with condescending attitude toward the "barbarian," Herodotus never approached Second Isaiah's conception of the majestic sweep of universal history. Similarly from a Virgilian perspective St. Paul's ideas of the importance of the Jews might seem quite naïve; but to any who have grasped Paul's (and the later Augustine's) realization of the universality of history and the transitory and partial character of all human empires, Virgil's Augustan messianism and glorification of Rome will be myopic provincialism.

Christian historians have often expressed this universalism in curious ways (by modern standards), when they have started their histories with the creation and fall of man and projected them forward until the Last Judgment.[18] But the significance of this universalism is evident when compared with the frequent tendency of historians and philosophers of history (including some notable ones along with the cheap pamphleteers) to assume that the only significant history is that which they know; or that history finds its focus in the achievement of some particular race, economic class, or nation; or that the past existed mainly to bring to birth the present. The point needs to be stressed in this age when, as a historian in one of our most famous universities reports, "Universalism has been very widely lost to the vision of history given college students."

Implicit in this universalism is the protest against any historical absolutisms. To God and his kingdom belong the only

---

[18] That Christianity actually effected a "Copernican revolution" on historical practice has been shown by Collingwood. See *The Idea of History*, pp. 49-50.

truly absolute significance. The conviction of the transcendence of God serves to show the merely relative claims to truth and power of all historical movements and institutions. Greek and Roman, bourgeois and proletarian, American and Russian pretenses are put in their places. Inevitably Hitler found in the Jews (by their very existence) and in faithful Christians (by their religious protests) a reminder of a universalism which undermined his whole conception of history and which he could not tolerate.

This rejection of all human and historical absolutisms has usually been considered as especially characteristic of Protestant Christianity. Reinhold Niebuhr, with his constant protest against all idolatries—whether political, economic, ecclesiastical, or anything else—has made it well known in American thought. But it is rooted deeply in Jewish prophecy. And it is by no means unknown to such Roman Catholic writers as Baron von Hügel, Theodor Haecker, Erich Frank, and (to a lesser degree) the historian Christopher Dawson.

2. Judeo-Christian historical analysis assumes a biblical doctrine of man. Three conceptions are especially meaningful for historical investigation.

a. *The creatureliness of man.* According to traditional doctrine man is created from the dust of the earth. His life is enmeshed with nature, dependent upon natural processes, subject to natural caprice. A biblically-grounded interpretation of history is ready to acknowledge whatever specialists determine about the influence of geography, climate, economics, and biology upon history. (There are more remarks about food-getting and geography in the Bible than in most sacred literatures.) The temptation of the "philosopher of history" is to ignore such influences. But there is truth in Pascal's comment that if Cleopatra's nose had been an inch longer, the course of history would have been changed.[19] Dean Inge writes that a microbe "had the honor of killing Alexander the Great at the age of thirty-two, and so changing the whole course of history."[20] Clearly this sort of reasoning can be overdone, but it is more likely to be overlooked. To the philosophical idealist such notions imply a "bankruptcy of historical method."[21] To others they imply the insult that man is not master of his fate. But historians must do justice to their truth. History is not independent of disease, famine, the cruelty of nature, and the biological life cycle which sets limits to the historical time of every man.

b. *The Image of God.* Biblical thought goes on to say that man's creation is in the image of God. Man is not merely a part of nature. He transcends the natural processes in which he is involved. Some of the marks of this transcendence are reason, imagination, love, and freedom. The historian who neglects these factors in the name of naturalistic and deterministic creeds falsifies history.

The Ionic word, ἱστορίη, originally did not differentiate between natural and human history. But since Herodotus, and especially since Christianity invaded the west, the word "history" has usually, in its precise sense, been reserved for human history. The current trend toward core courses in higher education has not usually resulted in consolidating the natural and historical sciences.

Nevertheless various interpreters of history have tried to submerge man in nature and interpret his history accordingly. Marx's dialectical materialism and Spengler's revival of Greek cyclicism built on the analogy of history and the biological cycle are famous modern examples. In both cases the result was, first,

---

[19] *Pensées*, No. 162. Cf. Bury's essay, "Cleopatra's Nose," *Selected Essays.*
[20] "The Idea of Progress," *Outspoken Essays*, II, 166 (London: Longmans, Green, 1932). Inge misses the Christian idea of history when he lets such observations persuade him to devalue history along Neoplatonic lines.
[21] Collingwood, *The Idea of History*, p. 80.

inconsistency, as these thinkers violated their own premises by recognizing important differentiae in human history; and, second, a warping of historical understanding due to deliberate neglect of important aspects of the human historical process. Similarly Herbert Butterfield, the Cambridge historian, shows:

Hitler in *Mein Kampf* pointed out that nature is ruthless since she is prodigal with individual lives and considerate only for the development of the species; and because he had taken nature as his pattern or first principle, because he envisaged primarily man-in-nature (and then transferred his conclusions or his inferences to man-in-history), he regarded this inhuman principle as one which was applicable to the human race itself. That attitude is more understandable, more dangerous, and more likely to recur than many people realize; for it is liable to be the facile heresy of the self-educated in a scientific age.[22]

Such are the weaknesses and dangers of historical studies which, by overemphasizing nature (or technology), overlook the typically human in man.

c. *Sin.* In biblical thought man, though created to love, is sinful. His historical existence is precarious, and in trying to make it secure he resorts to various stratagems in which he exalts himself and his institutions in defiance of God and his fellow men. The result is written large across the pages of history. Political institutions, which might serve useful purposes, become the expression of individual and group pride and will-to-power. Security measures develop into threats to security of others, and defensive institutions become powerful imperialisms.

As ancient prophets and modern psychologists have often shown, man is adept at devising rationalizations for his own errors. His inner flaws he projects upon his environment, attributing his failures to external causes. Institutions of private property and revolutionary communism, shortages of food and luxurious abundance, primitive helplessness and overdevelop-

[22] *Christianity and History* (London: Bell, 1949), p. 6.

ment of technology—these and many other causes have been blamed for human woes, and long books of history have been written on the basis of each of these assumptions.

In a biblical understanding of history the blame for man's troubles will not be projected upon any of these convenient scapegoats, although any may be recognized as contributing to or accentuating a specific form of trouble. An extra inch on Cleopatra's nose might have saved Marc Antony from some of his indiscretions, but it would not have made him a saint or have saved the Roman Empire. A change in economic conditions might mitigate many a difficulty in the world, but it would not redeem human nature. Judeo-Christian historical methodology, recognizing the depth of man's historical problems, will not become the tool for wistful utopians, who are unwilling to face the realities of evil, or for cynical dictators, who justify their power by pointing to the source of all evil which they are vanquishing. Knowing the universality of sin, the religiously-wise historian will not make the common and cheap error of attributing historical evil solely to one group (national, racial, religious, or economic). As Butterfield states it, ". . . the historian does not content himself with a simple picture of good men fighting bad, and he turns the crude melodrama that some people see in life into a more moving kind of tragedy."[23]

3. A consequence of the biblical understanding of human nature is the recognition that history is event-ful. It is made up of concrete, unrepeatable acts. Where there has been history there have been unique, individual events, creative or destructive. Whether the witness be the impact of a Socrates upon generations of human life, or the huge mystery-ridden stone figures on Easter Island, something unique has taken place. Emil Brunner writes:

[23] *Christianity and History*, p. 91.

The characteristic element in history is not that something happens—even in the clouds all kinds of things happen, but there is no history there—but that something is *done*. . . . History is made where decisions are made.[24]

History is not the unfolding of an eternal rationale. There is in it what Brunner calls the "irrationality of the absolutely factual,"[25] what von Hügel called "sheer happenedness."[26]

What this means to the practicing historian is indicated by Carl Becker, who quotes Rousseau's challenge: "Is it simple, is it natural that God should go in search of Moses to speak to Jean Jacques Rousseau?" Becker's disarming answer is: "Well, frankly, we do not know."[27] The answer does not mean that the historian should be gullible or neglect to sift evidence wherever possible; it does not even imply a predisposition to believe. It does mean that the historian cannot determine on an a priori basis what should have happened, and assume that such is what did happen.

This conception of the event-ful character of history belongs to the dynamic set of categories which Hebrew thought contributed to the west. It has repeatedly been shown how the Hebrew conception of time, replacing classical cyclical conceptions, contributed to the possibility of history as the modern world understands it. Collingwood has further shown how most classical thought, with its metaphysics of substance, made of change a lesser reality and thereby made historical understanding almost impossible.[28] Hebrew thought, with its basic categories of event, purpose, and activity, broke down the static conceptions and gave the impetus to modern historical understanding.

4. Despite the emphasis on freedom, biblical thought knows that history is not simply the result of a sequence of conscious

[24] *Man in Revolt* (Philadelphia: Westminster, 1947), p. 440.
[25] *Ibid.*, p. 436.
[26] *Essays and Addresses* (New York: Dutton, 1926), II, 108.
[27] *The Heavenly City of the Eighteenth Century Philosophers*, p. 46.
[28] *The Idea of History*, pp. 42-45, 47-48.

human decisions. Surely no one, including the admittedly wicked men of our age, planned the history we have lived through. Sometimes for better, sometimes for worse, the deliberate decisions of men result in events which were never decided upon. Decisions at Yalta, Potsdam, and around the world were made in a twilight where their outcome was invisible.

This aspect of history is overlooked by many purely rationalistic and voluntaristic theories. Yet surely its recognition is essential to historical analysis. It is not a uniquely biblical insight. The Greeks had their Fates and their mysterious *peripeteia*, the reversal of fortunes following *hybris*. The Hellenistic age had its *Tyche* and *Fortuna*. Shakespeare had his "destiny which shapes our ends"; Marx, his dialectic; Hegel, his "cunning of reason." Atomic scientists write of the events leading to Hiroshima with as vivid a sense of fate as can be found in Greek tragedy. Any of these conceptions, if used as a mechanical determining principle, can interfere with the understanding of history. But recognized as a symbol of the very processes of history, any can lead to understanding.

The crucial question for the over-all understanding of history is whether this nonvoluntaristic aspect of history is to be conceived as a blind, purposeless and meaningless congeries of natural and human forces; or whether it embodies some meaning and purpose. The latter alternative is the insistence of the Hebrew-Christian conception of providence—the governance of history which is hidden but meaningful and divine. The full faith in providence implies more than is sketched here; but the present endeavor is to show how one aspect of it, an aspect partially shared by some nonbiblical thought, may be helpful in the work of the historian.[29]

[29] This feature of history has been discussed helpfully by recent writers, Christian and non-Christian. See Morris Cohen, *The Meaning of Human History*, p. 127; H. A. Hodges, *Christianity and the Modern World View* (London: SCM Press, 1949), pp. 65-68; R. G. Collingwood, *The Idea of History*, pp. 53, 95, 116-17. Collingwood finds that Christianity made a dis-

IV. History and the Christian Assurance

The foregoing pages have suggested something of the relevance of biblical faith to historical understanding. An attempt has been made to state a few presuppositions which this faith offers to the practicing historian. It has not been suggested that the evidence of history "proves" these principles; nor has it been hinted that the historian should try to "demonstrate" them in his writing or teaching. It has rather been said that, when used as presuppositions or principles of interpretation, they give insight into history. Their relevance might be, and sometimes has been, recognized by those who have not accepted the Jewish or Christian faith.

The full content of Christian faith, as it relates to history, is of course something more. Christianity is not just a set of presuppositions; it is a gospel, a faith, an assurance of God's victory and man's redemption. In the words of the British Christian historian, Martin Wight:

History is not an autonomous process which secretes its own meaning as it goes along, like a cosmic endocrine gland. . . . History is a process with an author, who lies outside it. . . . It had a beginning and will have an end, both of them determined by its author; and it is only in relation to what lies outside itself that it has a meaning.[30]

The Christian believes that historical life is never utterly bereft of meaning, but that the disparate flashes of meaning, which sometimes illumine and sometimes are blotted out by history, find their only conceivable coherence in a source not contained within history. Any moment of history requires a past and a future to make sense. And the whole of history requires a larger context—a heaven above, a future ahead, or a

tinctive contribution to western historiography at this point. Butterfield gives an especially penetrating and creative analysis of the meaning for the historian of the Christian doctrine of providence; see *Christianity and History*, chap. V.

[30] "The Church, Russia, and the West," *The Ecumenical Review*, I (1948), 38.

City of God which is neither but something of both. It is God alone who can unite history, can complete it, can redeem it in his kingdom. There are within history evidences of judgment and of grace: evil is destroyed; wounds are healed, life is renewed, the chain of past guilt is broken by creative activities. But these are never complete; redemption awaits the future. *Die Weltgeschichte* is not *das Weltgericht*. God is the judge of history. And this God has revealed himself in the life of a man upon earth—a man who was crucified in history but who lives again and reigns. The faith can be stated only in the terms of New Testament eschatology, and the Christian thinker is wisely reticent in trying to probe its literal meaning too far.

Such profession of faith goes beyond the proper function of the historian *qua* historian. Yet it cannot but make a difference in his whole conception of his professional function.

It was Hegel who said that the one thing history teaches is "that peoples and governments never have learned anything from history."[31] It is more hopeful, and perhaps more truthful, to say that what people learn from history depends upon what they bring to its understanding. For the faith and the presuppositions with which they approach history will determine largely what they are able to see and what understanding they can reach. The purpose of Christian faith is not to make more competent historians; but the Christian historian may find in insights given by his faith the possibility for clearer and more profound understanding of history.

[31] *Introduction to Philosophy of History*, tr. by Sibree (New York: Willey, 1944), p. 6.

4

Religious Implications in the Humanities

Douglas Knight

I

THE last quarter century has developed a striking interest in humanistic studies—the languages and arts. At least there have been a vast number of public pronouncements made; and a great range of university programs has been developed to deal with these studies in a variety of new—and old—ways. Rather than recapitulate such well-known events, however, I should like to consider instead the implications of their appearance as a specific concern in many universities, and the way in which their best nature is to be understood.

Actually, of course, this emphasis on the humanities is only one of a number of prominent developments in our intellectual and spiritual life. The interest in religion on the part of people who in 1900 would have regarded it as a mere deterrent to social progress is another significant event of our own time. Equally striking is the ferment in thought about the proper view of literature, or about the significance of the forms of contemporary art.

These developments of interest and changes of attitude have a common core; they may involve different groups of people, but they also all involve an interpretation of experience quite distinct from that shared, for instance, in certain of its important aspects by Sir Isaac Newton and Mr. Julian Huxley. Indeed many of the recent controversies in literature and art have been—though the antagonists seem not always to realize it— precisely about the world view suggested by the work of Descartes and Newton, and elaborated into dogma by writers like Herbert Spencer and Thomas Henry Huxley.

In his sensitivity to the partialness of the view of reality developed by that dogma, Matthew Arnold is one of our immediate ancestors. He suggests constantly the pressure of its suspicion of the personal, the intuitively perceived, the other than rationalistically ordered—suggests that pressure, though by different means, as urgently as Wordsworth before him. Such a tension between the poet's world and the scientist-philosopher's is one meaning, furthermore, of the wistfulness of *In Memoriam*; and it is one aspect of the fatalism which finally destroys a novel like *Jude the Obscure*.

We are the inheritors, then, of a divisiveness in the senses and intellect whose implications have been developing for three hundred years. The nineteenth-century tug of war between science and religion was one natural outgrowth of this division, though not quite in the way one might assume. That struggle developed in good measure from the fact that religious thought had succumbed—as the poetic tradition had not—to the dominant concern for objective statements about a measurable universe. Controversies which continued through the nineteenth century over the literal acceptability of Old Testament statements about creation issued from the assurance of the previous century that Christian dogma offered statements of the same order and type of validity as those which were being erected into the dogma of physics. As the method of physics began to extend itself into geology and prehistory, this assurance broke down. Christianity had mortgaged its house, and now the new owner appeared to take possession.

Where religion failed in its attempt to assume the sanction of the scientists' metaphysic, poetry and the other arts were split many ways by the very existence of that metaphysic. Their area of operation was progressively narrowed to what is disparagingly called "the subjective"; society more and more denied them what Hobbes and Locke had denied from the start, a world of significance upon which and with which they could directly work. What began with the scientists as a metaphysical assumption about "reality" developed inevitably into a supposed statement of fact about all experience; and a situation like that of our own time was well started on its development. Poets were more and more separated from a responsible position in society, humored in their separation but ultimately castigated and ignored for it.

This very ostracism helped to create a solution, however. We see it foreshadowed in the French symbolist poetry of the later nineteenth century and even in the "art for art" concerns of late Victorian England as well as of the continent. The self-consciousness of the practitioners in both these groups is an indication of their fundamental desire to break with the hierarchies of value assumed by the rest of society, their wish to claim for painting and poetry a validity comparable with other orderings of human experience. The extreme to which individuals in both movements were willing to go is an indication of the seriousness of the battle they felt they were waging. A cult of aesthetes, like a cult of suffragettes, insisted through its exaggeration on the real importance of the object of the cult. Mannerisms were, among other things, a way of acting out—of dramatizing in the root sense—attitudes so unacceptable to society that without distortion they would never be considered at all. By their explicit rejection of the rest of the world, many artists set up their counterpressure against society's implicit repudiation of them.

Such suggestive extremism in the arts appeared as the forerunner of work which was to express the urgency of that extremism without its blatant self-containedness. The writings of Joyce, Eliot, Proust, or Yeats are a modification of, rather than a mere rebellion against, the world view accepted for two and a half centuries. Paralleling the work of philosophers and historians like Whitehead, Burtt, and Collingwood, they develop again the central insight that abstract patterns for experience, though they often interpenetrate the quality of individual events, cannot be described—in the words of a recent naturalistic writer —as "the conceptions that exact knowledge suggests to us."

As modern descriptive physics is making constantly clearer, exact knowledge as an entity in itself—or as much of an entity as one can make it—does not suggest anything at all. Either one accepts the comfortable chaos of the logical positivists or he accepts with all its complexities the fact that the order in experience, while obviously it does not exist as a mere product of the mind, no more plausibly exists as a series of events objective to and separate from that mind. The complex task of our time as the best artists of the twentieth century see it is the penetrating and understanding of this double universe of perceiver and perceived—and, even more important, the assimilation of it to one single view of experience which will include and display the interanimating richness of the mind which sees and the world which is seen.

This reassertion of their responsible position by painters and novelists, for instance, suggests a number of problems which the universities in their concern for the humanities must also deal with. The universities owe a unique responsibility to both present and past, a responsibility to explain and interpret the very series of events which I have outlined. For the loss by the arts of their proper place in society, and their rediscovery in this century of what that place should be, has profound implications for the university study of music or the classics, French or painting.

These implications have perhaps been most vigorously developed by the controversies of the last few years about the value of "historical scholarship" for the study of the arts. It is significant that history should be the focus of disagreement; one is not free of it in our society even in his attitude toward the most contemporary event. Economic and sociological interpretations of literature, for instance, place a concern with the history of the moment above their concern with the actual nature of any of the humanities. When we shift to the more orthodox form of history, of course, we find that the hope for absolute sanction expressed by the attempt to make exact sciences out of the various studies of society has also projected itself into our customary view of the past. Often we like to think that we can formulate description and assemble fact completely enough to give objective validity to our analyses of other times than our own.

The result of this view of history for the humanities has been a passionate desire to know, for example, what Homer was really like for the Greeks. The shift in the theory of translation between 1720 and 1850 is a brilliant reflection of this desire; Arnold could hope, as Pope could not, to reproduce in English the effect of Homer—the effect conceived as existent in the mind of a nineteenth-century Greek scholar, but not actually existent in and through Arnold's own time. Rather it was pictured as a true reknowing, the obliteration of twenty-five hundred years by the time machine of the intellect. Homer for the good Greek scholar existed not primarily as a book to be read but as a past to be re-created. He could talk about the meaning of the *Iliad* only if he could somehow give objective order to that meaning in terms of what he knew the Greeks behind the poem to have been. One started by asking how the Greeks saw the poem; he finished by refusing to grant anything for the poem which he did not find evidence for in the society which first read it.

II

Perhaps the most curious result of this procedure was that the quest for historical absolutes ended in the destruction of that prime historical fact, the developing present. Just as the scientist tried to enunciate his generalizations without reference to the full character of the actual events in time which were his experiments, so the historian and with him the literary man fled from the relativities and uncertainties of the present to the order of immobilized human events—events fixed in the amber of the past. One may well interpret one aspect of the nineteenth century passion for historical certainty as a flight from the present urged on by the same avoidance of direct experience characteristic of post-Newtonian physical science.

The twin of such an escape to the past was, of course, the escape to the future embodied in the myth of progress; the two forms of flight were mutually supporting, and between them the present tended to vanish. It was replaced by a sense of ceaseless motion in time, motion which combined past and future either in the hopeful determinism of a Comte or the hopeless determinism of a Spengler. In both cases the effectiveness and indeed the real existence of the present were denied. One dealt with the shock of immediate experience by regarding it only obliquely, by considering it as result or cause but never as complete event. The place for such events was in the changeless past, or in the inevitable future which resulted from that past.

Such a concept of history, then, turned almost inevitably into a scale of validity for various kinds of experience. Much of the suspicion of contemporary writing and painting still found in so many universities results not from a healthy desire to avoid premature praise, but from the usually unvocalized conviction that such work should not be thought about until it can be interpreted as some form of historical event. It is felt that the terms in which a poem should be criticized are those of origin, influence, cultural relevance—"place," in short—and that they can be developed only if one removes himself from it in time and thus puts it into a fixed context.

It is obvious enough that this view of contemporary writing or painting can often be a destructive one; but as I suggested a moment ago in speaking of Arnold it raises even more curious and complex problems if one is dealing with the arts of the past. Those are problems of which, in one form, artists have always had to be aware; and of which a line of great critics have always been aware. The completed work of art is not adequately bracketed by psychoanalysis of the artist or by the evocation of a context of events—or even of ideas—within which the work was originally produced. The questions which one must ask if he is to understand *King Lear* or Dürer's *Ritter, Tod und Teufel* must in some way be asked of the work itself. The necessary conditions for interpreting either of these pieces grow from its nature as a work of art, as much as from its place in time or from the web of psychological concerns which might lead an artist to be interested in trying to produce it.

Once we have said so much, and granted that a painting or a poem, though it must have a certain relation to these two sources, is not to be defined and limited by them, we can begin to understand why the recent critical disagreements are so important. For not only do they remind us that certain critics share the attitude which has enabled the best artists of our time to assert their right to deal with the full order of experience; these disagreements are equally important because they enable us to discover the proper way in which the humanities can regard and interpret the past with which they must be so largely concerned.

This does not mean for a moment, of course, that we expect to find one common form for the disagreement between so-called formalistic and historical criticism. But the host of minute factual and factional distinctions is far less important than the basic question of principle so often obscured or forgotten, a principle at heart involving nothing less than the nature of what one is to call valid experience. Is it only to be found in sensory or abstract events? Or can it possibly be found in the formal treatment of words or colors or shapes? If we incline to the second view, then what is the basic character of a work of art which gives it serious claims on us; and what are the implications of those claims for the study and teaching of the humanities? These, it seems to me, are the questions which underlie the critical controversy of which I have been speaking, with all its lengthy past development; and the questions which also underlie the new concern of the colleges with humanistic studies.

A work of art depends upon and at the same time evokes two kinds of order: that of tradition, and that of metaphor and symbol. These two aspects of it have much in common but above all they share the quality of existing fully within a given poem or painting and at the same time of creating a field of relationships beyond its strict limits of statement. This field of relationships takes with tradition the form of an independent and self-contained structure for a given work like *Paradise Lost*, but at the same time a structure which implies a whole range of other poems and establishes complex relations between them and *Paradise Lost*. These relations are temporal, though in a special sense, and they are finally significant as they exist within a given poem of the tradition rather than between the various works which embody it.

The temporal attitude of a living tradition differs from our ordinary idea of time because it constantly relates a living past to a living present. This has often been misunderstood, because tradition can so easily be lost between history on the one hand and convention on the other. As a word it clearly has connotations borrowed from both; and the result has all too often been the assumption that if one is traditional he is concerned with perpetuating convention out of the dead past. Such a definition fails to take into account the fact that the potential difference between tradition and convention is precisely the difference between life and lifelessness. By this I do not mean to be harsh toward convention in art and experience; but it should never be forgotten that convention at its best provides the material out of which something may be made. A conventional way of painting a picture or writing a love song may exist without the existence of any value in the works produced. All that is required is a consistency between the qualities of the so-called "new" piece and the already defined qualities of the convention. As a result we never have to ask where a convention leads, but only where it comes from.

A work which we have the right to call traditional, on the other hand, is not so because we can predict from the other works of the tradition what it will be like. It is so because it draws strength from those works without ever being merely dependent on their strength. It gives as much as it takes; the works behind it share in its success and become illuminated through its achievement with their common form. The relation between heroic poems, for instance, may be expressed in continuing conventions like the roll call of heroes or the extended simile from nature. But it derives its real significance rather from a continuing interpretation of experience, in which the various conventions participate. One could fabricate the outward shape of an epic, but not the use of that outward shape to body forth a persistent concern with man's struggle to create glory from his mortal infirmities. In contemplating and interpreting that struggle a late poem like *Paradise Lost*, for instance, learns enough from an early poem in the tradition like the *Iliad* so that it is not unfair to either work to say that Satan could not receive his full development without the previous development of Achilles. Such a fact modifies the independence of neither poem, while it does increase our interest in and our actual awareness of the earlier interpretation of destructive pride. *Para-*

dise *Lost* creates among other things a commentary on the *Iliad*, as well as on the *Odyssey* and the *Aeneid*. By being itself it enhances them, while in turn it could not be itself without them. This reciprocal relation is the heart of tradition, and it accounts for the special temporal connection between works in the tradition. It is a relation which could not exist without their occurrence in sequential time, but more significantly it is one which, as Mr. Eliot says, recognizes that "the whole of the literature of Europe from Homer . . . composes a simultaneous order."

III

This concept of order suggests why the relationships of the tradition are primarily within works rather than between them—as they would be if one were concerned with the history of the epic. Such relationships exist in order to place a single event—in this case a poetic event—within a context which will permit it the most heightened and at the same time the most inclusive significance. We know that the tradition is alive through our immediate experience with it, immediate within an individual work. And it is only by such immediacy that we are able to recognize the complexity of traditional art, a paradoxical complexity which by virtue of its very uniqueness reminds us of its relationships. Adam is no more to be confused with Aeneas than Hans Castorp in *The Magic Mountain* is; but neither Adam nor Castorp is known in his fullest nature unless we recollect through them both Aeneas' dream of devotion and his daily temptations away from that dream. The *Aeneid* actually participates in the other works. One does not say to himself merely that Hans is like Aeneas in certain ways; he says rather that the *Aeneid* is one aspect of what *The Magic Mountain* is about. If he wishes to, furthermore, he may with justice say the converse; *The Magic Mountain* is also in the *Aeneid*. The individual works are mutually illuminating, but more strongly than that they are mutually lifegiving. It is this sharing, this interpenetration to which we point when we talk of tradition.

Such an interpenetration produces, as the final characteristic of tradition, a special kind of objectivity—the objectivity of the community, of one mind working with the best of what other minds have done, not denying its individuality but triumphing over its isolation. The partialness of the personal is brought under control; the work of art is oriented, not toward what may happen to interest the individual artist, but toward what he is able to see as valid through the insight of his own mind fusing with that of others. The completed work is a common possession, and is judged by the extent to which it develops the common perception without departing from it. The traditional artist is protected by the company he keeps from falling to the mediocre average, but he is equally protected from wandering off toward the private or the eccentric. What he creates has the vigor of the personal and the authority of the communal.

These characteristics of tradition in literature constantly combine with its other chief discipline, that of metaphor and symbol. Together they are responsible for the fact of complexity as the central quality of a work of art—not complexity of statement, but complexity of implication and suggestion. One can make statements, and very complex ones, by a great number of other means. The characteristic of art is actually to create events, to reveal the fullness of something rather than to talk about it. This is why paraphrase fails with the arts; a reader cannot describe something which is only itself. This does not mean that he cannot establish relationships by means of it, or that he cannot understand it fully. But he cannot translate it into other terms than its own; he cannot value it merely as an instrument to be used.

If he is kept from doing so because tradition multiplies so enormously the possibilities of meaning within a given work of art, he is equally kept from stepping outside the work by metaphor. Where tradition suggests the one in the many, though ne'ver dominant so as to eliminate the many, metaphor suggests the many in the one. Its richness of suggestion results from the creation of a nodal point, a precise event in which a whole order of significance is implicated. Satan in *Paradise Lost*

> so endur'd, till on the Beach
> Of that inflamed Sea, he stood and call'd
> His Legions, Angel Forms, who lay intrans't
> Thick as Autumnal Leaves that strow the Brooks
> In *Vallombrosa*, where th' *Etrurian* shades
> High overarch't imbow'r; or scatter'd sedge
> Afloat, when with fierce Winds *Orion* arm'd
> Hath vex't the Red-Sea Coast, whose waves o'erthrew
> *Busiris* and his *Memphian* Chivalry,
> While with perfidious hatred they pursu'd
> The Sojourners of *Goshen*, who beheld
> From the safe Shore thir floating Carcasses
> And broken Chariot Wheels, so thick bestrown
> Abject and lost lay these, covering the Flood,
> Under amazement of thir hideous change.

Through the most complex sort of multiple metaphor the poem develops the nature of the fallen angels, and by implication the nature of what a fall of their sort is. "Thir hideous change" is a center for the associated images; they all deal with some form of it, and taken as a unit they develop the loss, the violence and the presumption which lie behind it. The three partial similes within the passage throw their emphasis upon these qualities in turn, but we are not permitted to separate them. The poem's rhetorical order demands that we take such varying aspects of the Fall together, as we take the similes together. One cannot ultimately separate the two; a basic consideration of the meaning of evil for *Paradise Lost* is implicit in the precise interdependence of parts which creates the complete simile.

Metaphor grows from a point, then, and develops its significance through the aptness of the point chosen. Like it, a symbol depends upon the precision of relationship between the event which is made the symbol and the event which is symbolized. The symbol has a further complexity, however, of including completely within itself both aspects of this relation. A metaphor of bare trees does not necessarily include old age; but the garden in *The Romance of the Rose,* if it is to exist at all, exists as the anatomy of a particular kind of love. Another way of making this distinction would be to say that symbols do not exist apart from a dramatic structure of some sort—whether implied or explicit. We may abstract them from an event, as the rose and cross have been abstracted, but we can do so only because they have had a full dramatic development to make them entities. Metaphor and simile unfold by description, and we judge them by the justice with which their parts—like the parts of a landscape painting—suggest one whole; symbol unfolds by action, and we judge it by the effectiveness with which the events implied in it lead to one inevitable end. Homer's comparison of the moving host of the Achaeans to a swarm of bees pouring out of a hollow rock is an archetype of the first, Milton's development of Satan a perfected form of the second.

Both symbol and metaphor share with the function of tradition as I have outlined it an emphasis on the fullness and immediacy of experience, an acceptance of a certain form, at least, of final reality as present in the particulars of art. Unlike the anthropologist's investigation of a symbol, the artist's use of it is centered in what it may become, not in what it may have come from. He does not pursue the origin of his materials, but their end. He asks what can be made; and he knows that the ancestry of a symbol no more than that of a man proves what is there. This power to become something—a power almost of life and growth—is equally the achievement of tradition, of course. The result of its fusion with metaphor and symbol in a completed work is a sense of the living presence of the constant and universal in the immediate and particular. The richness of significance possible through all these means is also a special order of significance not to be created in any other way. The lifeless structure of abstraction and the chaotic vigor of immediacy are made into one organism, the senses and the intelligence appear as an entity.

Faced with so complex an order, the critic—that is, the teacher of the humanities at his best—has a responsibility both toward the works of art themselves and toward the community he serves. The artist cannot maintain this double relationship. It is sometimes said that writers and painters are irresponsible; as I have already implied, such statements grow from a misunderstanding and implicit denial of the real responsibility of the artist. He owes his duty to the work itself, to the necessity of controlling into one whole the endlessly multiplying possibilities out of which the work must be shaped. But such a demand is obviously separate from that which emerges when the painting or poem has been finished; for we have no right to ask the artist to take account of the unevenness of his audience.

The critic, on the other hand, must take account of a great number of qualities characteristic of that audience. He must deal with the artist's work in such a way that its implications are understood without being falsified; he must deal with the artist's audience in such a way that it comes gradually to accept poetry or painting in their own terms. If he succeeds with these two inseparable responsibilities, justice for the work and justice for the reader, he will himself be a kind of creative artist; he will have produced an analogue to the mediation between subject and object which a painting or a poem creates. But he will be the artist at one remove, causing the work of art to open like a Japanese flower, unfolding in the minds of its audience possibilities which without his help would remain unregarded in the work.

Above all he must help that audience to overcome a desire

which he must also fight in himself—that of having the comfortable pleasure of a great poem without the overwhelming shock and pressure of it. The true critic and teacher must root out the mere aesthete in us all, the desire to stop with art as with religion at the pleasing relationships of the surfaces of things. He must help to make clear instead the necessity of facing and mastering the almost intolerable revelations of the *Iliad* or *Ulysses*. He must really bring together two ways of seeing life—that of our daily experience of the world and that of the work of art.

The two are, of course, in one sense not separable; if the work does not have certain relations with what we already know, then we cannot penetrate it. But life and art can no more be identified than they can be separated; the perception about human existence which we say we find in a poem is more accurately to be described as the poem itself. If we paraphrase the poem, we lose the insight which was to be the purpose of the paraphrase. A work of art is not experience, but it animates, informs, and actually transforms experience. By means of an illusion of experience it reveals the things which are the meaning of experience, which may be half sensed but cannot be fully grasped until they have their proper and complete form. The critic constantly struggles to point out, as the artist does not have to, the complex relationships which are understood only through the ordering of art—the interpenetration of love and blind anger in *Othello*, of modesty and prudery in the *Hippolytus*. He tries to show that the meaning of a work is not what it can be made to say but what it helps to organize as perception and insight.

The teacher of the humanities, then, owes his major responsibility to a particular means of apprehending reality. It does not matter whether he teaches the classics or the history of painting or the theory of modern poetry; his basic concern is for the techniques of the art with which he deals, as those techniques can be shown to create a consistent significance for some area of experience. If he fully accepts this concern, furthermore, then he is sooner or later in contact with religious as well as artistic insight. For when religious formulation and artistic order operate in their proper areas and ways, their chief means and certain of their chief ends are held in common. If either succumbs to supposed naturalism, the two then become hopelessly disparate; but though they must not be identified they normally and properly shape human existence in analogous ways.

IV

There is perhaps no more obvious indication of this sharing than the Hebrew-Christian tradition itself, which has at its core a dramatic structure starting with the symbolic event of the creation and concluding with the perpetually recurrent life, sacrifice and Resurrection of Christ—the whole making possible an attitude toward experience which constantly guides us from the literal to the symbolic, and from the once perceived to the generally understood. As with an artistic tradition, the historical past disappears in favor of a constantly enriched present—or at least of a present which may constantly be enriched. The individual within such a tradition, furthermore, is enabled by it to transcend himself without losing himself—that is, to achieve within a religious order the same kind of objectivity which we have already seen in traditional literature. Just as in the experience of love one becomes more his true self as he gives himself to others, so through the wisdom of the tradition one possesses his personal understanding more validly since its communal quality shelters him from his potential solipsisms.

A religious life of this sort, in making the past present just as the life of a work of art makes the past present, is no more bounded by the mere present than by the mere past. In both aesthetic and religious experience one transforms the temporal even while his awareness of the urgencies of his immediate experience is heightened. He is freed from the concept of time which dominates our society—a moving time whose chief attributes are novelty and exhaustion, where newness is virtue and constant alteration therefore a necessary condition of life. Instead he can accept time as a constant present, a present which offers the recurrent opportunity for decision and therefore the constant possibility of building toward certain absolutes—both operations implicitly denied by the interpretation of time as motion.

An analogous modification of sequential time is one of the most significant aspects of religious symbol. Where tradition reshapes the past by making a relationship from a sequence, symbol reshapes the present by embodying in the immediate event a coherence which reaches beyond it. The tradition of religious thought helps us perceive with a common intelligence; the symbol of religious faith helps us see and sense ourselves within the common existence. Its dramatic nature concentrates our understanding in as well as beyond the inescapable qualities of human life which follow from our centrally paradoxical nature—that nature which receives its basic expression in the story of the Fall and the Resurrection. The ego-centered aspiration which ends in self-destruction is a permanent fact of experience; religious symbol is the only means of holding all its implications in a properly kinetic relation with one another. The emphasis of this active relationship, furthermore, is on a kind of development which is not the outgrowth of time but rather of the precise nature of the situation with which the symbol works. The birth of Christ prefigures his death; the significance of his life exists, not as the abstract of a series of events in time, but as a simultaneous whole whose nature demands each of its parts and in turn justifies each of those parts. The religious symbol, like the literary one, creates a permanent and nontemporal order for insight which we have only in a fragmentary way within time. Symbolism is an indirect but therefore complete means of fashioning the significance of direct experience.

A realization of this continuity in means between religious formulation and the basic nature of the humanities puts the greatest demands upon a teacher. He is responsible for the re-establishing and encouragement of attitudes which make religious faith possible as more than an incoherent longing. He is responsible for the reaffirmation of the fact that vigor and accuracy of mind need not necessarily—or even centrally—be associated first with the supposedly "objective" studies. And as a result of this reaffirmation he is in a position to guide us again to a recognition of the perceiving mind as an aspect of the event it perceives. The other great disciplines order the universe around and within society, but only the humanities reveal man alive within and inseparable from the order.

It is for this reason that theology remains in many aspects the archetype of humanistic studies; it considers an order which places man in his fullness within the fullness of outer experience. When J. S. Whale remarks that "the only really good man is the pardoned man, since he alone has been set free from the self-centeredness which underlies all sin," he suggests the irreplaceable function of a doctrine like the Atonement in permitting one to recognize a sought-for inward state—freedom from self-concerned and self-devouring evil—together with an outward Presence from which the possibility of that freedom must come. We are purged of our pride by an admission of it in objective terms; in providing these terms the Atonement allows us to understand the nature of the weakness with which it helps us to deal. It is not merely a projection of inward unrest, nor merely a commitment of faith, but the two in complete interaction.

The difficulties faced by theological thought today, of course, are those which result from its desire to present such complex views in the face of far simpler dominant modes of thought. But that identical complexity is accepted and sometimes mastered by the artist, with whom as with the theologian lies the responsibility of making a whole world again, of redeeming a fragmentation of experience at least as disastrous as the blight of political separativeness. The technique of dividing knowledge so that one might master its parts has been a valuable servant of our past, but one feels too often that it is the master of our present. It is the task of the humanities to break categories which exist in logic rather than experience, and to replace them with perception which has the richness of that experience together with a completeness lacking in any individual's contact with it.

The absolute thus created by the humanities or by theology is not constructed in a linear fashion like the postulated and abstract absolutes of the physical sciences. Rather this absolute exists in full recognition of the fact that what we call the final in art is not so; but it exists equally in recognition of the fact that art possesses a quality of the final which pragmatic data by themselves can never claim. The literal and pragmatic, after all, can by definition never be ultimate; they belong to a world view dependent upon endless sequence, and one sees its philosophical consequence in Mr. Julian Huxley's remark that God becomes less useful as we come to know more and more about the universe. The traditional and symbolic, on the other hand, are final in the sense that their central issues are not those of time but of the meaning in certain relationships; the action of the *Iliad* like the action of *The Magic Mountain* has as its end the creation of ordered insight in which intuition, reason, and imagination fuse to one whole. The view of things implicit in the work of the artist, as of the theologian, includes this complex order together with the knowledge that it is a human approximation, a human penetration of order which lies beyond the human. The sense of mystery, almost of miracle involved in the proper study of the humanities results from a recognition of the way in which the known exists within the unknown, suggesting how one may regard that unknown but never usurping the place of deity by pretending to be the sum of things. The absolute of the humanities has humility at its root; its bases must be the most complex of human perceptions wedded to the humblest kind of faith. They must be and are the bases of mature religion.

5

Norms and Valuations in Social Science

Walter G. Muelder

AS THE social scientist looks out upon his world today and
seeks to make his contribution to the solution of its most
pressing personal and group problems, he finds changing presuppositions and the quest for valid universal norms the order
of the day. In their capacities as citizens religious leaders and
social scientists have developed a marked consciousness of responsibility. Indeed, the conception of the responsible community is a touchstone both in religious circles, such as the
World Council of Churches, and in scientific associations.
Definitely discredited, though not entirely eliminated, is the
dilettante. To some extent cultural relativism is still a factor to
be reckoned with. A deep sense of seriousness has settled upon
the community of scholars and with it more understanding and
rapprochement between religion and social research. Values
have become not merely curious entities to be described in various settings but are viewed as powers capable of creating an
emerging world culture and providing tolerable justice and satisfaction the world round. Such values are pressing the scientist
to go beyond his traditional Comtean positivism into more ad-
venturous and difficult perspectives. He is moving from antireligious presuppositions into a realm more friendly to Christian
faith.

Thus social science reflects in part its own social environment and the world cultural crisis. In America the past twenty-five years have seen three major challenges which have profoundly affected social studies, the Great Depression, World War II, and the United Nations. In the present chapter we cannot hope to outline all the great developments in contemporary social research. We are selecting those changing perspectives and conceptions of human nature, social responsibility and value norms which are especially relevant to the function of religion in American education. There is to that extent an admitted bias in the selection of material and pointing up of issues. The bearing of the discussion upon the responsibilities of instruction and research in our institutions of higher education will be evident to the reader throughout.

I. Social Science and Citizenship

American social scientists have long noted the critical dilemmas of the nation, but not until the Great Depression did they come into their own as citizens and public persons. The caricature of the professor in government with his academic cap presiding over a bureau, pulling fantastic ideas out of the air while practical men of affairs looked on with helpless despair, is a familiar symbol of this sudden new role. Though initially the butt of sarcasm and even of angry jokes the specialist was there to stay. Economists, sociologists, anthropologists, and political scientists came into their own, with the campuses of the nation turning attention somewhat from physical technology to social engineering. Since the significant and critical problems of business cycles, unemployment, morale, racketeering, labor organization, industrial violence, public works, social security, agriculture and the like took the center of the stage, social science was forced into new directions. There were not only the special problems of limited interests but the problem of the economy as a whole. From the static assumptions of a complacent "neo-capitalism" men turned more to social dynamics and to logical tools adapted to conflict and social planning. The theories of Keynes and Marx and Lenin made an abrupt entry into the classroom and gained the public ear. They represent here a shift in all fields.

If the Great Depression with its predominantly economic and emergency governmental emphasis gave to the social scientist new roles and to social engineering a new significance, World War II made heavy demands on psychologists and anthropologists in addition because of the challenge of racism and the defense of democratic values and ideals. Scientists were called upon to commit themselves and their science. Is one racial group inferior to another? What of the dignity of man as man? Is democracy merely a conditioned response, a mere social relativity with no claims transcending nations? Is democracy practical or is it merely a luxury for wealthy free-enterprise nations? Is freedom merely what Americans want or ought it have a rightful place in the lives of men and groups suffering from totalitarian regimes? The problem of universal norms could no longer be side-stepped in what many had tried to keep as value-free domains of scientific inquiry. Significant social problems drove the scientist beyond traditional positivism. We shall develop this conception more fully below. Gunnar Myrdal's book, *An American Dilemma*, may be taken as symbolic of the frank commitment to certain personalistic values on the part of innumerable social scientists.

The legacy of World War II has challenged social thought to envisage and guide mankind into some viable world community. To set nations, religions, economic patterns, languages and the like side by side in a neutral row of differentiated entities, or even to show their interrelations abstractedly, no longer suffices except in purely preliminary phases of study. Today the anthropologist is called on to state, if he can, what culture patterns will work in a universal frame of reference. What of cultural pluralism? What of the future of minorities? As the present writer views the problem we must all ask: Are the values and social goals of the United Nations' Charter anthropologically sound? Is the "Universal Declaration of Human Rights" adopted by the General Assembly of the United Nations really to be the group of social purposes canalizing the social energy of the whole world? Social scientists had their share in drafting this Declaration. Anyone who reads it recognizes its western slant. Social science in all its branches has much work laid out for itself if it is committed, along with the General Assembly, to the following:

> The General Assembly proclaims this Universal Declaration of Human Rights as a common standard of achievement for all peoples and all nations, to the end that every individual and every organ of society, keeping this declaration constantly in mind, shall strive by teaching and education to promote respect for these rights and freedoms and by progressive measures, national and international, to secure their universal and effective recognition and observance, both among the peoples of member states themselves and among the peoples of territories under their jurisdiction.

The question which religion on the campus and the social scientist alike face is whether they really regard these values as the basis of a new world culture. In any event the situation emphasizes the role of social goals and value norms in social science.

From the standpoint of religions like Christianity and Judaism the personalistic values of the Universal Declaration of Human Rights may well appear to be only natural implications of the ethical monotheism of the Bible. The special significance of the situation is that these values and ideals are now projected as inductions from anthropology and other social sciences or as social engineering goals which anticipate their confirmation in further social research.

II. BIAS IN SOCIAL SCIENCE

There are explicit and marked indications that social scientists have a concern for induced social change today. When sociology and economics made their debut as organized scientific societies in America late in the nineteenth century, they expressed concern for social reform. Indeed, there was an intimate connection between their aims and those of the rising social gospel. Richard T. Ely, for example, viewed economics as an application of the second great commandment of Jesus. Early papers in the journals of sociology often favored quite explicitly some form of Christian socialism. It was not out of keeping with the general spirit of much social science for the first encyclopedia in the field to have been edited by a clergyman, W. D. P. Bliss, and called *Encyclopedia of Social Reform.* But soon the dominant *laissez-faire* spirit of the nation and the desire to emulate mathematical and physical sciences made themselves felt. Non-normative, purely descriptive objectivity was the ideal. Purposes and values were eschewed. Interest in social reform was for moralists preachers, and philosophers who had not yet reached the maturity of scientific insight into law. However, this perspective gave way substantially in 1929, when, as some say, the nineteenth century came to an end. That year President Hoover appointed a committee to make a study of social trends in the United States. In the report which was issued in 1932 this major query was posed: "How can society improve its economic organization so as to make full use of the possibilities held out by the march of science, invention and engineering skill, without victimizing many of its workers, and without incurring such general disasters as the depression of 1930-32?" The answer was implied that only through planning and conscious control could a better adjustment between man and his material culture be achieved.

Some leading scholars were quick to point out that the previous training of the scientist included "no awareness of the social consequences of his work," while the training of the statesman and administrator had no provision "for the potentiality of rapid scientific advance" with "no prevision of the technical forces which are shaping the society in which he lives." Not only public officials but certain learned societies and foundations turned attention to the relation of science to society. The Social Science Research Council, the American Council on Education, the National Academy of Sciences, the Carnegie Corporation, the Laura Spelman Rockefeller Foundation, the Falk Foundation and others, played important parts in assisting in the new direction of research. In 1937 at the American Association for the Advancement of Science the current movement was described as "an effort to shift from science for science's sake to science for the sake of humanity."

The concept of social engineering has largely replaced the earlier notion of social reform. Scholars now recognize that there has been a bias in social science against induced change, especially against all attempts to assist social change through legislation. The supposed validity of Sumner's conceptions of "folkways" and "mores" has been challenged. Gunnar Myrdal argues:

> By stowing the commonly held valuations into the system of mores, conceived of as a homogeneous, unproblematic, fairly static, social entity, the investigator is likely to underestimate the actual differences between individuals and groups and the actual fluctuations and changes in time. . . . Sumner's construction contains a valid generalization and offers a useful methodological tool for studying primitive cultures and isolated stationary folk-communities under the spell of magic and sacred tradition. . . . The theory is, however, crude and misleading when applied to a Western society in process of rapid industrialization. . . . It conceals what is most important in our society; the changes, the conflicts, the absence of static equilibria, the lability in all relations even when they are temporarily, though perhaps for decades, held at a

standstill. The valuation spheres, in such a society as the American, more nearly resemble powder-magazines than they do Sumner's concept of mores.[1]

In much past social research the ideological tendencies have been biased in a static, *laissez-faire*, do-nothing, and conservative direction. Such valuations which are masked behind descriptive objectivity really serve to injure the disfavored groups in society.

With the increased use of social engineering the fact-finding, the scientific concepts, and the theories of social causation will themselves be instrumental in planning social change. Because of the New Deal, the War and the challenge of the present crisis the scientist will more and more become familiar and competent with planning concepts and with practical action. He is himself an actor in a drama in which he wishes to be participant observer. He will never again be given the opportunity, says Myrdal, "to build up so 'disinterested' a social science" as he once conceived to be his "ideal." In the search for knowledge and control of social causation the environmentalist trend in science is bound to continue. Along with it will continue to go the traditional American faith in human beings. Accompanying it also is the view, which we shall elaborate later, that "human nature" can be changed and the confidence that human deficiencies and unhappiness are, for the most part, preventable.

In developing a concern for normative sociology and for social engineering, the social scientist completes the full cycle and returns approximately to the practical position held by the leaders in the Christian social gospel movement of fifty years ago. The theological frame of reference is, of course, absent. There is, moreover, no well-articulated metaphysics of value, no Christian theism, which provides an ultimate ground of norms and persons. Neither is there a fully developed philosophy of social science with a system of theoretical ethics coherently integrating these

[1] Gunnar Myrdal, *An American Dilemma* (New York: Harper, 1944), p. 1032.

sciences into a moral whole. Yet there is some evidence that social scientists are working with norms consistent with a Christian philosophy of society. There are, of course, resources and insights in Christianity which have not been fully exploited by scientific hypotheses. Our concern here, however, is with the internal development in social science according to its own autonomous and practical logic. It is this internal logic and the interactions of research projects with the social situation which drive the scientist beyond spectator description to participant decisions. Social scientists differ radically as to what is involved in responsible participation from the scientific viewpoint, some holding that the scientist may depict the social consequences of possible decisions; others going so far as to include valuational commitments in science itself.

There are dangers in the emphasis on the practical applications of science and social engineering. Some of these will appear more fully later in our essay. It should be noted here that in social engineering one cannot emulate the exactness of the physical technologist. The social engineer cannot assess with any such assurance as the latter the strains and stresses, the reactions of human beings to the measures he may advocate as can the civil engineer. "Should he therefore," asks MacIver, "as social scientist, refuse to advocate any?" MacIver replies, "That would be the denial of the validity of the knowledge he possesses." "If the social scientist does not use [his knowledge], having first acquired it, is he not denying his social responsibility without thereby vindicating his title of social scientist?" The risk of inexactness must be taken.

A second risk also is unavoidable. The objective of action is itself the product of a value judgment. MacIver along with Myrdal rejects the old stereotype that the social scientist must eschew value judgments. Here are two vital considerations:

[1] The danger of bias besets the social scientist in every kind of investigation and his problem is to guard himself against it, in short to

maintain his scientific-mindedness, and not to shun areas of knowledge where he may be susceptible to bias.

[2] Applied science is in all fields the concomitant of pure science, and to it we owe all the civilization that man has built—why should it not be so in the social field? In this respect the social scientist is in precisely the same position as the chemist, the bio-chemist, the biologist, the physicist, and all the rest.[2]

Beyond these negative considerations there are on the positive side serious scientific considerations emphasized also by MacIver, Myrdal, and others like Linton and Kluckhohn.

The social scientist who seeks to avoid bias by complacently refusing to investigate issues that are infected by it is not thereby saving his scientific soul. He is like the saint who would guard himself against temptation by abjuring the world where temptations abound—and then is beset by new and more insidious temptations in his retreat. His boasted objectivity is apt to develop into indifference or into a not too secret satisfaction with the *status quo*.

There is frequently a bias in refusing to deal with biases. Moreover, the scientist may shut himself off from large fields of social reality which are of the greatest importance to his fellow men. That is a puny type of social science which does not grapple with axiological issues in the value-loaded and emotionally charged areas of human experience. Avoidance of bias is self-defeating. "His disinterestedness is likely to be or to become the expression of an interest, and he cannot protect himself against *that* bias because he proudly proclaims it to mean the absence of all bias."[3] Moreover, bias is not inherently bad. If there is truth about values, such truth deserves to be known. The truth in Christianity may be difficult to establish scientifically, but the value which biases argument may be true, nevertheless.

There are also certain ethical considerations which the scientist has to face in a democratic culture. The anthropologist as

[2] R. M. MacIver, *The More Perfect Union* (New York: Macmillan, 1948), pp. 273-75.
[3] *Ibid.*

citizen, says Kluckhohn, is morally obligated to look at the world. "For the essence of democracy is that each individual offers to the thinking of the group those insights that derive from his special experience and training."[4] Thus beyond the fact of involvement in bias is the necessity of making a choice among ends and programs based on research to be promoted. There is thus the need to go beyond traditional science to philosophical study of norms. Even scientifically speaking it is better to accept this ethical dilemma than to evade it. "Research workers should realize," says MacIver, "that their large preoccupation with such subjects as housing, public opinion, crime and delinquency, unemployment, tariffs, and so forth, is itself directed by the social importance of these areas of investigation and that if they refuse to draw inferences regarding preferable policies they are like investigators of public health conditions who refrain from recommending what should or should not be done about them." Social responsibility links research of the most critical and objective sort with profound ethical choice. If the social scientist "refrains from making practical applications he is the more apt to divorce his particular ethics from his scientific faith and to make judgments as a layman, as a human being, without the regard for evidence he insists upon as a scientist." MacIver concludes: "The social scientist cannot move the world, but he may be able to learn the secrets of how the world is moved and so furnish aid and special directives to the forces on one or another side of the eternal struggle to move it this way or that."[5]

MacIver[6] takes issue with Myrdal on how the ethical valuations are to be related to the factual knowledge which science provides. Myrdal emphasizes the aim of practical research to be that of showing "precisely what should be the practical and political opinions and plans for action from the point of view of

[4] C. Kluckhohn, *Mirror for Man* (New York: McGraw-Hill, 1949), pp. 264 f.

[5] MacIver, *op. cit.*, pp. 276, 279.

[6] *Ibid.*, pp. 276-78.

the various valuations if their holders had also the more correct and comprehensive factual knowledge which science provides." Myrdal thus wishes to make bias explicit. He would show what values imply by way of consequences. He would expose the assumptions behind and the conflicts between social ideals and practices. This pragmatic approach has many supporters among social scientists. MacIver would go somewhat farther, for the cause is not won when rationalizations are simply exposed in the light of social science. The exposure of prejudice and its consequences alone does not assure the triumph of the larger ideal. Prejudice and rationalization are too fecund for that. In relation to the study of the Negro in the United States in *An American Dilemma*, MacIver asks, "Why need he [Myrdal] study the nature and social consequences of inter-group discrimination exclusively in the light of certain presumptively dominant creeds of the discriminating group?" The investigator may find that the consequences of discrimination are detrimental to social well-being, as he understands it. "If in the judgment of the investigator the consequences are undesirable it becomes for him a task wholly consonant with the principles of science to examine in turn the available methods for mitigating or removing their source."

The social scientist can also contribute much by moving analytically into the center of social movements and showing how old values are linked with new behavior, how leaders can manipulate the people with old symbols filled with new content. The methods of social science are able to show whether the adaptation of behavior to presumed demands of value systems is based on a valid or false linkage.[7] Moreover, once published and publicized, research becomes one of the social forces making for change along with changes in the techniques of production, of communication, and of consumption, to name but a few. Like these, scientific ideas force individual and group revaluations.

[7] *Ibid.*, p. 279.

The spread of knowledge, moral discussion, and political propaganda are integral factors in an interdependent system of causation. Ideas have a momentum of their own and enter often into the breakdown of old myth patterns and the emergence of new complexes of value-impregnated beliefs. It makes a significant difference, therefore, whether the social scientist believes in the efficacy of social engineering, of democracy, of the American Creed, of Christian brotherhood, or whether he is a cynic, a fascist, or a mere ethical relativist. In the sense of commitment to ultimate values the question is thus both ethical and religious. Religion as a valuational process which rallies mankind to universal ideals and to the possibility of social amelioration guided by the objective love of truth and respect for personality is thus not only a live option for the development of social science, but a fruitful prospect. And meliorism, the belief that this is the kind of world that can be made better—a view natural to the social engineer—rests on a teleological assumption which opens the door to metaphysics of religion. Other chapters in this volume explore this aspect of the problem more fully than can be done here.

The rationalism and moralism which are presupposed in the faith which holds to the possibility of induced social change are not to be confused with the older doctrine of progress which played so large a part in the eighteenth century and which thrived in the optimism characteristic of much social Darwinism. Meliorism and automatic progress are poles apart, if indeed they can be placed in any common scale of social causation. Anthropologists at work among the many cultures of mankind, sociologists of religion analyzing primitive and historical communities, economists at work on the business cycle and on comparative economic systems have largely liquidated, out of scientific necessity, any view of inevitable progress. Cultures do not recapitulate each other. Religions have no fixed sequence of evolution. No unseen hand guides self-interest and cut-throat competition into the haven of the general welfare. Social engineering and social planning for freedom amidst a world where democratic and spiritual values are admittedly precarious are holding out to mankind a more serious assignment in social responsibility than proponents of necessary progress ever conceived of doing. Indeed the "old" doctrine of "progress" is today so dead in social science as not even to be a whipping boy of the innovator in social theory. At the same time the general term "progress" is not entirely outmoded, except among those who deny any standard of value. There can, for example, be no question that the potential resources of human culture generally and of most cultures have steadily increased. Anthropologists incline to view the triumph over human misery and degradation as having a spiral character rather than that of an unbroken climb. There are discontinuities. There are troughs and crests. Cultures are always in the making. The possibilities for a significant life for mankind are exceedingly great, but not predestined. Christian and scientific criticisms of the dogma of progress present stimulating challenges to the social theorist and to the social engineer. Higher education is thus today at a stage where conflicting frames of reference in religion and science illuminate the problems of social change.

III. VALUES AND INTEGRATION

Social engineering requires the integration of many disciplines. The TVA was as significant for its inclusive approach to the problems of a region as for its use as a yardstick by which to measure the exploitation of utility companies. In the social sciences there has grown an appreciation for multicausal and cumulative causation methods as over against the monocausal schools of thought such as economic determinism. This has meant that anthropology as an inclusive cultural science has been coming into its own. Its marvelous progress has made an important impact on all the special social sciences. Whereas the sociologist and economist, for example, had carried on their investigations almost entirely within the narrow frame of reference provided by western and American culture and society, the ethnologist was compelled to view societies and cultures as a whole. Whereas the special disciplines took for granted the presuppositions characteristic of western life in the last few centuries, it has been necessary for the anthropologist to realize that these are not an invariable accompaniment of social living. Such presuppositions are of relatively little value in a period of rapid social change and conflict and in a period when world community, embracing all previous histories of nations and societies, is the assignment of mankind. An economist whose generalizations were based on the American business cycle of one hundred years can hardly use these as a basis of world trade. Much wider ranges of data are needed in a day when generalizations must be coherent with global movements. The "correlation of the social problem" states the contemporary issue.

In one science after another there has been a shift from the assumption that the individual is the cultural unit and that society is composed of a sum of identical and interchangeable units. Anthropology is dependent on the work of special sciences but has had to modify them in the process of meeting holistic demands. As Ralph Linton has pointed out with respect to personality psychology:

> It concentrated upon the individual and at first, under the influences of the natural sciences, tried to explain all individual similarities and differences on a physiological basis. Although the importance of environment in personality formation soon became apparent, this was used, at first, simply to explain individual differences. . . . The discovery that personality norms differed for different societies and cultures came as a shock and one which necessitated a basic reorganization of many of their concepts.[8]

The interaction of psychology and ethnology has been very fruitful.

[8] Ralph Linton (ed.), *The Science of Man in the World Crisis* (New York: Columbia University Press, 1945), p. 13.

There has come about a reconsideration of the integrative factors of heredity, physical environment, the family, the small group, social values, and institutions. Whereas the nineteenth century social philosophy was still largely determined by the hereditary point of view, and whereas under the impact of the American scene an extreme environmentalist viewpoint sometimes made itself prominent, there is ample evidence today for an equilibrium between these two opposing standpoints. Moreover, cultures must be approached not only from without descriptively but in terms of their inner meanings. Anthropology is no longer an assemblage of curious differences among the habits and artifacts of primitive men, but a holistic discipline seeking comparative laws with predictive values. Kluckhohn writes:

> Each culture is saturated in its own meanings. Hence no valid science of human behavior can be built on the canons of radical behaviorism. For in every culture there is more than meets the eye, and no amount of external description can convey this underlying portion of it. Bread and wine may mean mere nourishment for the body in one culture. They may mean emotional communion with the deity in another.[9]

In bringing together the representative problems and generalizations of anthropology in the volume called *Personality in Nature, Society and Culture*, the editors, Kluckhohn and Murray, take what they call the "field" approach. They say:

> We regard the conventional separation of the "organism and his environment," the drama of "the individual *versus* his society," the bipolarity between "person and culture" as false or at least misleading in some important senses. Knowledge of a society or a culture must rest upon knowledge of the individuals who are in that society or share that culture. But the converse is equally true. Personal figures get their definition only when seen against the social and cultural background in which they have their being. . . . Although those who study culture and society are primarily interested in the similarities in personality and those who practice psychotherapy and investigate individual psychology have their focus of attention upon differences, the two sets of facts are

[9] Kluckhohn, *Mirror for Man*, p. 202.

inextricably interwoven. One defines the other. In actual experience, individuals and societies constitute a single field.[10]

This field concept, as outlined above, does not eliminate any of the factors biological or cultural, but it does bring them into a new relationship. Franz Alexander's criticism of Freud may illustrate in part the need to be self-critical in these matters. Freud, he says, was too biologically oriented.

> He postulated a too elaborate, biologically predetermined instinctual structure which, in its main features, unfolds in a more or less autochthonous manner, like a flower. He recognized, possibly even overemphasized, the importance of those early experiences which arise in family life, but he overlooked the fact that the parental attitudes themselves are strictly determined by cultural factors. This neglect is the basis of a significant error. . . . Freud declared the personality structure of the European and American of the nineteenth century to be the universal human nature.[11]

There are limits to the adaptability of the biological constitution to cultural demands. To put it absurdly, there are no cultures in which the men bear the children. In no society do the cultural pressures override and eliminate all aspects of personal individuality. On the other hand, no society is a mere *Und-Summe* of individuals. The first and basic task of a child's ego anywhere is accomplishing the continuous adjustment to those biological changes which rapidly succeed one another in the processes of maturation. And yet, cultural factors, including parental attitudes, powerfully influence the child's readiness to accept the ongoing maturation. Moreover, cultural constellations reinforce or bring to the foreground certain emotional mechanisms, though they do not introduce any basic dynamic principles into human nature.

In cultural conditioning there are, then, both continuities and discontinuities. Ruth Benedict says:

[10] C. Kluckhohn and H. A. Murray (eds.), *Personality in Nature, Society and Culture* (New York: Knopf, 1949), pp. xi-xii.
[11] *Ibid.*, p. 330 f.

The anthropologist's role is not to question the facts of nature, but to insist upon the interposition of a middle term between "nature" and "human behavior"; his role is to analyze that term, to document local man-made doctorings of nature, and to insist that these doctorings should not be read off in any one culture as nature itself. Although it is a fact of nature that the child becomes a man, the way in which this transition is effected varies from one society to another, and no one of these particular cultural bridges should be regarded as the "natural" path to maturity.[12]

The reciprocity of individual and cultural factors as noted in contemporary sociology is enriched by the contributions of psychiatry in case work and by the newer sociology of the family. Case methods and clinical relationships point up the sources of individuality differences. Family studies indicate that the immediate group environment composed of parents mediates largely the demands of the culture. An intimate study of family life brings to light the need of recognizing the specific influence of the parents and not to neglect this while concentrating on the larger cultural whole. There is a dialectical interplay of biological heredity, family life, and the dynamic patterns of culture in the biopsychosocial whole. On the one hand, the fundamental directions of childhood training do not derive from the inborn nature of persons but anticipate the roles which men and women will eventually play as they fulfill society's ideals. Methods of child rearing and education which are divorced from the general emphases of the culture will finally alter the emerging adult personality. The spirit of the culture is permeative. Desired changes in adult personalities require an inclusive approach to all phases of social life. "No man is an island." No family is an island.

On the other hand, personality structure cannot be deduced from general social ideals alone. The child's inherited constitution reacts and responds to an enormous range of individualities as represented by many personalities along with their parents in the many relationships into which they enter. Especially in a

[12] *Ibid.*, p. 415.

changing civilization like our own, with a great variety of trends and pressures, intricately interwoven in complex patterns, the child selects what it needs. What is selected depends largely on emotional needs developed in family life under the influence of the particular personalities of the parents. There thus emerges a profounder appreciation of the family, "its function and destiny," than was the case several decades ago. Ruth Nanda Anshen, summarizing the views of a number of leading authorities in *The Family: Its Function and Destiny*, says:

> The contributors to this book have further attempted to show that the family is an integral and indispensable entity in the life of man; that the present collapse of marriage and the family is a perverted triumph of a profaned passion which in truth now largely consists in a reversion to abduction and rape, divested, however, of the ritual that surrounded such violence in some primitive societies; that the dissolution of the modern family is tantamount to the gradual profanation of the fundamental myth which at one time bestowed meaning and sanctity upon family life now converted into mere rhetoric, and finally dissolving the rhetoric itself through the complete vulgarization and secularization of its contents; that *eros* is love which demands to be loved, whereas *agape*, the all-embracing, descending principle of love, is the redemptive good will which asks only the joy of selfless service to the beloved, and that it is for lack of this latter love that the world is dying; that morals and politics are identical and are embraced by the same rules which govern the organization of the family and the organization of the state.[13]

In other words, the family is not only an essential cultural unit within culture as a whole, but social scientists view its conservation as one of the principal tasks confronting our civilization. Adequate family life is a functional necessity for a healthy culture.

The "field" approach, then, includes due recognition of the intimate relationships obtaining in the person-family-culture continuum. John Gillin has shown that definite correlations exist

[13] Ruth Nanda Anshen (ed.), *The Family: Its Function and Destiny*. (New York: Harper, 1949), pp. 426-27; cf. also p. 17.

between the sociocultural constellations and the type of person one becomes as an adult. He credits Malinowski with probably being the "first to recognize that the influence of the family configuration and social organization determines the form of the conflicts and resulting 'complexes' of the personality and that, since social structures differ from society to society, psychological complexes do also."[14] Malinowski also laid the basis in comparative ethnology for much of the "neo-Freudian" theory today which sees the "source of many neuroses in the socio-cultural situation surrounding persons in their formative years." In all of this work today it must be emphasized that the person is not dissolved into the cultural continuum. This is of the utmost importance for the religious conception of the sacredness of personality. This present emphasis can be traced from several angles, as we shall see.

David Bidney, combining philosophical and anthropological competence, points out that logically "there need be no contradiction between the organic or personalistic and the impersonalistic or superorganic views of culture, provided it be kept in mind that we are dealing with different levels of abstraction and that organic or personal culture is logically and genetically prior to superorganic culture."[15] Culture as a concept is not to be hypostatized into a transcendental force. Bidney believes that George Mead, John Dewey, Charles H. Cooley, Ellsworth Faris, Auguste Comte, and Ernst Cassirer overemphasized the thought that the nature and mind of the individual can be understood only through the society of which he is a member. Hypostatization of culture, he thinks, is an error in Hegel, Comte, Marx, Spengler, and Sorokin, all of whom allegedly made culture the primary, impersonal "agent" and man a passive vehicle. Bidney may go too far here in some of his negative criticisms but he is

---

[14] Kluckhohn and Murray, *op. cit.*, p. 167.
[15] L. Bryson, L. Finkelstein and R. M. MacIver, *Conflicts of Power in Modern Culture* (New York: Harper, 1947), p. 183.

right in cautioning against "the fallacy of 'misplaced concreteness.'" He brings out a valid relationship of personality to culture when he concludes:

> If we bear in mind that culture, in its primary sense, is logically and genetically an acquired attribute of human nature and that it is for us to determine which cultural heritage is to be conserved and which is to be allowed to wither away through desuetude, then we shall be rid once for all of fatalistic delusions concerning the cultural superorganic.[16]

That the determinate nature of man "is manifested functionally through culture but is not reducible to culture" is illustrated and partially verified in the study made by Allport, Bruner, and Jandorf of a number of cases of persecuted persons under the Nazi regime. It was a study of how the persecuted adult defends himself psychologically against catastrophe; of how far catastrophic social disorganization disrupts basic personality integration; of how political attitudes change under the impact of catastrophe and the like. We are here concerned to show what the psychologists found it important to emphasize as psychological mechanisms came into play to protect against catastrophe. Gordon Allport says:

> (1) *Persistent goal striving* is the indispensable postulate. Families to defend, children to educate, business to foster, friends to help—in short, the conservation of personality structure and all the major values of life call for tenacity. (2) Such differentiated goal-striving demands the *retention of a structured field.* Migration into a new and strange life-space removes the "behavior supports" essential to the pursuit of long-established goals. In adulthood, our data show, such a catastrophic change in frames of reference, values, and supporting habits meets with active resistance.[17]

Very rarely, he goes on to point out, does catastrophic social change produce catastrophic alterations in personality.

> Neither our cases nor such statistics as are available reflect any such number of regressions, hysterics, or other traumatic neuroses as the

[16] *Ibid.,* p. 185.
[17] Kluckhohn and Murray, *op. cit.,* p. 353.

gravity of the social crisis might lead one to expect. On the contrary, perhaps the most vivid impression gained by our analysis from this case-history material is of the extraordinary continuity and sameness in the individual personality.

Thus, while induced social change is frequently stressed by social scientists, while the possibilities of planned and manipulated personality development are very real, the adult has a persistent basic structure of personality. Despite disaster the established goal striving, the fundamental philosophy of life, skills, and expressive behavior are amazingly the same. "When there was change in our subjects," writes Allport, "it did not seem to violate the basic integrations of the personality, but rather to select and reinforce traits already present."[18]

We can bring this section of our survey to a close by mentioning the person-in-community or individual-group discoveries made in a very different field by Elton Mayo, namely, that of industrial relations. Here we note again the basic shift from an earlier atomistic individualism to the communitarian personalism of the present stage of research. Much of the social insight found in Mayo was already present years ago in the social gospel writers and theorists like Gladden, Stuckenberg, Peabody, and Rauschenbusch, but it did not have much of a place in social science. Clinical research in industrial relations as reflected in the studies by Mayo over a quarter of a century may be symbolized by noting the shift in emphasis from *The Human Problems of an Industrial Civilization*, published in 1933, to *The Social Problems of an Industrial Civilization*, published in 1945. In the first study methods were developed of analyzing and securing better understanding of individual workers in relation to their jobs and of ways to improve their sense of well-being in industry. Later research revealed the importance of social groupings and of teamwork as well as of the individual. Though not

[18] *Ibid.*, p. 365.

excluding the individual, Mayo stressed the importance of groups and methods of understanding the behavior of groups, whether formally organized and recognized by management or self-constituted, informal organizations. He showed that it is within the power of industrial administrators, amidst technological changes in the plant and social chaos in the community outside, to create within industry itself a partially effective substitute for the old stabilizing effect of the neighborhood.

Mayo rejects what he calls "the Rabble Hypotheses" which grew out of the Manchester School's development of economic principles. He notes also that the profit motive as a basis of business organization failed completely. The conception behind individualism in economics that society consists of a "horde of unorganized individuals" misses social reality entirely. Contrary to much politico-economical theory which would ground democracy on the "rabble hypotheses," the real outcome is that of Hobbes's Leviathan. Democracy must make group life and adaptive behavior a basically different conception from all this. Clinical work in industry, with knowledge-of-acquaintance of the actual event and intimate understanding of the complexity of human relationships, "ran headlong into illustration of the insufficiency of the assumption that individual self-interest actually operates as adequate incentive."[19] Given the opportunity of communication and collaboration amongst themselves, the workers in a "problem" department of a textile mill greatly increased their efficiency and the labor turnover dropped from 250 per cent to 5 per cent. Experiments led to the conclusion that "associative instincts overshadowed material conditions as determinants of productivity. Where individuals became a team, not only did their productivity increase, but their personal outlook and their ability to collaborate changed for the better." Mayo's work is but one of many new inquiries in the rapidly developing field of

[19] Elton Mayo, *The Social Problems of an Industrial Civilization* (Cambridge: Harvard University Press, 1945), p. 59.

communication research. Without communication there can be no community. Irrational hates, hostile groups within industry and among nations, challenge both the theory and the practice of adaptive society, with the theory and art of communication and co-operation a central project.

IV. THE PROSPECT OF UNIVERSAL NORMS

We have not been able adequately to sketch the great areas of social inquiry being developed along many constructive lines. Especially should more be noted concerning the newer studies of political units, the state and social control. Propaganda and the mass-communications problems are receiving much attention. But we must turn our thought to the present concerns for values and for norms which transcend nations and cultures, concerns which have been basic to monotheistic religions for centuries and now confront the sciences. Over and over again the social sciences bring us to the threshold of a universal axiology. Without the critical knowledge of the anthropologist, integrating the work of special researches, it is presumptive for religion or philosophy to attempt any concrete or empirical formulations of religious life in the future. But there need be no longer any disjunctive alternative of "science" *or* "religion." In all cultures religion's functions are symbolic, expressive, and orientative. It grasps the whole meaning in anticipation. Every culture has its myths, its value-impregnated beliefs, and must define its ends as well as its means. Scientific investigations of the technics of society do not provide the symbolic expressions of ultimate values. Ultimate norms, moreover, often condemn facts which are described by science and demand change. On the other hand, there is no intrinsic reason why ultimate values should be incoherent with known fact or proven theory. Since, moreover, as J. S. Huxley says, the emancipation of natural science from considerations of value is a fiction, and since some of the most important data with which social scientists deal connote values in some socially approved hierarchical order, the problem seems to be to find norms which will provide the most rationally coherent realm of ends intelligently integrated with the means appropriate to their realization.

In the transition from pure to applied science many scientists have discovered the inevitability of bias and values. We have noted how Myrdal and MacIver relate social engineering to values and social responsibility. Social psychologists like Wayland Vaughan connect intimately the "science" of psychology with the "art of living." During the last fifteen years there has been a marked growth in the social psychology of values and of intelligent social control. E. Freeman, O. Klineberg, S. H. Britt, G. W. Hartmann, E. C. Tolman, E. L. Thorndike, R. S. Lynd, G. W. Allport are but a few of the men working in the field who have come to grips with the problems in the borderland between traditional psychology, sociology, and ethics. G. W. Hartmann in 1939 speaking to the Society for the Psychological Study of Social Issues argues for "Value as the Unifying Concept of the Social Sciences." He held that "Values are both the basic data and the explanatory tools of all the social sciences." In 1940 before the same group E. C. Tolman, who has devoted many years of study to animal behavior, pledged as follows:

> Our fellow human beings today all over the world are giving up their lives in the name of new loyalties. And, if we psychologists here in America don't preach our own sermons, we shall be caught by theirs. If we don't say our say, not merely as to how to detect and measure and tabulate social change, but as to what good social changes would be, then we shall deserve no better fate than the one which otherwise undoubtedly lies in store for us.[20]

The values to which the American social psychologists quickly turned were those of democracy and personality. The moral kin-

[20] W. Vaughan, *Social Psychology* (New York: The Odyssey Press, 1948), p. 110.

ship between science and democracy is natural to the scientist. Democracy fosters a process of open discussion which exposes more and more of the interests, facts and valuations of the community. Democracy and science foster a free, open, and critical participation of the members of a group. Democracy brings under the light of mutual criticism the varying perspectives of the participants. Public discussion properly conducted has a purifying effect and is part of the moral education of the people. Science fosters a community of disciplined thought and criticism in which enlightened proposals of experimentation and hypotheses for the solutions of problems are subjected to public examination under commonly accepted postulates and tests in continuous intercommunication among researchers. The exploration of values by social scientists seems on the whole to have driven them to greater loyalty to democratic values. Our multigroup society with its wide range of interests plays its part too. For democracy stresses not one single absolute value but thrives in the interpenetration of a subtle and intricate multiple of values. It finds its path of least resistance, intellectually and morally speaking, in an adaptive process in which interests and institutions are wont to be balanced in a dynamic equilibrium. It may not be going too far to say that democracy is a way of life in which personality builds itself ever new institutions more suitable for its own self-realization.

America feels herself to be humanity in miniature and hence almost takes for granted that the perfecting of democratic ideals and values here has universal applicability in the long run. As a matter of fact there is genuine continuity between the American Bill of Rights and the Universal Declaration of Rights adopted by the General Assembly of the United Nations.

In this quest for general valuations, we note a significant shift from much early anthropology to present practical and theoretical concerns. No longer is the emphasis on curious differences, on demonstrations that "anything goes somewhere in the world."

The older work frequently fed not only cultural relativism but moral relativism. Today we may say that it is not relativism but relativity which is central. Cultures are meaningful wholes. The objective behavior differences of one culture as compared with another are not grounds for irresponsible conduct in one's own culture. Cultures have internal logics. The economic theory, the political theory, the art forms and the religious doctrine of each society are expressive of coherent elementary presuppositions. The amoralism of ethical relativism finds no support in the serious study of cultural relativity. That value to which cultures are relative from a comparative point of view is the actualization of personality. Knowing how personality develops in its various cultural settings, and knowing the vast potentialities of personality expressions, and the means of social control and education, the future depends indeed on a genuine personalistic axiology.

The convergence of the social sciences on the questions of intrinsic values and objective norms is new. But the coherent convergence is becoming philosophical in spirit and in method. There is much to be gained in this new development. Instrumental values can now increasingly be tested. Intrinsic values and universal values are only slowly emerging from the inductive and comparative studies of cultures. One anthropologist goes so far as to say:

> Some values appear to be as much "given" by nature as the fact that bodies heavier than air fall. No society has ever approved suffering as a good thing in itself—as a means to an end, yes; as punishment, as a means to the ends of society, yes. We don't have to rely upon supernatural revelation to discover that sexual access achieved through violence is bad. That is as much a fact of general observation as the fact that different objects have different densities. The observation that truth and beauty are universal, transcendental human values is as much one of the givens of human life as are birth and death.[21]

[21] Kluckhohn, *Mirror for Man*, pp. 285-86.

A generation more of co-operative study will greatly enlarge this list in all probability. Some scholars believe that the common ethical findings are already considerable.

We have indicated above some of the high values which must today be placed on the family. As Ralph Linton says, "In the Götterdämmerung which over-wise science and over-foolish statesmen are preparing for us, last man will spend his last hours searching for his wife and child."[22] Has not Ruth Nanda Anshen perhaps anticipated tomorrow's science by her philosophical observation:

When it is conceded that man believes in a universe of law, of reason, of love, only then will half truths, evasions, indirectness, self-abasement, and falsehoods be understood for what they intrinsically are; sickness of the soul derived from that miasma which poisons love and life while it clouds the spirit. Knowledge, the possibility of truth, is a *sine qua non* of every conscious act, and the primary importance of knowledge is proved by the fact that in order to criticize knowledge it must be presupposed. And a knowledge of the good is the foundation of all reality, of society, of the family, since it is the *ratio sufficiens* of existence.[23]

In conclusion we may note that there is an organized convergence of science, philosophy, and religion which has been an active process in America for about ten years. In 1940 there was convened the First Conference of Science, Philosophy, and Religion. These conferences which are an ongoing process are centered about the validity of democracy as a social value and the dignity of the person. All who participate agree to the aim of increasing appreciation for the supreme worth and moral responsibility of every individual human person. Social scientists have freely contributed to this normative discussion along with philosophers and religionists. This is itself one of the major demonstrations of changing presuppositions and antipositivistic

[22] Anshen, *op. cit.*, p. 38.
[23] *Ibid.*, p. 435.

tendencies in the social sciences. For many have come to realize that the crisis in civilization is in large part capable of being phrased in these terms: whether we are to have a world community and a world culture in which untrammeled social science can be responsibly applied to the problems of that crisis.

PART III

The Academic Community

6

Liberal Learning and Religion in the American College

Victor L. Butterfield

W E SHALL here attempt a general appraisal of the state of liberal learning, of the humanities, and, particularly, of religion in the American college classroom today, and, by getting at the sources of their weakness and strength, seek to suggest more effective ways and means of nurturing their health. We shall first consider the attitudes of students and "laymen," of teachers and administrators, toward these areas of study, particularly as reflected in postwar reforms. We shall then proceed with a general analysis of American learning and scholarship particularly at the graduate level, and examine their significance for the two areas indicated in our title. Finally, we shall suggest ways in which the religious, or spiritual, enterprise can be academically fostered by those most interested, whether as individual teachers and scholars or as members of groups particularly concerned with the liberating spiritual growth of college students.

I. Student and "Lay" Attitudes Toward Liberal Studies

The undergraduate's attitude toward learning has improved somewhat during the last several student generations. Student interest in the humanities, and especially in political, artistic, and spiritual problems, is more genuine and intense than it was a decade or two ago. The Depression naturally tended to make students somewhat more earnest, and certainly we all were impressed with the seriousness and maturity of the veterans as they returned from the war. A fair degree of this intensified motivation and interest arose from the most practical of concerns—the desire to get the degree and to have a good record as a recommendation for a job. In many instances, the amount of genuine curiosity or increased sensitivity to fundamental human problems was not great. In many cases, however, such concerns and sensibilities were real, and there was enough of this deeper drive on most campuses to improve notably the tone and atmosphere of the whole community. There was an increased concern for moral and political issues, and even for spiritual ones. Many a student in his war experience had been driven to ask seriously about man's fundamental place in this world and universe, and how ideals and spiritual forces might ease the problems of life, make for happier adjustments, and inspire men to proper deeds. This underlying concern has, however, in our Protestant groups at least, been accompanied by an *increased* suspicion of traditional or institutionalized forms of religious and spiritual expression. It is without doubt an excessive skepticism, but in many instances it has a healthy basis and is fundamentally a promising sign.

With the passing of the veteran our campuses lost, indeed, much of this matured curiosity, but one can well doubt whether the pendulum will swing all the way back. Certainly, if the colleges and universities do their job as they should, there ought to be some permanent gain of attitude among the younger, more inexperienced students who are now coming to us. In addition to the partial contagion of the veterans' attitude, the continued maladjustments and anxieties of society will help this greater seriousness to persist.

The attitude, however, of the nonacademic world toward liberal learning, and especially toward the humanities and at least the *intellectual* aspects of religion, does not seem to have changed markedly for the better. There is a profound and persistent contradiction in the American people between an extraordinarily blind and sentimental faith in "general" education on the one hand, and an unconscious but very deep-seated suspicion of learning and the use of reason on the other. We annually spend millions on our public and private educational institutions; yet at the levels of man's most fundamental experience, very few Americans really believe that books or ideas are a source of much help. Whereas we believe profoundly in the use of knowledge and logic in all our so-called "practical affairs," when it comes to matters of creative enterprise, to morality, and to religion, we tend to rely *almost exclusively* on inspiration, will power, sentiment, and blind faith. As a result, we get very widespread public support for general education, especially when it has apparent practical value; but at the college and university level there is a strong tendency to discount the importance of learning unless it is "practical," particularly in the fields of literature, the arts, history, philosophy, and religion. The "lay" mind tends to think of them as frills or hobby pastimes for leisure hours, and in their intellectual aspects, at any rate, as essentially irrelevant to any important human problems.

Despite this curious and obstructing contradiction, there is little doubt of generous public support of our colleges and universities for the long run, notwithstanding the current widespread suspicion both of the intellectual's political attitudes, and of the private as opposed to the public institution. We shall have to fight some of this contradictory attitude by direct frontal attack, pleading and working for liberal studies as such at every opportunity. For the most part, however, we must resort to the slower but sounder method of winning students to the experience of finding learning and thought not only attractive, but also powerful instruments in the guidance and control of their lives, as individuals and members of society.

II. The Nature of Curricular Reforms

So much for the briefest of reports on the attitude of the student and the layman toward religion and the humanities on the campus. What about our faculties and administrators themselves? The ferment of reform that has existed on our college campuses during and since the war is nothing short of astounding. We quite properly had a bad conscience about the job we were doing, but certainly none of us can complain of the amount of sheer effort put forth in the early postwar years to do a better job. Nearly every college in the country has made some degree of revision in its approach and offerings. *The real questions, however, are two. First,* how significant on the one hand is all this reform in terms of anything really fundamental? Is it for the most part simply a recasting of the patterns of knowledge, the handling of which will not be materially different from times past? Or does it reveal a fresh insight into the relation of learning to the growth of the mind and the spirit? *Second,* to what extent is this ferment at the college level provoking a change of attitude or reform in the basic source of our learning and scholarship, that is, the graduate school itself? This institution is on the whole a highly conservative one with a deeply ingrained tradition. Furthermore, in the last analysis, albeit unconsciously and indirectly, it supplies the undergraduate curriculum with its premises of both ends and means. Let us explore these two questions in order.

In answer to the first question, there are grounds for fearing that the reforms *are* for the most part superficial. Despite much apparent variety in our new educational programs, a vast and disturbing uniformity in the movement persists *in the sense that learning is still largely thought of in surface dimensions only.* Usually the pattern follows the Columbia or Chicago plan, though in varying ways: a general education for the first two years in the three great fields—humanities, social studies, and science, the latter often being broken down into the physical and biological sciences. The preoccupation of most reformers within these broad categories is largely one of selection of such material as will give the student a "comprehensive" and perhaps "integrated" view of the "field." The traditional "major" or "concentration program" still prevails in most places for the last two years, and here the traditional justification in most instances persists—namely, to give the student "a sense of mastery of a limited field."

In many places where this new general program is in force, there is also, to be sure, a growing concern with the problems of method and technique. How the student can be motivated and how he can better learn to think and express himself are matters of more conscious preoccupation among many teachers than heretofore. Up to a point there is a real gain in this phase of the reform. Here again, however, the goals tend to be limited to the development in the student of sheer intellectual facility and power. There seems to be relatively little awareness that in the last analysis the growth of sound judgment is dependent upon an increased sensitization to basic standards and principles of social, moral, aesthetic, and religious experience. We are in danger, from such a limited emphasis, of training sophists at best and fascists at worst.

Even the reformers who reach for goals more profound than those of developing mental power often seem confused as to what is basic in that depth. There is, for example, the growing movement of "integrated education," but I am not sure that the concept itself is being very carefully examined. One kind of integration amounts simply to the process of reducing information to some kind of coherent pattern. I cannot see that a great deal is to be gained by simply setting up another pattern of knowledge for the student. Our fields of learning are the traditionally integrated patterns, and, whereas we might gain something by keeping the pattern shifting, we shall never by such a device develop any greater power in the student to do his own integrating. As long as the student is presented with any organized body of knowledge and is expected merely to apprehend and remember it, his own capacity to organize will not grow. A second type of integration refers to the ability of the student himself to marshal material into some kind of coherent pattern and ultimately to mold his knowledge and experience into some coherent philosophy of life. These are both important, the latter vital, the former already in many places an element in our traditional "major programs." The second, the building of a philosophy of life, is dependent on more than four brief college years, and it is dependent upon a third kind of integration which seems to me central and basic; namely, the habit of relating knowledge or ideas to percepts, or appreciations, or aesthetic and other values of experience that bear upon man's fundamental problems. Again, however, it is this last type of integration which is seldom discussed in our reform movements.

One can hardly talk about educational reform without some mention of the famous St. John's Program, particularly as an excellent illustration of what is here being discussed. If its proponents had been somewhat more tactful and courteous, this program would have received far more general attention than it has, despite the fact that it has proved suggestive to many teachers and educators. It may have its limitations, but it also has at least one enormous merit, the program of reading in "great books." William James was being fundamentally serious when he advised women of the American Alumnae Association that the business of a liberal education is to "help you to know a good man when you see him."[1] The most important single thing that liberal education can do is to expose the student, as James says,

[1] William James, "The Social Value of the College Bred" from *Memories and Studies* (New York: Longmans, Green, 1911), p. 309.

to human excellence in every type of important achievement. The great masters of interpretation, namely, the "great books" in *all* fields, are the first and primary source of liberal education. This fact St. John's has recognized. Yet I fear the program has not fully capitalized on its opportunity, because of too much emphasis on philosophic dialectic and too little on empirical reference and on the perceptive and aesthetic side of the learning experience. There was little doubt in the visitor's mind, at least a decade ago, that St. John's students develop great dialectic dexterity, but they do not impress one as students who try to connect their concepts with the vivid perceived details and values of concrete experience. If one might put it thus, they seem like men who can think but are not really thoughtful. Perhaps one of St. John's difficulties has been in requiring too many great books. As my old teacher, Professor Lane Cooper, often maintained, a few great books carefully studied and fully tasted and *felt* are far better than more of them less fully digested. As an illustration of this principle, he used to point to Abraham Lincoln, whose diet was the Bible, Shakespeare, and Euclid until he started reading in law.

Neither can one talk of college reforms of the type that concern us without mentioning the "Progressive" colleges. I regret never having had a chance to pay a substantial visit to some of these campuses, but from the reports of others whose judgment can be trusted they have often succeeded in establishing in their students a degree of intellectual freshness and vigor, and a sense of creative study and thought that does not characterize many of our better established but conventionally-minded colleges and universities. The risks, of course—and they are often recognized and perhaps corrected by the colleges themselves—are first the risks of creation or expression without grounding in knowledge or careful thought, and second the risk of an intellectual or cultural narrowness determined by the limited personal interest of the student. Yet in so far as the "progressive" program succeeds in making the learning process a rich one, tying observation, appreciation and reflection into a total organic experience, it has reached to the heart of the educational problem—at least psychologically. When such a process is also concerned with great human and social issues, the seeds of liberal wisdom will really sprout.

So much for reform movements at the undergraduate level. One cannot deny genuine gains in educational reform since the war, and even before, on some campuses. In general, however, one questions whether the reforms have been as significant or meaningful as first impressions would indicate, since the general attitude toward knowledge and its function in life has not significantly changed. It cannot change dramatically until there is much more awareness among our intellectuals of our social and psychological need for a more profound moral orientation.

May we now turn therefore to the second question, namely, the extent to which this educational ferment at the undergraduate level is tending to effect changes of attitude toward learning in the graduate schools. Here again there are signs of some slight reform. These changes, such as they are, are being brought about partly by internal criticism, but largely I suspect by virtue of external pressures taking shape these days in the form of a rather widespread demand for more effective "teacher training." Whereas one can be happy about the pressure on the graduate schools to do something or other about the situation, I do not find myself particularly sympathetic with the teacher-training movement. Here again most of the thinking concerns matters of technique. What is needed above all else in our teachers is this experience I have mentioned of a deeper insight from learning and of a keener devotion to it. Without these it is almost impossible for the teacher to help his students make any significant discoveries, but with it, his own enthusiasm and example can carry the battle single-handed a good share of the time. The failure of the graduate school, however, to place much premium on its own teaching is doing untold damage to the teaching profession as a whole. The greatest of the German scholars of the last century took as much pride in their reputation as teachers as in their fame as scholars. Our graduate schools have not, in our general imitation of German scholarship, emulated their masters. Apart from the unfortunate attitude toward teaching, there is, in addition, the traditional attitude toward scholarship itself, a tradition which in many respects has serious and unhappy consequences for liberal learning at all levels of our education.

As a premise to this criticism, may we clarify briefly a fundamental premise of liberal learning. If liberal education is to justify all the faith and money that are going into it, many of us feel that it cannot stop short of its capacity to stimulate the growth of individuals in such fundamental ways as to give markedly increased meaning to their lives. Historically it has had this effect on many lives and, in doing so, it has, in combination with other forces, lifted the race on various occasions out of barbarism to appreciable heights of civilized culture and harmony. Where learning takes serious hold, however, it does so because of its appeal and inspiration. This appeal comes from its capacity to give us meanings, insights, and experiences which cater to our deepest urges and needs whether rational, social, moral, aesthetic, or spiritual.

In the face of this obvious truth I should like to indicate some features of current American scholarship which betray this fundamental function. I need hardly point out what has traditionally been the disposition of vast proportions of our undergraduates—namely, the feeling that learning is a necessary evil, a thing to be escaped except for the requirements of examinations and the degree. College faculties have long doubted whether more than a quarter of our college graduates ever again read an important book after they have left college halls. These proportions may have improved some in recent years, but the picture is still far from what it should be. What is even more disturbing in the situation is the reaction of the old guard, conservative scholar. Relatively few seem to think more can be done about the difficulty. They regard educational effort as a matter of will power and self-discipline. You can lead a horse to water but you can't make him drink, and if he won't make himself drink, there is an end of it. They also overrationalize the national attitude toward learning, and feel that young men and women coming to us from homes with little cultural background can hardly be expected to take to "culture," no matter how great the inspiration. The forces of the Philistines are too blinding to permit the student to discover meanings in his education even if given the chance.

There is something to be said for these complaints, of course, but they are overargued, as further factors in the picture will indicate. Early in World War II, the father of one of our students asked that his son be switched immediately from his major in literature and fine arts to mathematics and physics, since the boy was planning to enter the navy and wanted to be prepared. One could not question the desirability of some mathematics or physics, war or no war, but one could question such a major shift, especially when the student's program had originally been so carefully planned to meet his basic needs and interests. When the wisdom of the move was questioned, however, the father protested that he did not "see what business a boy of service age had these days in fiddling around with art and literature." The irony of the situation lay in the fact that this father was a highly reputable professor of literature in one of our leading universities. Apparently he had not himself found sufficient spiritual resources in his own field to be able to justify it for his own son at a time of either personal or national crisis. Unfortunately his counterpart can be found many times over. In contrast I think of our undergraduates who took copies of the

New Testament or of Plato's *Republic* off to the wars with them and read them most when the going was toughest.

Another story to point up the same picture. A college dean in a leading university, the man in charge of seeking freshman counselors from among the graduate students, says that the men he interviews from the medical school, the law school, the engineering school—all the professional schools—are almost to a man finding their professional training not merely challenging but positively exciting and absorbing. By contrast it is a rare and occasional graduate student from the college of arts and sciences who is finding much meaning in his graduate studies. They are proving a relatively tedious and dull experience, a necessary apprenticeship to a future job in which he hopes his activities will be more interesting. The unhappy fact, however, is that a discouraging proportion of them never find it so. The thing that has impressed me more than any other in my last half dozen years of teacher scouting has been the extraordinary number of men one meets among younger teachers on our university campuses (excluding perhaps the scientists) who have no real or vital feeling for scholarship. The pressure to publish finds them in a false position. They are not writing articles out of any inner compulsion, but are gradually habituating themselves through external pressure to the routine of production. They will eventually reach the point where it becomes bearable but hardly creative in any important human sense. As they obtain their positions, they will only add their weight to the pedestrian leadership in learning, and in their turn, and in the name of "rigor" and "soundness," will help to shackle the minds of the next generation. The meaninglessness of current scholarship to many *able* people is probably the greatest single indictment of our whole enterprise of professional learning, and until it is substantially corrected it will be very difficult for the undergraduate liberal colleges to have the effect, either personal or social, which is potentially theirs.

III. The Dimensions of Liberal Scholarship

What is the trouble here? Why should we be caught in this curious contradiction of professing an enterprise of enormous human significance on the one hand and finding on the other that large proportions of very able people are incapable of getting any real inspiration or meaning from it? We can revert to typical aristocratic notions that learning is meant for only a very select few. In that case, however, one would guess that our graduate schools even in normal times are vastly overcrowded, and we are wasting a lot of money and energy. Furthermore, if we revert to this rationalization, we refuse in advance to try to "activate" the potential which learning has for a democracy. We shall never solve the democratic problem by putting learning in the hands of a small and exclusive proportion of our population on the theory that they alone can set a civilizing tone. We must find some way of spreading the appreciation of learning more widely if we are to expect any substantial moral support or appreciation for the important insights which the ablest of our scholars can provide a society. Finally, partly for personal and partly for objective reasons, I have an intense conviction that learning can and does in various important ways mean a great deal to people with I.Q.'s below 130! Moreover, this stems from broader considerations and from a more varied exercise of our mental powers on the material of learning than is normally credited or encouraged in professional scholarly circles.

Specialized learning has been attacked time and time again as the source of our difficulty. Some of us doubt the charge that concentration on a given field is necessarily a limiting experience. Surely any field, particularly such a one as history or literature, has potentially within it a vast amount of meaning; and indeed those fields that the so-called humanists most malign, such as science and economics, are certainly not without great resources for liberal or humanistic experience. The fault does not lie in the material of the field but rather in the limited number of avenues by which it is understood and appreciated. Typical, for instance, is the usual scientist's refusal to admit either the history or philosophy of his subject as an integral, legitimate, indeed necessary part of the "field" for full and adequate understanding. Knowledge of a body of facts and emerging principles, and operational facility with them, are the earmarks of professional learning. Liberal learning cannot dispense with such competence, but it cannot be "liberal" or "humanizing" without benefit of further avenues of understanding. The method, the criticism, the implications of science for man as man, indeed the beauty of science, are the necessary conditions of a fully trained and liberal spirit. It's in the cloth if we will only cut it right, but our refusal to do so is continuing to give us scientists of great professional competence but with little or no training in the modes of thought by which we handle other human problems, either personal or social.

In the same way, and with double irony, fields such as literature or history, which are spoken of normally as the "humanistic" fields, have been at least partly damaged for liberal purposes by a similarly limited intellectual treatment. The relative indifference of many literary scholars, for instance, to the psychological and particularly to the ethical, religious, and philosophical features of poetry or drama accounts in large measure, it seems to me, for the lack of appeal that these fields often have for normal, intelligent, and sensitive students and laymen. To summarize my position, though I am not sure that it clarifies it, I am completely Whiteheadian in my criticism here, and take my cue from him in feeling that the difficulty with our scholarship is that we tend to establish a "given set of abstractions"[2] by which we handle a field. We fail to give a book or a body of knowledge the wealth of treatment, either in terms of aesthetic perceptions or general

[2] Alfred North Whitehead, *Science and the Modern World* (New York: Macmillan, 1941), p. 283.

ideas, which is necessary if our minds are to develop that capacity for understanding or that creative power, or indeed that interest in knowledge and reflection, that is the business of liberal education. "There is no groove of abstractions which is adequate for the comprehension of human life."[3]

IV. VITALIZING RELIGION THROUGH VITALIZED LEARNING

What bearing have our findings thus far on the problem of a more effective education in the humanities generally and in religion in particular? We have stated in effect that students will probably hereafter find these areas of greater concern than they have in the past but that their chances for profiting from them substantially can be increased only by a substantial change in the very nature of liberal scholarship itself. How can we help to bring about this shift and make the connection between learning and religion more vital?

It is an exceedingly subtle and difficult problem since it involves a shift in the half-conscious or unconscious premises of many scholars and teachers. These are hard to change. Just as individual growth, however, proceeds by the necessary shifts in our fundamental attitudes, so, too, does the effectiveness of institutions depend on the constant rediscovery of their fundamental methods and aims.

It is only fair at this point, however, and very helpful in finding solutions, to make clear that my criticism of graduate scholarship reflects no quarrel whatever with the principle of research which is one of its two primary functions. My quarrel is with the nature or quality of the *average* attitude of those pursuing it. My criticism is made, moreover, with full awareness of the many men in the profession who are notable exceptions to the average. Every college and university, whether graduate or undergraduate, is blessed with some men who take a vast pride in teaching well, who take a sincere interest in their

[3] *Ibid.*

students and show a genuine respect for them,—men whose minds are fluid, open, imaginative, sensitive to the variety of principle and appreciation that liberal scholarship calls for. These men are not only the chief forces of liberal learning in our colleges and universities, but basically the soundest allies of the cause of religion in these institutions, whatever their particular theological or philosophic beliefs. We should capitalize on their leadership and help at every opportunity, seeking them whenever possible for our active partners in the cause.

Further suggestions depend in part on that connection between religion and scholarship which we have been discussing. The connection may still not be clear. Yet, if we think of religion in individual and spiritual terms rather than in terms of theology and institutions, the connection should be more apparent. There is a close alliance between the fundamental function of learning and religious insight and growth, at least so far as the Protestant tradition is concerned. Each of us, if our religion is to be vital and meaningful, must seek his moral and spiritual values and his God in his own way through his own discoveries. If liberal learning is committed to the proposition that through searching into the lives and experience of the race, and particularly into the insights of our great thinkers and prophets, we can find ideas or meanings upon which to draw for our own insight and growth, and if we include in these searches all areas that have been fundamental in the experience of the race—scientific, political, psychological, aesthetic, moral, and religious—we are then placed in the most strategic position possible for all spiritual insight and discovery. From such sources, meshed as they must be with our own immediate experience and problems, we stand an excellent chance of a vital religious growth. The other two principal sources of such meaning are the authoritarian, on the one hand, and the purely emotional, on the other. Neither is consistent with principles of liberal learning nor can either yield so adequately to most of us the sound deep-seated conviction which this less dramatic process can achieve. It has the perpetual freshness of discovery, the solidity of reason and thought, and it is as commensurate with faith as any form of philosophy of life.

If this basic assumption is correct, then our function as educators and teachers becomes clearer. Those of us most concerned ought in any case to continue to talk about religion in higher education and to further it in every obvious way that we can. We should encourage its discussion among the faculty and administration; we should urge stronger departments of religion in our universities and colleges; we should help with the work of religious organizations; we should continue religious publications and further other forms of propaganda. We can also do more to make clear to our colleagues that religious issues and ideas have as important a place in western tradition as any, and an educational community that neglects them is simply *refusing* to look into a fair share of the inherited experience of the race— a refusal which is an antiliberal attitude if ever there was one. Religion must assume the place in liberal studies that historically, in men's experience, is due it, if the colleges and universities are honest in the purpose of their profession.

It is not merely a matter of "being fair" to the "field" of religion, however, simply because it has had an important share in human experience. It has done so because it has had a probable or certain validity in the lives of sensitive and intelligent men and has provided them with both moral standards and moral drive. If ever history was in need of both, it is today. I should hardly need to add that for most religious men in western history, religion has meant some form of Judeo-Christian faith, and for both reasons the study of this particular tradition is central in any program of liberal education. I am fully aware of the so-called "emancipation" of many scholars and teachers from forms of religious doctrine or institutions which they could not in conscience accept. But many of our most sensitive and able teachers seem to have thrown out the true with the false, the articles of reasonable as well as unreasonable faith, and to have fallen into the limiting though equally dogmatic and faith-founded position of strict scientific naturalism. This has resulted, unconsciously in many instances, in a refusal to consider most intangibles, as falling outside the realm of scholarly concern, and has given students the impression that matters of standards or of quality are either unimportant or, at best, matters of taste. The need for moral and spiritual rediscovery in committed intellectual leadership is desperate. The scholars' return to what has been a vital source of our moral strength is called for. Understanding and appreciation are just as surely the product of study in this realm of values as in any other realm. One can never quarrel in a liberal community with an honest skeptic so long as he personifies the meaning of the word "thoughtful." But one can quarrel with the mind that has closed itself to all further consideration of the basic human issues in art and politics, in psychology, ethics, and religion. Wisdom has never emerged from such refusals.

So beyond and beneath the active support of the usual agencies of religious education is a more basic and, for the long run, an absolutely essential foundation stone; namely, the effort by one device or another to push the meaning of scholarship into richer or more vital channels, to encourage in the training of graduate students and in the teaching of undergraduates a more varied and more creative treatment of the material with which they are dealing, making sure that all the basic human concerns, religious as well as political, ethical as well as economic, philosophic as well as psychological, artistic as well as scientific, be somehow incorporated in all scholarly and teaching enterprises, no matter what the "field."

This basic need points up the problem. There are numerous ways of trying to solve it. The graduate schools could help enormously, apart from placing more emphasis on good teaching, by insisting that their students cover a greater variety of important aspects or wider dimensions of the field. College administrators can help by insisting on the selection of teachers committed to this richer understanding of their material and to the students' deeper understanding of it. General faculty concern for the method and purpose of liberal education can help. The more these matters are studied and discussed by those directly responsible for teaching, the more effective and vital the teaching will become, particularly if all or most will acknowledge the basic principles involved; namely, that learning must tie in vitally with all that is best in human experience.

Lastly, perhaps the most important single device for the college campus remains to be mentioned and fully exploited. As has been suggested, there is on every campus a certain number of scholars and teachers whose concerns are fundamentally moral and spiritual, whatever their theological or philosophic positions. These are men sensitive to the adventure of the human spirit, whether for themselves or their students. Such men are often willing, if encouraged, to gain further knowledge and wisdom from authors and colleagues of different fields and different modes of thought. Wherever smaller groups of teachers and scholars on any campus can meet with this fundamental purpose in mind; and can gradually initiate programs of instruction as independent enterprises relatively free from the restraints of the larger group; and where they can do so in a spirit which is committed in part to their own growth in intellectual variety and creativity, we shall begin to establish focuses of revitalized education. At these points a significant vigor should develop which to a surprising degree would lend ferment to the lives of our graduate and undergraduate students. Its contagion, grounded in the perpetual personal discovery of fresh and important insights and meanings, should carry in it the seeds of a significant spiritual revival in our centers of learning.

7

Religion and the Mind of the
University

Bernard M. Loomer

THE nature of religion today and the nature of education today are such that the problem of "religion in higher education" is surrounded with almost insurmountable obstacles. The context of this problem has developed from a long and complicated history extending over a period from three to four centuries. There is certainly no basis for hope in any fundamental solution that is going to remedy the situation in a short time. Possibly the most that the present generation can do is to become clear about the nature of the problem and to make a beginning attack.

In attempting to define the nature of the problem concerning "religion in higher education," we should have some definition of the nature of the university situation in which this problem must be worked out. In what follows I have tried to clarify this picture by describing the nature of the university mind. With some qualifications, generalizations that are true of universities are also applicable to colleges.

I. Attitudes toward Religion

The first observation that can be made about the university mind is that it is in general ignorant and illiterate with regard to an adequate conception of religious faith. Even those university faculty people who are favorably disposed toward religion are in the main immature and uncritical about their religious faith. They are as naïve and uncritical in this respect as they are critical and sophisticated in their own specialized studies. Their religious faith usually consists of that religious attitude and understanding which they have carried over from their childhood. Religion for them is something fundamental and simple, and they would prefer not to be forced to rethink their understanding of it. Seldom is there any critical, organic relation in their minds between their specialized disciplines and their religious beliefs and practices. They would be disposed to support a vigorous defense of the validity of religious faith, but not if this defense were to necessitate a radical reorganization within themselves. They feel that religion should be accorded a recognized status within the university, but they would be incapable of stating the intellectual justification for this feeling.

There are others within a faculty who also interpret religion in terms of something they experienced in their childhood and adolescence. But this group feels that it has outgrown any concern with religion. They identify religion with certain beliefs, practices, and observances which in their process of maturation they have reacted against and denied. Therefore religion in its conventional sense can be ignored or dispensed with, and more reasonable and sophisticated substitutes can be found. On the whole they are not violent in their opposition even though they react emotionally against conventional religion and are convinced that it has no intellectual justification. In fact they exhibit an amused tolerance toward those of their colleagues who seek or apparently require the "consolations of religion." They regard the religious concern of some of their colleagues as a rather pathetic form of eccentricity. From their point of view, most of us have peculiar twists in our personalities; we are addicted to various forms of escapism and infantilism such as alcoholism, sex, and religion. These several forms of addiction are minor vices. A mature and sophisticated intellectual ideally ought to be able to get along without them. But unless these and kindred eccentricities take the form of grand passions they should not be criticized too severely. The fact that a colleague resorts to these various forms of indulgence does not disqualify him from membership within the community of scholars. For this group, a religious orientation is superfluous for the life and thought of the scholar, whether he be student or faculty member.

Another group in the faculty is much more strongly negative in its attitude toward religion. Members of this group regard religion as something that is not only a block but a positive threat to many of our most precious rights. They feel that religious people and institutions have imperialistic designs and motives operating under the guise of benevolent concern. After all, was it not the Christian faith which controlled all those studies that later became distinct and separate academic disciplines? It was only as these disciplines escaped from the iron hand of Christian faith that they were free to pursue their inquiries for truth in an untrammelled manner. For these people, religion is not only the opiate of the people, but it is also the great barrier to creative and independent intellectual effort.

Those who are concerned with the furtherance of the religious enterprise must grant at least the partial truth of this latter contention and recognize the real danger that these people are insistent to point out. For the nature of religion is such that it is either fundamental, central, and basic or it is nothing. In the nature of the case, religion cannot be a peripheral concern and discipline. Yet an adequate religion must not result in dogmatism or uniformity of thought. It is precisely at this point that many faculty have their fears. Religion as they have known it does connote something dogmatic, leading to the loss of freedom and independence of inquiry. It has been too often true that the centrality of religion has tended toward an emphasis upon uniformity of thinking. Therefore with regard to at least conventional interpretations of religion many faculty people understandably prefer an atomistic, pluralistic, and essentially unorganized university. As long as the university remains atomistic and pluralistic, there is freedom because no group is in a position of power to dictate on matters of fundamental intellectual importance. By and large this group has not encountered interpretations of religion which do justice, on the one hand, to the fundamental centrality of the place of religion in life and thought and which preserve, on the other hand, the fundamental rights of freedom and independence.

In all fairness it should be added that there is another group of university faculty, small but increasing in number, whose members are seriously concerned and spiritually prepared to give religion a hearing. They do not think of religion in unsophisticated terms nor do they view it as a neurotic obsession or as a problem to be overcome. They regard it, critically but sympathetically, as a (or the) possible resource in dealing with fundamental issues. They read and understand good theological works and they are heartened and encouraged. Yet they are cautious. They await greater constructive efforts on our part.

It follows from all this that a great deal of education concerning religion must be carried on even in our highest centers of learning before a fundamental attack on the problem of religion in higher education can make much headway. The illiteracy, immaturity, inertia, indifference, and antagonism of faculty people toward religion constitute serious obstacles to the religious enterprise in education that will not be easily or quickly overcome.

II. SPECIALIZATION AND ITS CONSEQUENCES

The second observation is that the university mind cannot be understood unless it is seen in the context of the departmental structure of the university. It cannot be overemphasized that the

basis of university life is to be found within the various departments of which the modern university consists. This observation
is trite enough. But several human consequences of this fact
should be noted.

In the first place each department with its constituent field
of specialized inquiry constitutes a world of its own. It has a
language all its own, and it has its own unique outlook on life.
The unique technical language and outlook of a department are
such that the members of other departments cannot even spell,
let alone understand, the meaning of the words that are used.
Administrators are placed in the unenviable position of having
to make decisions about research projects that they do not comprehend. This general situation gives rise to an inferiority
complex that is shared by university faculty and administrators
alike.

When the university is defined as "a community of scholars,"
it should be understood that the word "community" is used in
a very loose sense. One might think that a university would be
a place where the greatest communication of ideas occurred.
But as a matter of fact a university is an institution where very
little fundamental communication takes place, particularly between members of different departments. There is no common
language of discourse or any commonly understood set of ideas.
The attempt at communication by faculty members from different departments usually results in a feeling of mutual frustration.
The member from one department wants to carry on the discussion in terms of the most important and advanced ideas in his
own subject matter. But to make these points clear to his own
satisfaction he inevitably falls back upon the use of a vocabulary
that is special to his department. In order to discuss the content
of these ideas he must assume that the person from the other
department will follow the discussion as easily and logically as
he himself does. He does not want to embarrass himself or to
insult the intelligence of the person from the other department

by beginning his presentation with an introductory and elementary discussion of words and ideas. The listener from the other department may honestly want to hear this presentation, but he secretly wishes that the introductory and elementary discussion of words and ideas were possible. And yet he does not want to embarrass himself by asking for an elaboration of what must appear obvious to the person from the other department, nor does he want seemingly to question the importance of the other person's subject matter by requesting such a preliminary and beginning statement. Consequently the whole attempt is usually unsatisfactory to both concerned. The speaker comes to realize that the other was willing but incapable of following the discussion and that a lot of confusion and misunderstanding cannot be overcome without a long and tedious setting forth of elementary facts and considerations which at this point he either does not have time to undertake or does not want to bother with. He also comes to a conclusion regarding the illiteracy of the other and realizes that the world has a long way to go before his own contribution can be understood by the general run of men. Yet at the same time he senses his own inadequacy in not being able to simplify and clarify his meanings. The other person comes to resent what he feels are the inadequacies of the speaker because he thinks that important ideas in any subject matter ought to be capable of being expressed in nontechnical language. He may even classify the other as a purely technical scholar with severe limitations, and conclude that ideas which require extreme technical competence for their understanding may not be so important after all. Thus while both leave the discussion somewhat dissatisfied for different reasons, each leaves the discussion enhanced in his own eyes. Each builds up his sense of superiority at the expense of the other.

The fact of departmentalization not only means that each man specializes in some particular area of study, but also that each person comes to look at the world through the eyes of his specialization. This is true in the general sense in that an economist, for example, is likely to look at things from an economic point of view. Similarly the religionist defines the world from the vantage point of his particular concerns. This fact has implications for the attempt to interrelate two or more departments. The economist relates economics to religion by considering religion in terms of its economic implications. The reply of the religionist is that the economist's viewpoint does not do justice to fundamental religious concerns. The same situation would hold if the example were to be reversed. Therefore all specialists are extremely wary of any attempts to integrate various departments, because each anticipates a feeling of resentment and dissatisfaction with the way in which his own particular subject matter will be handled within the integrative scheme. The economist may be aware that his field has moral, political, and religious implications. But he is inclined to think that these implications do not and cannot constitute the essential substance of his own peculiar subject matter. Economics must be allowed to speak its full content and only an economist is equipped to convey its full weight.

In the academic world, a university post is a highly coveted possession. Its achievement is a universally recognized symbol of intellectual success. It is an honor that carries a great deal of prestige. But this prestige is purchased at a frightful price. One might think that the attainment of this goal would result in a feeling of great freedom and security. But actually at the very moment of attaining the top rung of success in his profession, a professor is subject to great personal insecurity. He knows that he is surrounded by people whose intellectual capacities are as good, if not better, than his. He knows that he can maintain his sense of security only if he remains within the confines of his field of specialization wherein he has achieved some mastery and competence. He knows that if he ventures beyond his field of competence he may be severely criticized and be called naïve or stupid. A university professor may be relatively indifferent to being insulted in all sorts of ways. But he dare not be called naïve or stupid. His very position and his prestige, as well as his own self-evaluation, depend upon his being recognized as a person of critical intelligence. He cannot afford to run the risk of losing this recognition by venturing beyond his field of specialized competence.

Therefore a university professor shows great hesitation in even attempting to relate his field to other fields of specialization. He develops an almost structural quiver when he is asked to appear before a group of faculty outside his own field and to relate his own special discipline to theirs. He knows that he is risking his very professional life in such a venture. Consequently a university professor will not disclose to others that part of himself which goes beyond his specialized competence. At least he will not do so unless he is very sure of the persons to whom he is speaking. By the very nature of his situation, he is not a trusting person. He feels that his own sense of personal worth and integrity is dependent upon his not disclosing himself to others who may not appreciate his competence. He is defensive. Many times there are good intellectual reasons why he dismisses criticisms of his work that are made by men outside the field of his competence. But these good reasons are always intertwined with his own defensive reactions which are ever-present because he implicitly feels that he himself is being attacked. His own world of meaning is threatened, and his place in the community and his self-esteem are in jeopardy. Academic discussions about intellectual topics are never as objective and disinterested as those of us in academic circles would like to believe and would like to have others believe. Some may feel that the university professor is guilty of pretentiousness in the form of intellectual pride. Undoubtedly there is some truth in this contention. But it can be said with equal and possibly greater justice that the university professor is a fearful creature who knows that his sense of security and well-being hang on slender threads. The god of the university professor is specialized competence. His whole intellectual life is defined in terms of it and all the rest of his life is dependent upon it.

This whole picture is evidenced in terms of the criteria that govern the choice of appointments to be made to the faculty. If, for example, the choice is between a first-rate scientist with no concern at all to relate his field to other fields in the interests of intellectual wholeness and no ability to do so, and a technically second-rate scientist who is able to relate two or more specialized fields, inevitably the decision is made in favor of the former. Intellectually and humanly speaking, the consequence of this policy is that competence is rated as a more important qualification than intellectual integrity, where "integrity" means "wholeness," "unity," the denial of fragmentation or the absence of compartmentalization. Even those few who are concerned with intellectual integrity will usually insist that competence in a specialized field is the first and basic requirement for faculty membership. Even in their eyes integrity is something that goes beyond the call of duty. They think that integrity may be realized after one has achieved competence or that it may come naturally in the course of events and without conscious effort. They do not seriously entertain the idea that competence may not be the essential prerequisite for integrity, and that competence may be as dependent on integrity as they feel integrity is dependent on competence.

To be sure, intellectual integrity cannot be achieved on the basis of incompetence. But there are levels of competence. The highest or the deepest achievement of competence within a specialized field is rooted in a concern for integrity.

The emergence of independent and autonomous departments came about as a means of furthering the progress toward truth. This was a valuable step forward. But the present-day departmental organization of the university operates as the greatest single collective defense mechanism for the members of a university faculty. To the degree that this characterization is true, the university mind is not a free mind. The saying that "you shall know the truth and the truth shall make you free" is not to be taken in an unqualified sense as applying to the truth involved in specialized inquiry.

From a religious point of view, one of the profound consequences to the university mind of specialized intellectual discipline is the loss of a more deeply human kind of perceptiveness. One great possible danger of concentrated and prolonged specialized discipline is the atrophy of a sensitive awareness to the fundamental and pervasive features of everyday life. Specialized inquiry aims at knowledge rather than at wisdom. Wisdom is the result of a penetrating analysis of the obvious, of common everyday experience. Whitehead has said that it takes a very unusual mind to elucidate the obvious. Indeed it is this very elucidation of the commonplace that stirs the hearts and imaginations of people, even the intellectuals. The great themes of life are the themes that deal with the basic and foundational character of day-by-day existence. The great religions and the great philosophies are those which disclose the greatness and profound resources to be found within very usual occurrences. The specialized point of view has a tendency to become blind to these features and resources. It tends to deal with the unusual, the uncommon, and the extraordinary. At its best it fails to perceive the greatness which is so near to all that it may appear insignificant. It thereby tends to forget or to lose sight of the concrete basis of our intellectual life, and even of our specialized disciplines. To this extent, the academic mind too often becomes irrelevant to the great human issues. By definition knowledge is abstract. And to the extent that it is abstract, it is valuable. But its value is lessened if the discoverer of knowledge too long forgets the concrete ground from which abstractions are made. Knowledge can be and too often is purchased at the price of wisdom. And today one of the decisive questions that confront the university mind is the problem as to whether this is too great a price to pay for knowledge.

It is a commonplace idea in the minds of many people outside academic circles that the university is the prime illustration of the ivory tower. This characterization usually means that university faculty live a peculiarly irresponsible type of life, and that they are relieved from the burdens and pressures that constitute real life outside the university. But from what has been said above, it should be clear that university life is just as real and troublesome and dynamic as life outside. Any administrator knows that faculty people are beset by the same trials and tribulations that are common to most people. They have most of the worries, frustrations, anxieties, and defeats that make life difficult for people beyond the bounds of the university. It is true that university faculty are relieved from some of the pressures that businessmen, for example, must live with. But it is also true that the university professor who takes his job seriously is subject to pressures that no other group of comparable men endure. The pressures and efforts of hard intellectual work take their own toll. The process of attempting to become intellectually self-conscious is to be sure rewarding, but it constitutes a very uncomfortable, disturbing, and searching kind of experience. The demands of this process result in intellectual and spiritual labors that most people are glad to escape. The practice of having the results of your efforts subjected to the constant, vigorous, and many times unsympathetic criticism of your colleagues results in psychological and physical pressures that do not characterize the lives of most people. The ivory tower is not a place where; it is rather an attitude of mind and spirit. There is an ivory tower life that some university people live. But there is as much ivory tower living in the business world as there is in the university. The conclusion to be drawn from this consideration is that no class of people is entitled to look down its collective nose at any other class. Intellectuals are as guilty of this practice of snobbery as any other group. But this attitude only furthers the divisiveness that is all too characteristic of our society. It usually involves an attempt to enhance one's self at the expense of others. And it reflects an insecurity wherever it may be found.

III. LEADERSHIP AND INTEGRATION

The third observation is that there is no intellectual leadership in a university. I mean by this that there is no sense of intellectual direction that characterizes the university within itself. Consequently the university furnishes no intellectual direction for the rest of the community. The reasons for this state of affairs are quite obvious.

On the whole, top university administrators are not appointed primarily because of their intellectual endowments. Those who can think don't have time to. Or, to put it more fairly, they have to think about too many matters. Their energies are used up by all kinds of important activities, especially the all-consuming need to raise money. If they are not exhausted by the effort to meet this inescapable pressure, their time is taken up with a variety of other almost equally urgent tasks. Dr. Robert Maynard Hutchins, former Chancellor of the University of Chicago, has aptly characterized the life of the administrator by saying that he has to do so many all-important jobs that he does not have the time to do the one thing he ought to do. The one thing he ought to do is at least to suggest the fundamental intellectual direction in which the university should move. Consequently, the university is actually a pluriversity, a collection of independent and autonomous departments, each with its own concerns and policies. There are not, even within any one university, commonly accepted criteria whereby the various academic ranks are to be distinguished. There are not any commonly accepted criteria of adequate and really competent scholarship. And, apart from financial considerations, there are no significant principles in terms of which the expansionist tendencies of universities can be curbed.

Because or when the chief administrative officers of a university do not and probably cannot provide intellectual leadership of the university, it is somewhat unrealistic to think that the faculty will undertake this task. At best the faculty, or some part of it, might assume this responsibility if it were absolutely sure that the administration would be sympathetic. But if the administration is felt to be negative or at best neutral in this regard the faculty will not accept the burden of this task for fear of going out on a limb and having it cut off.

In any event, the attempt on the part of a portion of a faculty to establish the intellectual direction in which the university should move is almost bound to meet with failure. This is so because a faculty's proposal would not constitute an official and binding policy. It would not constitute an official pressure that had to be encountered and taken into account by the rest of the faculty. It could safely be ignored by those who either disagreed or were not interested. It would not be binding upon the administration and would not be a decisive element of policy with regard to faculty appointments. The pressure necessary to make this decision significant would not be generated by the faculty itself. To be finally effective pressure must assume the form of power, and power to be decisive must be official.

As a consequence of this basically human impasse, there is at present no concerted and sustained effort to make a university out of the pluralistic and atomistic departments within the so-called university. There is no official pressure to attempt to integrate in any effective way the various disciplines that pursue their independent careers. The administrator may talk about the need for integration, and may urge that something be done. But faculty members can remain secure within their departments because they know that this is only talk, at best the expression of a somewhat vague and unrealistic hope. The larger the number of departments, the larger the faculty, the more vague, unrealistic, and sentimental this hope becomes. Integration is a luxury and not a necessity of academic life. It will not become a necessity until it becomes an inherent part of administrative policy. The culture may cry for integration and a sense of intellectual direction. But this cry will go unheeded because administrators are incapable of responding to the cry and the faculty are not compelled to answer.

The god of the faculty is specialized competence. This god cannot or at least usually does not respond to the cry of the troubled soul which seeks human and intellectual integrity. The god of the administrator is efficiency, and the law of that god is compromise. Consequently important distinctions, judgments, and criteria are blurred because of conflicting forces and interests. These idols may not always be consciously chosen but nonetheless they are inevitably served. The institution is preserved in its mediocrity. The letter of the law is observed. But the spirit becomes enchained. As Whitehead has observed: "The art of persistence is to be dead."

IV. Competence vs. Integrity

The fourth observation is that the moral, intellectual, and spiritual standards of universities are not very high. On the whole modern American universities exist in terms of a capital of inherited ideas, but there is no concerted and sustained effort made to replenish the capital fund of these ideas. Universities have more or less assumed a justification for their existence, and they have also assumed the validity of this justification. But it is precisely the fact and validity of this assumed justification which are being called into question today. In terms of the kind of work that goes on in modern American universities, one might say that they have practically no good grounds on the basis of which they can criticize what happened to German universities with the coming of Hitler to power. If, contrary to the whole process of historical development, one could conceive of this country's being suddenly and seriously threatened by powerful reactionary forces, it could not simply be assumed that our universities would constitute a strong bulwark against these forces. Or at least one might say that the strength of the universities in this projected crisis would be derived more from the general American culture than from the resources of the universities themselves.

There are after all rather few constructive and creative minds in our universities. The intellectual level of most of our work is to be seen in terms of historical, critical, and analytical studies. Competence is measured in terms of this critical and analytical type of labor and not in terms of genuine creative effort. The greatness of creative work is not the normal or usual standard. The creative scholar is the exception and not the rule. True creativity is for the most part welcomed but the implicit policy of the university is that general academic life does not require it for its proper functioning.

Another way of putting this same point is to say that an insufficient number of university professors are intellectually alive. The labors of their research do not issue into results that have intellectual consequences. Too much of their work deals with facts of many kinds but not with ideas as such. Or at least the ideas dealt with lack penetration and generality. The professors are apparently incapable of generalizing the results of their inquiries in such a way that their relevance to other subject matters can be seen. Consequently most professors feel that they really need not take into account the results of the intellectual labors of their colleagues.

This means that there is no sustained intellectual communication that goes on in a university. There is too little intellectual passion exemplified. Professors do not go to each other's classes because it would be mutually embarrassing and because each must prepare his own lectures on specialized topics and carry on research in specialized areas. There is very little discursive discussion of ideas in general and of their relation to various disciplines. There are very few opportunities for one man to present the results of his inquiries to others. He writes for a specialized audience and his writing is published in technical journals. He is not required to relate this research to a wider area of thought and his colleagues are not required to take his results into account.

The point at issue can be related to our discussion of the university as an ivory tower. The university is an ivory tower for those within the university who do not believe in the value of, or are not seriously engaged in, fundamental intellectual pursuits. There is the life of the mind which issues into the products of the mind, such as scientific discoveries, works in fine arts, humanistic and social understandings of man. This life and these works are important if man is to understand himself and his world. Great works of the mind quicken the imagination and the sensitivities, widen and deepen the range and depth of appreciation and understanding. High civilizations require great works of the mind. These works are in part at least the justification for the intellectual life, and the place of the intellectual in our society. But too often the modern university professor does not believe in this kind of justification, or at least his labors do not exemplify it.

A university is usually defined as an intellectual community. But the content of the word "intellectual" is defined in terms of specialized competence. The larger ideal of intellectual integrity is lost sight of or becomes an expendable ideal. To be sure, we usually assume that the competent scholar is an honest scholar. But intellectual integrity is more than competence or honesty. It may presuppose these. But intellectual integrity involves the idea of wholeness, of unity, wherein the several disciplines that make up a university are synthesized. The ideal of integrity involves synthesis of the various aspects of man's experience with his world because they are aspects of any one individual. If we required a prospective faculty appointment to be concerned about intellectual integrity, we would be asking him to relate two or more fields of specialized inquiry. But all we ask for at present is that the prospective professor be competent. We imply thereby that the professor as a divided or compartmentalized self can be both an adequate member of a faculty and a true representative of the intellectual life. Some administrators would like to invoke the ideal of integrity in evaluating prospective members of the faculty. But for various reasons they operate in terms of the minimum intellectual standard, namely, competence. In this fashion universities support and even further the mediocrity that is so characteristic of our society.

This mediocrity has its moral roots and implications, only one of which need be cited here. In order to carry on independent intellectual work the faculty must be free to pursue its inquiries. Freedom of thought is a necessity and not merely a dispensable convenience. Most faculty members presuppose that they are free to carry on their inquiries and that they are not too subject to coercive pressures. This is trite enough. And yet standards of faculty membership do not explicitly require that each faculty member should be concerned actively to support and protect the freedom of inquiry of his colleagues in other departments.

This fact would seem to indicate that universities are not sufficiently aware of the theological and philosophical bases of their existence. The right of freedom of inquiry is grounded in either the fundamental principle of Protestantism or its secular equivalent. Most non-Catholic universities are aware that they are not Catholic. They know in a general sense what they are against. But they are not aware of what they are for, or of the principles in terms of which their character is justified. Few if any universities can set forth a meaningful statement of goals and purposes that would withstand careful scrutiny and be relevant to the needs of our culture. At best such a statement would involve the ideas of freedom of inquiry and the pursuit of specialized truth. But the definition of freedom would be stated negatively in terms of "freedom from" rather than positively in terms of "freedom for."

V. Conclusion

This general picture of the university mind has several implications for those who are concerned with advancing the cause of religion in the realm of higher education. What follows is not an attempt to present a constructive solution or to be definitive, but rather to state an outline of general principles in terms of which an answer may in the course of events be found.

The most obvious consequence is that the presentation of religion must meet the basic requirements of intellectual respectability. This is a large order and it is an important condition. But, important and fundamental as it is, it is still minimal and preliminary. Some people seem to think that the cause of religion has achieved its goal when a department of religion has been established in a college or university, especially if it can be claimed with any justice that the faculty in the department of religion is as strong as the faculty in any other department. This is a solid advance, but it marks only the beginning.

A more advanced stage is to be seen in terms of the requirement that religion must be presented in such a way that its relevance to other disciplines can be seen not only by the religionists but by the people in these other disciplines. The problem of the relevance of religious inquiry to other academic inquiries is a difficult one. But one of the most important facts about academic inquiries is that they covertly contain implicit religious outlooks operating in the form of assumptions, presuppositions, methodologies, and guiding principles. Therefore one of religion's first obligations is to recognize this fact and to make it explicit. The possible relevance of an adequate religious faith and theology cannot be seen by people in other disciplines until they are made aware of the implicit religious assumptions in terms of which they have been operating. The actual relevance of an adequate religious faith and theology cannot be made clear until the implicit religious premises of these other disciplines have been shown to be inadequate. A constructive and adequate theology must prove itself to be such in terms of its more fruitful intellectual implications and consequences for other academic disciplines. If this cannot be accomplished, those faculty members who are concerned about religion have no ultimately persuasive reasons for complaining about their colleagues' lack of interest in things religious. They will have lost the battle on intellectual grounds, too often the vulnerable, soft underbelly of theology.

Religion can never be a peripheral matter. It is a central and ultimate concern that constitutes the core of an individual's life and thought. Implicitly or explicitly it is the foundation for that organization of values and meanings which form his personality. It cannot be an extracurricular activity. Nor can the presentation and discussion of it be confined to a department of religion in a college or university. It must constitute the heart of a curriculum. Undoubtedly a department of religion is necessary for the more intensive study of religion. But religion must also be conceived in such a way that at least some phases of it can be dealt with by other disciplines as disciplines and not as something extraneous to themselves.

This more advanced requirement places a great burden upon religious intellectuals. They must not only know their own subject matter as competently as other faculty members know theirs; they must also know their subject matter in relation and as relevant to other disciplines. But the fulfillment of this obligation will become a real possibility only to the extent that the academic representatives of the religious enterprise believe in the value of intellectual disciplines as such. They cannot compromise their devotion and vitiate their contribution by wondering whether they are really serving the church in their intellectual labors. They cannot afford to be swayed from their singleness of purpose by appeals from ministers and misguided laymen to make their work relevant to the so-called practical needs of the church. In one sense the fundamental intellectual issues of our time are the pressing practical problems of the church. The attempt to find adequate answers to these issues demands the devotion of men who regard the intellectual life as a calling. It is not an escape. It is not less real. And it is not a luxury for the church.

I have indicated that there is no intellectual leadership in our universities. I have tried to show why a faculty will not assume the burden of providing this leadership. Yet the process of constructing a university out of a miscellaneous group of independent departments must begin with some group in the faculty, however small and unpromising the beginning may seem. The nature of religious faith is such that it must of necessity seek for intellectual integrity, for one intellectual world. It must concern itself with the problem of intellectual direction. Part of its business is to try to make sense out of the various intellectual outlooks of the several constituent departments of a university. One of the main obligations of a divinity school or a department of religion, therefore, is to be the university within the university. This must be undertaken not from a feeling of superiority or condescension but out of a sense of humble courage. It can best attempt to be the university within the university by exemplifying the intellectual standards of competence, integrity, and freedom in its own intellectual labors. Its work must illustrate the interrelationship of various specialized disciplines.

For many years the work of professors of religion has aped the standards of other disciplines. This process of imitation was necessary because in so many instances religious scholarship did not compare favorably with scholarly standards of other departments. But the time has long since passed when professors of religion should be content with measuring their work by the standards of others. They should attempt to remain true to the genius of their own discipline, not as religious inquiry in proud isolation, but in organic relation to other types of intellectual inquiry.

It follows from all this, almost by definition, that a university is as strong intellectually, morally, and religiously as its divinity school or department of religion (or those members of a university faculty who are doing what a divinity school ought to be doing). The failure of modern universities is in large part the failure of religion. This is true in spite of the excellence of individual scholars within a university. Divinity schools are admittedly weak intellectually, morally, and religiously. Universities are therefore correspondingly weak in these respects. Unfortunately no divinity school or department of religion in any university has seriously assumed its full obligations to the university. By and large this failure is due to a lack of intellectual and religious manpower which is not to be easily or quickly remedied. It has been several hundred years since the best minds of western culture have centered their intellectual concern in theology. But the challenge and the opportunity are present.

In the last analysis, however, religion is more than an affair of the intellect. It may well be in the long run as well as in the short run that religion's greatest contribution to higher education will not be exclusively or even primarily intellectual. The university is usually defined as an intellectual community. In its narrowest definition this implies that an individual is a member of a university faculty in terms of his intellect, and not in terms of his whole being. This definition of a university unwittingly seems to provide the justification for the contention of scholars who maintain that as members of a faculty they are not responsible for the moral, social, and political consequences of their research.

But however that may be, it must become ever more apparent

to those members of a university faculty who are seriously concerned about religion that a university must be defined in more than intellectual terms. The definition must run deeper than that. This something more is needed if the intellectual tasks themselves are to be carried on most fruitfully. The intellect must feed on something more fundamental and elemental than itself. The lack of intellectual vitality and power in our universities today is not due simply to a decrease of intellectual ability. The failure is more profoundly human. The psychological and spiritual conditions of frustration, rebellion, anxiety, and emptiness of many faculties are living evidence of a need for a university community which is more than an assemblage of competent intellects.

The university is not the church. To take one obvious point, membership in a university faculty involves the meeting of certain intellectual standards which do not apply to membership in a church. And yet the kind of community that is needed in a university if members of its faculty are to realize their intellectual goals may perhaps more closely approximate to the community which is the church than we have realized or admitted. This is not an attempt to solve our intellectual problems by an evangelistic appeal. But certainly one obligation of the faculty of a divinity school or a department of religion is to exemplify, at least within itself, that kind of community which allows and encourages the type of self-disclosure and trust essential to the achievement of intellectual self-consciousness and integrity.

The conclusion of this discussion is that we shall not have better universities until we have better theology, and that we shall not have better theology until we have better universities. The implied corollary is that we shall not have better universities until we have better churches, and that we shall not have better churches until we have better universities.

8

The Teaching of Religion

Virginia Corwin

RELIGION has been taught in one fashion or another in the colleges and universities from the beginning. From having been considered a central concern of the college the teaching of religion passed through some decades in which its place was uncertain and ambiguous. The objectives, the methods, even its existence in the college have been affected by the intellectual and social forces which have borne upon all religion. At the middle of the century the situation seems to be clearer than it was. Religion is widely recognized as a subject worthy of serious study, and its relation to the central goals of education is again being discussed.

I. Background of the Present Situation

The second quarter of the century has seen genuine improvement in the teaching of religion. Departments of religion in most colleges are modest in size and in the number of offerings, but unless size be taken as the sole measure of health the teaching of religion must be said to be in a sounder state than some other fields, and in much sounder condition than it was in the middle twenties. Courses in religion are far more numerous than they were. By 1940 all church-related colleges, 85 per cent of the independent colleges, and 30 per cent of the state institutions had departments of religion. Several of the universities in which work had been allowed to lapse have recently re-established or strengthened courses and departments. Princeton in 1938, Yale since 1947, and the University of Pennsylvania in 1949 are among these. New York University established a department in 1950. Furthermore, during the past twenty-five years standards have been steadily improved. Departments are by and large staffed with people holding the same academic degrees as their colleagues in other departments, and the level of competence in scholarship and teaching is presumably equal to that in other fields. Student response is hard to measure, but in many departments over the country there is lively interest. Princeton, for example, after beginning with one professor of religious thought and two courses in 1938, now has a department of five men, and six year-courses. This advance could be matched in other places. Perhaps most significant of all, the relation of religion to the total educational goals of the colleges is again being widely discussed. Most of these matters call for further examination, but taken together they indicate a healthy upswing in the teaching of religion, even if no more than a beginning has been made.

In the twenties the situation was very different. The required courses in religion which represented the expression of religious conviction at the founding of the independent colleges had fallen on evil days. The progress of the elective system was pressing hard on any specific requirement at all. And in far too many places courses in religion were taught by preachers rather than by scholars and teachers. Courses were frequently stronger on edification than on intellectual content. Professor Charles Foster Kent of Yale, in his vigorous campaign in 1922 and 1923 for the wider and more effective teaching of religion, put first the need for persons really prepared to teach. Since most colleges had been founded by denominational bodies and practically all the rest by men and women of religious convictions, the teaching of religion in the earliest days tended to be frankly doctrinal, a pattern which it was difficult to change. The intent of this teaching had been to produce Christian beliefs and life in the students, but by some time early in the century that objective was no longer consonant with the strictly intellectual interests of other departments in the colleges. Charles Foster Kent underlined just those factors when he said that religion courses were not more widely offered because religion was associated both with denominational interest and with doctrinal authoritarianism, resistant to new literary and historical methods.

Different types of colleges have perforce taken different attitudes toward the introduction of teaching in religion. The independent and church-related colleges, by virtue of their religious heritage and their freedom, have throughout their history had the largest proportion of departments of religion, and the best-developed programs of courses. The teachers colleges have done least in this field, and in 1940 only 10 out of 149 of them had departments. For them and for the state universities the legal problem has presented a persistent difficulty. The question has been whether public and land grant institutions, receiving tax money from all the people of the state, could rightfully establish teaching in religion. During the earlier years of the century policies of caution prevailed, but in the twenties there was an increasing demand from various quarters that students be able to study religion at the university level.

During the twenties "schools of religion" were founded by denominations at the gates of a number of the state universities, and some thirteen of them still continue. These schools were of several types, some more successful than others. For instance, in the University of Texas in 1922-23 sixteen semester hours in religion were offered by the university, twelve by the Association of Religious Teachers, six by Newman Hall, ten by the holder of the Presbyterian Bible Chair, and twelve each by the incumbents of chairs supported by the Disciples of Christ, the Church of Christ, and the Methodists. The University of Illinois had a not dissimilar arrangement. It is obvious that it would be difficult to produce a well-integrated program of courses of high standard under such circumstances. It is also clear that charges of sectarianism could hardly be avoided. The University of Ohio tried and abandoned that plan. The experiment at the University of Missouri met these difficulties rather better. The Bible College of Missouri was established by the Disciples in 1896, but in 1914 they invited other denominations to join with them in providing teachers of religion, and by 1929 the Disciples, Methodists, Presbyterians, and Jews each supported a faculty member. Denominations paid the salaries, and maintained control through members on the board of trustees of the school of religion but the course offerings were planned by the collective faculty of the school. Under that, or somewhat similar arrangements, well-planned courses might be offered to students of the universities, who were allowed to elect a stated number of hours to be credited toward a degree. At the same time state money was not spent for "sectarian" teaching. There is the possibility that in the future such schools of religion may be associated more closely with the undergraduate colleges of arts and sciences. Thus, the School of Religion in the State University of Iowa, which began to offer courses in 1927, by 1939 had been accepted as a department of religion within the undergraduate college. The university carries administrative expenses, but money for the salaries of instructors, who are Jewish, Roman Catholic, and Protestant, is provided from private sources, individual and denominational.

It is not only in that way that the problem is being met, for it is becoming clearer that even in state institutions the legal difficulties are not insurmountable. Although in 1940 only 30 per cent of the state institutions reported departments of religion, a total of 80 per cent offered courses in religion of one sort or another under university auspices. In many cases the offerings in religion consisted of only a few hours, but that they were there at all suggests the possibility of expansion. The objectives of the teaching of religion have undergone a change since the earliest years. Originally colleges were founded in part to educate ministers, and in part to produce religious-minded laymen. The Protestant churches wanted men who could study the Scriptures intelligently, for the Word of God was the proper study of man. Courses in evidences of Christianity were added to studies in classics and mathematics and most colleges would have accepted wholeheartedly the view suggested in the Wellesley catalogue of 1886 which stated that "the systematic study of the Bible is pursued through all the courses." The colleges really supplemented the work of the churches, and although the methods of the two were different their goals were the same: the formation of a Christian mind and character, and that a Protestant one. Most of the teachers were ministers, and it is not surprising that long after the general faculty ceased to be members of the clergy presidents of the institutions and professors of religion still were. The Christian character of the colleges was unmistakable.

By the eighties and nineties strictly intellectual interests began to forge ahead. The ferment of the philological and historical disciplines in the German universities began to affect American colleges. One of the first results was the organization of the colleges into more departments than had been felt necessary until that time. Among them, in the independent colleges, were departments of biblical literature, or of Bible study. In the year 1892-93 both Wellesley and Yale founded such departments, and during the next decade many more came into being. But more important than the founding of departments of religion were the basically new objectives and methods introduced into the teaching. The religious literatures of Christianity and of other religions became objects of strictly intellectual investigation, unhampered by doctrinal restrictions. The liberal movement was under way, with the inevitably resulting opposition that did not come to an end until the middle twenties.

The first of the new disciplines to take hold was a strict kind of philological study. One must suppose that a course in St. Paul's epistles to the Corinthians described in the Yale catalogue of 1888-89 as "not a theological but a philological interpretation of St. Paul" was of this sort. Courses in Arabic and other Semitic languages were added to those in Hebrew and Greek, and study of the scriptures of other religions became available in departments of oriental languages. But alongside the philological studies historical and literary methods were adopted. Yale's department in its first year offered such courses as the study of parts of the Old Testament in Hebrew, pre-biblical and biblical history, the Minor Prophets (studied as history and literature), Old Testament Psalm and Wisdom literature, and a course in the epistles of St. Paul, described as a "study connected with the development of the thoughts of the writer." If it seems on first sight that this is a return to the older doctrinal teaching it is a false conclusion. Literary and historical techniques were coming into their own. The word "literature" in this connection should not be taken to suggest an aesthetic interest of any sort, but rather the literary source analysis which gained so great an influence.

It is hard to be sure whether the objectives of the new "modern" study of religion were fully recognized. It is clear that intellectual understanding was a prominent goal. Christianity was a field of study worthy of investigation. But a perhaps more fundamental motive was the continuing hope that religion might be served by the new methods. It was widely believed that accurate and objective knowledge could be obtained of the formative periods of Old Testament and New Testament thinking, and that by this means religious reverence and experience would be deepened. Thus the intellectual interests were placed hopefully in the context of a larger faith. Part of the enthusiasm arose because the new studies were independent of the older divisive denominational interests. This optimism of the whole interdenominational liberal movement was expressed in the years after World War I by many of the men who pressed for more departments and new courses.

The late twenties and the thirties were a period of conflicting views about religion, and these inevitably bore on the teaching of religion in the colleges. It was the uneasy equilibrium of liberalism between faith in the methods of objective study, and belief that loyalty to Christianity could be served thereby, that inevitably brought the teaching under attack both from the right and from the left. Conservative church circles pointed out that the optimism of the liberals was not justified. The sectarian faith of many students did not in fact survive the new teaching. Historical methods were charged with being destructive. This criticism arose partly from conservative fear of any change, but partly from a true, if inarticulate, perception that Christianity was not identical with the oversimple rationalism of many of the liberals. The attack from the left came from the suspicion in naturalist circles of continued acceptance of the Christian idea of God. Objective study seemed to them to dissolve the older supernaturalism, and they attacked the liberal movement because it did not go far enough. The early version of pragmatism associated with naturalism criticized much teaching of religion because it was preoccupied with the historical traditions, which belonged to the past, rather than with the problems of new adjustments called for in the present; a problem-centered, rather than a Bible-centered, curriculum was called for. Character-training seemed to some people to be the truly important objective of the teaching of religion.

While these criticisms came from without a certain amount of basic criticism was going on within. Teachers of religion, impelled to look at their work by developments in the philosophy of religion and in depth psychology, were becoming dissatisfied with the intellectualism of the older historical and literary studies. Religion was obviously more deeply grounded in individual experience than such approaches as source-criticism would suggest. It also closely reflected the communities of faith out of which the writings came; it was in part a *social* product, conditioned by its times. Furthermore, it was becoming clearer that religion is never a system of ideas nor a cult practice alone, but is expressed equally in the intuitions and choices of the good which are integral to vital religion.

Finally, it was increasingly recognized that teaching in the colleges would have to adjust to the new group of students. A program of courses designed for a fairly homogeneous Protestant group no longer fitted a student body of which Roman Catholics and Jews comprised an ever-increasing proportion.

Meanwhile, the pervasive effect of all of these influences and many more, social and intellectual, were at work not only changing the climate in the colleges, but affecting the assumptions and habits of the population as a whole. An increasing proportion of people had membership in churches, but religion to a lesser and lesser degree formed their minds. The result has been that students coming to the colleges have a very different background from those earlier in the century. Their "religious illiteracy" is frequently deplored, and the phrase does in fact describe an amazing lack of knowledge of facts about the Christian or Jewish faiths to which they nominally belong. More important still, they have no experience of religion as a mature commitment, which draws all aspects of life into a meaningful whole. But along with an increasingly tenuous association with religion has come a very widespread interest in studying it. The close of World War II and the uncertainty about the future forced upon thinking people the mood of self-analysis, and skepticism about the sufficiency of material values. There has inevitably resulted greater earnestness in the search for a religion to give direction and stability to life.

II. OBJECTIVES

The objectives of the teaching of religion today must be stated somewhat differently from the ways which seemed adequate twenty-five years ago. A statement of objectives will vary in emphasis from one individual to another, but perhaps many would agree that there are both proximate and further objectives, and that neither may be ignored. Of the possible proximate goals three seem to stand out: first, that the teaching must make clear the nature of particular historical religions, underlining the intellectual structure of concepts and insights, the basic non-rational experiences, and the way in which the religions have functioned in society; second, that the teaching must help to develop some norms as to what is sound and mature religion; and third, the philosophical assumptions and theological issues involved in holding a religious position must be made clear in relation to competing philosophies in our own day. The further objectives are still more important, but they differ from the others because probably by their nature they cannot or should not be tested. The teaching of religion must help a student to understand the underlying values and goals and assumptions of his own culture, and that of other cultures past and present. And it should clear the ground so that if he will a student may go on to develop religious thinking, and to commit himself to a religious faith. Conversion is not the business of the classroom, and decisions of this sort are individual matters. But the nature of the historical religions, and the issues in making the venture of religion are matters wholly appropriate to the classroom, and necessary preliminaries to adopting or deepening a faith. Each of these objectives must be defined more fully.

Of the three proximate objectives it is perhaps easiest to present the nature of the historical religions, but even there one meets trouble. There has been in all fields too much teaching of facts which in themselves are interesting and important enough, but which the student grasps as bare facts without seeing why they are crucial or revelatory. He has no knowledge or experience into which they fit. In the study of religion this inability to see beyond the façade of ideas is particularly unfortunate, for it means that the nature of the religion is not grasped at all. The student may know the names and functions of the Vedic gods, and fail to see what in the polytheism of the early Aryans may have led on to the magic- and priest-ridden *Brahmanas*. The teaching must make as clear and solid as the sources permit the pedestrian facts about a religion. They can in no way be dodged. But it must also help the student to see what the fundamental affirmations are, for example, about the nature of reality, what the good is that is worth striving for, the potentialities and limits of the men who strive—in short, the intellectual structure of the religion must be shown as the living and flexible attempts of men to adjust in a world which offers inescapable perplexities and temptations. The student may see in the most unified periods of history, or in the lives of the creative founders or leaders, that these fundamental insights have been related in a unified world view that has illuminated all aspects of experience. But whether he sees a fully developed world view or an abortive attempt at one he will see the rational structure of the religion as attempting to throw light on the ultimate meanings of life and death and the search for truth. He will never be deceived again by that widespread misbelief: that religion is primarily assent to a series of propositions which are only remotely related to the real problems of living.

More is involved, however, in apprehending the nature of a religion, than merely to see its intellectual framework, however richly and subtly this may be related to the process of living. For man's understanding of his world, and his checkered attempts to live a life consonant with his aspirations and insights, are spread out before us in every religion. He tries to know, but he also has to act. There is more than one significant way of being related to the world. The intellectual always hopes to understand fully before he acts. Since that is a luxury which life almost never affords, men are forced in the last analysis to act on faith, a faith which judges what is deeply true and important. This continuing attempt to understand the world and at the same time to act within it is the basis for all meaningful relation. It is nevertheless a process dimly understood by most people, if at all. In the historic religions there have been many ways of highlighting this crucial nonrational life of man, in which he chooses sin or goodness, worships God or forces his own egotistic power on the world by magical devices, opens himself to the grace of God and of his fellows, or tragically closes himself off in self-absorption. Commitment, faith, the moment of worship of the *Sanctus*, the conviction of Gautama that life need not be flawed by suffering—all, and many more, are examples of this nonrational aspect of life. The nature of religion cannot be understood without exploring such experiences. And that any forms that religion may take in the future will not ignore this aspect can be seen in the prominence of myth and symbol in the newer pseudo religions which compete today for men's loyalty. These areas are as yet but imperfectly understood by either the historian or the psychologist, and there is tremendous need for further clarification. But even with the present inadequacy of knowledge new experiments need to be made in ways of making clear to students these nonrational elements.

To understand the basic conceptions of a religion and what kinds of experience, rational and nonrational, comprise it, is still not enough. Any study must also deal squarely with the fact that from some points of view religion is a part of social experience. A study of its nature must therefore shed light on the various roles it has played in society, whether to unify culture, or to set every man's hand against his neighbor, to sanctify the *status quo* or to judge it and prod society into new life.

The second of our proximate objectives must be to develop norms by which religions can be judged. In the abstract, religion may be neither good nor bad; but as we see religions operating in our own time, or in historical periods, they take on strong color, whether for good or evil. They operate on the side of angels, and of devils. It is imperative that students see that fact, and be helped to judge what intellectual and ethical qualities would mark a healthy, vigorous religion.

In the third place, the teaching of religion should make as clear as may be what the crucial issues are in our own day. There is much inside and outside the colleges that attacks all religion as false superstition, or as unnecessary hypothesis, or as socially irrelevant, or on many other counts. And there is much in society that simply ignores religion by placing the emphasis on the material and selfish enjoyments available to the man who will grasp for them. The basic disagreements on crucial issues should be made clear to students, so that they may see where the issues lie.

One might suppose that these objectives that we have called proximate ends would be enough to absorb any teacher of religion. But beyond them lie two further objectives which must be considered still more important. Both of them are crucial for the development of a deeply educated person, and are therefore peculiarly related to the education which the liberal arts college strives to give.

The teaching of religion must be directed to the ways in which religious assumptions shape cultures. In fact, no culture can be deeply understood unless the operation of religious assumptions within it is recognized. Until religious illiteracy became far advanced we were not sharply aware that without religious knowledge men could become orphans within their own culture. The sciences may inhabit worlds of their own, but in all the humanistic disciplines the essential ways of thinking in our time, and the problems and convictions which we discuss are shaped by Christianity. One might give examples almost at random. Sculpture and architecture and painting in the west were during long centuries concerned with expressing religious meanings in symbolic form. A study of English literature loses many of its allusive overtones if one lacks a knowledge of the King James Bible. The forms in which ethical problems present themselves to our minds, and the tangles of our human relationships, are inaccessible apart from the teachings of Christianity. It is not that there are no nonreligious influences; a study of technical architectural advances, or of the social and economic forces in Elizabethan England, remains important. But Christian assumptions and conceptions are central to all forms of our cultural life.

In similar fashion knowledge of the non-Christian religious traditions is important. For all the deep agreement within the Hebrew-Christian tradition, in this country Jew and Roman Catholic and Protestant frequently find themselves estranged. Prejudices, springing in part from religious, in part from social and economic roots, thwart the operation of democracy. Religious institutions bring powerful pressures to bear, and it is essential to see how some of the most inexorable pressures are connected with deeply ingrained piety and belief. Such understanding would not substitute romantic approbation for the prejudices of ignorance, but it would develop a point of view at once realistic and interested. Clear-cut opposition might remain, but the tensions of prejudice would be undercut.

If we are to live in a world in which India, and China, and Japan, and the Arab peoples play increasingly important roles it is imperative that we appreciate what they prize. We shall need to study their history, their art, and their forms of government. But since the basic values and goals of a people are expressed most articulately in their religion we must read their sacred books and study the patterns of life which seem to them ultimately worth while if we wish to understand the springs of their action. Only so will men of the east and the west move toward unity at any deep level.

Finally, and most important of all, the colleges will do well if they can lay the groundwork on which the student can build a mature religion. Without presuming after the fashion of the nineteenth century to *teach* a religion, it is wholly appropriate to respect the worth of a mature religion. The goal of education, toward which the formal education in colleges is directed, must be such a *total* and *unified* relation of man to his total world. The scattered disparate deposits from different "courses" held together by unrelated attitudes and memories which for too many people substitute for an education certainly are not what enlightened educators would desire. Most colleges may not nurture any particular religion, but they would do well to foster an atmosphere in which students can be religious because religion is respected. The teaching of religion can help to clear away misunderstandings about the nature of religion, and to develop a view at once critical and appreciative of the great traditions in their greatest exponents, instead of judging solely by their pitifully small interpreters. The mysterious facts of suffering, and sin, and death face all men, as do problems of relating themselves to other selves and to God. Students in college may have only a partial experience of the pressures which life can bring to bear, just as they usually have little basis for intuiting the experience out of which Beethoven's last quartets emerged. But these are the elements of life which they will some day face, and they may well make an initial acquaintance with men who dealt with life in its more tragic or rewarding moments. Departments of religion should the more surely offer such an opportunity since there is so much in other courses in the college and in secular society which belittles religion, either by direct attack or by the erosion of embarrassed silence. Students have every right to judge for themselves what resources religions have for dealing with real problems, individual and social, and what intellectual issues are involved in the holding of such a commitment.

At the middle of the century there is far wider acceptance of the unique, because time-conditioned, nature of most experience. Along with this goes a radical recognition that in all religions, as in all cultural traditions or time-spans, there are important elements that are "objective" only in small part. People are conditioned by their traditions. The simpler optimism about the ease of achieving a universal agreement has faded. It was the expression of eighteenth-century rationalism. One must therefore accept the fact that students come to college Jewish, Roman Catholic, or Protestant, or unrelated to any tradition, and that for most the actual choice lies in an intelligent and critical understanding of their own religion, or a cutting loose from all. Only a few have the intellectual vigor to work out a new pattern. The problem is whether they will evaluate, and accept or reject, religion fearlessly and intelligently or merely out of ignorance.

It must be made abundantly clear that the frank hope that students may achieve a mature religion must not be confused with direct teaching to bring that about. The universities and colleges may not in our day play the role that was defensible when they had a unified student group. They may not proselytize for any form of religion. A course in religion in college is not a substitute for a church service or a student religious conference. In the first place, it confines itself to the effort to understand— to understand even some of the factors which elude rational categories. And in the second place, the critical and the appreciative must be held in balance. A sentimental admiration for all forms of religion can as little be tolerated as ignorance. But teaching should not be merely critical in the interests of a false objectivity. An appreciative attitude is as appropriate in the study of religion as in the study of art or music. Religion by its very nature may involve the student in that further step of becoming a participant, committed to religious faith and action whether within one of the great traditions or outside them. But he must take this further step by himself. To put it another way, this must be a by-product of classroom teaching, not its end. It is for individual Jews, Catholics, and Protestants, or for individuals who do not find themselves drawn to any of those camps, to go on from religion as an object of study to religion as an expression of worship and commitment. That last does not belong in the classroom.

III. Courses and Methods

If these are valid objectives for the work in a department of religion we might well ask ourselves how these objectives may be and have been implemented. What trends can be observed over the last quarter century? What courses are taught and ought to be taught? What interesting experiments are being made in content and in methods of teaching?

One of the obvious changes is a decline in the relative importance of biblical courses. From having formed the core of the teaching of religion they now take a substantial, but certainly not dominant, place. Interest has grown in the general history of religions, and in courses entitled "contemporary problems in religion," or philosophy of religion, to name only a few, so that biblical courses have by comparison fallen into the background. There are various reasons, aside from the competition of rivals, for the decline. In fewer institutions are Bible courses buttressed by requirements; it is now true usually only in church-related colleges, and even in these there is apt to be the possibility of choice among several ways of fulfilling a requirement in religion. New experiments are clearly called for. It has become obvious that the older historical and literary approach seems irrelevant unless the student has a considerable previous experience of religion. Nevertheless it cannot be ignored. Nor is the new archaeological knowledge, important as it is, useful by itself for most students. They learn more about artifacts than about the nature of religion. Meanwhile, because of changes in the convictions of biblical scholars certain courses can no longer be given. For example, because the gospels are recognized as documents expressing the faith of the Christian community they cannot be used except with caution as objective sources for reconstructing a "life" of Jesus. There is need for new experimentation in courses which will take full account of the results of scholarship without making them the end of the study, but rather a means for placing in true perspective the ideas and actions of the Hebrew and Christian communities which produced the Bible, wrestling as they were with real issues and decisions.

Courses which presented the Bible primarily as literature have been popular. Since no taxpayer can rebuke the student of literature, they fit appropriately into the offerings of English departments in universities which hesitate to found departments of religion. There are also less practical reasons for this vogue, for the historical approach has in many ways been unimaginative and heavy handed. Such literature courses have been concerned with literary types: poetry, whether dramatic or lyric, the story, wisdom, the epistle, and so on. They have also considered the techniques by which Hebrew poets achieved their effects, the economy of the storytellers and the genius for concrete imagery that the Hebrew language forced on its users.

There have been gains in recognizing the Bible for the literary masterpiece that it is. But there are decided limitations to many courses that emphasize literary value exclusively, for much that is essential to the Bible is omitted or slighted. If one looks through some of the books used as texts for such courses one is struck by the great silences. The prophets might almost never have been, the crucial if dull legal codes are unmentioned, and the New Testament writings appear splintered in appreciations of the parables, the lyrical passages in St. Paul, and the liturgical choruses from *Revelation*. The truth seems to be that neither an interest in the way by which effects are gained, nor in types of literature is a measure great enough to encompass the massive *fact* of the Bible. It is great literature, but it is great thought first, and finally. The literary approach to it is excellent as far as it goes, but it is doubtful whether that net can take its quarry.

Another great group of popular courses might be called histories of religious thought. Earlier they were taught as "comparative religions" or "histories of religions." Neither title exactly fits now. The comparative element remains inevitably as one tries to understand comparable elements in two religions: such as the concepts of Brahman and Tao, in the *Upanishads* and the *Tao Tê Ching*. The historical element persists as the sound insight that religious traditions change during the centuries. Generalizations about "Hinduism" or "Christianity" must be made tentatively as acts of the historical or creative imagination— important to attempt but daring and many times unsound. The interest now is in reconstructing the dominant ideas and practices of the greatest periods—an approach which emphasizes on the one hand teaching about man, God, the experience of fulfillment, ethical patterns, and so on, and on the other the concrete ways in which religions have expressed themselves in liturgies, temples, family ceremonies, and myths and stories. Such courses run the serious danger of superficiality, but if the selection of material is rigorous they may show how central religion is to other aspects of culture, and something of the ways in which men have tried to understand and adjust to their world, human and divine.

Allied to the general histories of religion, which include most of the great religions of the world, are courses in more detailed study of the great traditions. There are not many courses yet for undergraduates in Hinduism or Buddhism, but they exist here and there. There are large numbers of separate courses in Judaism, or the history of Christianity or of Christian thought, and these have an important place for students in acquainting them with the forms of thought and society and with the problems of religion of their own or another tradition. One field connected with the increasingly popular American studies is the study of religion in America.

Two kinds of courses widely taught which may be grouped together are the philosophies of religion and courses in contemporary religious thought. The concern with the philosophical basis of religions is indicated by the titles. Others which have been experimented with here and there may for want of a better description be said to present the religious traditions of our American scene. The content of one such course has been a historical study of the Hebrew-Christian tradition from the Old Testament period on, concluding with study of modern intellectual problems placed before the religious man by the development of psychology, naturalism, and scientific methods. Another has begun with a study of the beliefs and practices of present-day Judaism, Roman Catholicism, and Protestantism, and has gone on to a consideration of matters with which all of the great religions are faced: religion in the life of individuals, the fact of change in religious ideas, and the operation of religious institutions and ideas in society as a whole. For courses of this sort there can be no single pattern; the problems which might be considered are too numerous. They may serve as excellent introductions to the nature and functions of the religious traditions which are living options in the west. And there is reading available which can make courses like these quite as rigorous an intellectual discipline as any of the more standardized courses.

Still other courses which are less generally offered may be grouped together. Religious education courses appear in many lists of offerings; in western colleges they are very numerous. The study of religion in society is popular in other places, sometimes taking the form of a sociology of religion or again emphasizing the ethical aspects of modern community and religious problems such as those connected with the family, group prejudice, war, church and state. These courses are inevitably shaped by the instructor. In other catalogues appear great books courses, or studies of the biographies of religious leaders. There are psychologies of religion, and one could go on listing other types of courses which here and there are very successful.

In much of the teaching today there is a frank recognition that in a subject like religion a secondhand knowledge leaves much to be desired. Whenever possible, spokesmen of the faith being studied should be introduced to state their own convictions and to interpret. A similar kind of exposure to worship services of different faiths is important, and to the liturgies, and visual symbols which can be seen in churches and in museums. For example, an analysis of the structure of the mass, an understanding of the sacramental system and detailed acquaintance with the missal may precede a visit to a Roman Catholic mass. Even though much confusion and wonderment may remain unrelieved by a single visit such study does something to underline the importance of the climactic point of worship in the life of a Roman Catholic. To observe worship and devotion is surely a necessary step in trying to understand a religion. The methods of direct exposure cannot be used profitably without careful preparation, for if they are, nothing but a confused sentimentalism will result. And the danger that the speaker, or the service, may confuse the situation rather than illuminate it, is real. A speaker may present very individual views, or a synagogue service may be so atypical that it gives a quite false impression. But a class can be helped to evaluate such a situation and to take it for what it is worth. The experience, moreover, of seeing, and in small measure of participating in, faith in action, makes it possible within the limits of classroom procedure to realize that religions are never merely systems of ideas, and that faith as a lived experience is something other than knowledge. A wider and bolder use of such experiences of direct exposure is desirable, so long as methods are devised for understanding what is observed, and of relating it to facts gained by other means. The method is similar to the study of musical form, through hearing music and playing and writing it, or to the comprehension of problems of composition in art by experimenting directly with composition in various media.

Courses like the ones described above certainly have their place in liberal arts programs, and some of them might well be among the offerings in technical schools. For the great majority of students they will serve as parts of general education, but for some they will prove to be so interesting that they constitute a major. By the nature of the subject an interest in religion can be a focus for allied courses in art, in philosophy, in history, or in sociology. It is a broad and inclusive interest that finds little alien to it. One must wonder whether the theological schools that advise against a major in religion for students coming up to them know as much as they might about modern majors in religion in undergraduate colleges. It must also be asked whether they consider the loss to the field of many able students who as a consequence of that advice immerse themselves in the interests of some other field, and at the end of four years have forgotten their undeveloped interest in religion. A major in religion that puts courses in the field at a minimum, and lays stress on related courses in other departments, would surely send up to the theological schools students who were ready to do solid graduate work, because they had made a beginning of study in the field of religion and had worked seriously at relating it to other human interests.

One important problem that an institution faces, as we have seen, is how courses in religion should be grouped and administered. It seems clear that religion is a phenomenon worthy of being widely studied. It is equally clear that its ubiquity in human history makes it less easy to treat in isolation than, for instance, chemistry or any other of the sciences. But in this respect religion does not differ from art, or philosophy, or history, and the question as to whether there should be a department of religion is no different from that of the usefulness of departments in these allied fields. In most of the independent colleges, as we saw above, departments of religion were introduced when that way of organizing the intellectual interests of the colleges was being brought into this country. The danger of departmentalizing knowledge is that a student will identify education with "taking courses" in sharply delineated fields to one or more of which he devotes himself. That is a very real danger in our day. But surely the danger is to be avoided by recognizing that departments are not ends in themselves but means for furthering the work of the college which can be done only where there is a flexible, living core of scholars and students, engaged in tasks of analysis which may not stay within the conventional lines.

Most of the colleges and universities of the country have adopted departments of religion but there are notable exceptions, among them Harvard and the University of Michigan, where there is an articulate defense of the values of decentralizing the teaching of religion. In both of these institutions courses are widely scattered among departments of English, philosophy, oriental languages, sociology, psychology, and the like. A faculty committee at Michigan has defended on two grounds its decision not to establish a department of religion: first, that a department would be peculiarly subject to pressures from outside, and second, that scholars trained in religion are not usually sufficiently well grounded in, for example, psychology or philosophy, to teach courses in the psychology or philosophy of religion. Neither of these objections is particularly impressive. It is hard to see why a department should be more vulnerable than individuals. And in any case departments exist in other fields subject to heavy pressure, as, for example, economics. The second objection is not convincing because it is undiscriminating. It is obvious that a person trained in theology is not *ipso facto* prepared to teach psychology of religion, but neither is a specialist in abnormal psychology. Psychology, philosophy, and religion are fields of knowledge so inclusive that specialization within them becomes inevitable, and a person broadly trained in religion may well have done competent special study in one of the fields which bridge two disciplines.

From the point of view of the student there is much to be said for the establishment of a department of religion. Richness of offering and variety of approach can be achieved without centralization. The question must be raised, however, whether without a department most students are given enough help in relating the courses which they take, which may represent very contradictory assumptions and be concerned with most unrelated aspects of the field. Within a department such balance and integration can be handled more surely.

The university or college also stands to gain by having a department. It will be obvious that a department is more satisfactory than an allied school of religion since the university can control the standards of teaching and the type of offering far more effectively. If the choice is the more typical one between offering courses in various departments or in a united department of religion it would seem that the weight of advantage lies with the second plan. An instructor trained in the field of religion can be expected to have a basis for comparisons that is not ordinarily at the command of the scholar whose specialized interest is primarily that, let us say, of the sixteenth century or medieval history or literature, just as the student of the history of art has advantages over the person whose knowledge of art is confined to that of a limited period. If there are persons teaching in other fields who have special competence in religion, they may well offer courses in the department of religion. Furthermore the university has the advantage in making appointments. It can determine what aspects of religion it wishes to present and can then appoint men and women in those fields. When a small number of appointments is to be made there may be difficulty in getting the precise combinations of fields of scholarly competence needed, but the difficulties on that side will be as nothing compared with the problem of getting, for example, an eighteenth-century English scholar who is prepared to teach English Bible, or a specialist in rural sociology who is also competent in sociology of religion. Furthermore it will be easier to balance the philosophical points of view of the staff of instruction if the department plan is used, so that there may be proper variety and yet sympathy. Finally, the college is more apt to hear an articulate interpretation of religion if the teachers and scholars in the field are closely associated. They know each other, and they share the conviction that the study of religion is an important aspect of education. They are likely to be strengthened in their individual work by their association and to do a better job in interpreting the field to their colleagues and to the students.

IV. The Teacher

The teacher of religion is faced with a challenging opportunity, and it is one which makes rigorous demands upon him. On the one hand he should have a kind of understanding of religion which will most naturally be his if he is a person committed to a religious position. On the other he must have the objectivity which recognizes that for reasons which must be respected others may differ profoundly from him. Some institutions, apparently holding that objectivity is impossible and that a balance of traditions is the best that can be achieved, have followed a policy of dividing appointments among Protestants, Roman Catholics, and Jews. That there are some advantages in this arrangement no one could deny. Karl Adam, for example, in the lectures presented in his book *The Spirit of Catholicism* presented Roman Catholicism as no Protestant or Jewish scholar could have done. He conveyed the emotional overtones because he spoke as a believer. But the dangers of such an arrangement are very real. The question may be raised whether the sole obligation of a teacher is to present his material in the most persuasive way possible. Such a method suggests either that conversion is a proper goal of classroom teaching, or that undergraduates have knowledge enough to make a critical analysis by themselves. Neither would seem to be true. Sectarian teaching has the underlying aim of conversion, and it is not made more appropriate because in a department there are several brands from which to choose. It would seem to be especially important, therefore, to have persons appointed who are first of all scholars, and who are able to make a distinction between a personal religious loyalty and an obligation to show more than one side of a controversial issue. Students of very different faiths, and of none, will be gathered together in every class, and the teacher, whatever his personal commitment, must be free to help them all.

It is clear that the teacher of religion faces certain difficulties not faced in like degree by all his colleagues, but certainly by some, e.g. the economist who is committed to a capitalist or to a socialist point of view. On certain levels in the study of religion, as in the study of economics or literature, there can be a close approximation to objectivity; controversial questions are not raised. On the levels where there is deep disagreement about the interpretation of facts the teacher has an obligation to his students to make clear the opposing sides, and to show as honestly as he can what the issues are. Roman Catholics and Protestants disagree about some of the important facts in the history of early Christianity. Naturalists and theists likewise disagree both on the level of what things are true, and about how facts on which they agree should be interpreted. By presenting both sides the teacher can help his students to consider the issues at stake.

If he goes only so far and no farther he will have fostered the belief that where there is controversy decision becomes impossible. As we have suggested above, it is important that the teacher be not only a scholar, but also a person himself committed to a religious position. And he must make his students aware of his bias. If he is genuinely respectful toward other ways of interpreting experience, and at the same time tough-minded in pressing the important issues where differences lie, he should be able to help students whether or not they agree with him. He should as far as possible exemplify the fact that commitment is not incompatible with a critical mind and with willingness to learn. It is precisely this combination that has been characteristic of religious persons in periods of vital and flexible faith. Anyone who holds as his goal the achievement of intellectual competence, with due humility and spiritual perceptiveness, will find that students of very different backgrounds will draw from the same materials different personal conclusions. The task of the teacher is not to convert but to make understanding possible. And if he is interested in human beings he will find that beyond his relationship to his students as teacher stretch vast opportunities to be pursued outside the classroom of helping them as human beings to understand their predicaments and decisions. In fact, he will be embarrassed by the greatness of those opportunities, which will threaten his persistent need to pursue his own study.

Another opportunity facing the teacher is that of serving as the interpreter of religion in the general college community. He must be hardheaded in recognizing that many of his colleagues because of the specialized nature of their own education may know little about religion, and be relatively unaware what the contemporary religious issues are. He in turn may know little or nothing about some of their fields. In so far as he and they together can work to understand each other, and to see where fundamental agreements and differences lie, the gaps between areas of special studies will be bridged. If a naturalist and a theist can expose their fundamental disagreements their students will be the better able to deal with different assumptions which elude thought when they are submerged. Persons with this interest are invaluable for the teaching of interdepartmental courses, and the planning of joint majors, on the edges of two fields. Some, certainly, of the teachers of religion in any college should be able to carry on this kind of interpretation, and in our day when confusions are great and a general synthesis is not to be hoped for, such yeoman's work along the frontiers of our thinking may aid both the understanding of religion and the over-all task of the college. The two are very close together.

The nature of religion itself will force the teacher of religion to take an active role in the college. And he should do this not apologetically, but with a sense of the vital importance of what he has to say. Education will not be truly effective unless students unify their experience—unless their growing understanding of the nature of the world is linked with a sense of obligation to act responsibly in it. There may be nonreligious views which can serve as the basis of this unity for individual students, but the claim of the religions remains unique. The great religions, and some philosophies which have profoundly appealed to the minds of men, have served as the centers of experience for many generations. Rightly understood they will continue so to serve. And the department of religion should be counted on to present the importance of such a unified view more than any other department, with the possible exception of philosophy, although today more and more philosophers are concerned with method to the exclusion of world views. In somewhat similar fashion the social sciences have sacrificed inclusiveness when in the interest of being scientific they limited their method to description and analysis. The problem of ethical obligation is either ignored, or is brought in surreptitiously. The teacher of religion has the right and even the duty to press the claims of a genuinely unified education. Toward that end he must be willing to criticize inadequate or partial views, and to raise questions about the objectives of teaching in fields other than his own. He will not be alone in this, for many of his colleagues recognize the importance of a unified and comprehensive education even when they conceive narrowly of the functions of their field. The teacher of religion will with them have the courage to challenge narrowness and any ignoring of the morally, or socially, or intellectually responsible life.

It will follow from this that he will in turn be challenged. These are controversial matters, not areas in which there is placid agreement. The university in our day must become the arena in which the claims of differing ideologies and philosophies and religions are argued and espoused. And the scholar in religion who is also the believer must be vigorous in defense and in attack. This argument will be of a kind congenial to the college, and as far as may be from cynical propaganda. It will seek to give light, not heat. But it will not acknowledge neutrality on fundamental issues. Clear thinking in the second half of the century will have to take place in the presence of vigorous oppositions. Teachers of religion cannot simply be scholars competent in remote fields if they are to serve the generation ahead. In other words they may not escape being touched by the insights of their own discipline. Vital religion has always acted to judge the false and the narrow in the interests of a life which is open, and ethically sensitive, and devoted.

9

Worship in an Academic Community

WILLARD L. SPERRY

O F THE many problems which arise in a college or university, having to do with the presentation of religion,
that of communal worship is so difficult as to be all but insoluble.
To put it in other terms, the problems of the curriculum and
the classroom are much simpler than those of the chapel or its
cultural equivalent.

The act of worship, when true to itself, is, as the word itself
implies, an ascription of worth to some objective reality. It is an
instinctive and spontaneous dedication of oneself to that which
is so in its own right. St. Francis' "Canticle to Brother Sun" is a
perfect example of this thesis. Self-consciousness of a too subjective and introspective kind is at a minimum in any genuine act
of worship.

Let me cite two or three nontheological, nonecclesiastical instances of these propositions. In one of his works Ruskin describes his reaction to his first glimpse of the eternal snows of
the higher Alps in the Bernese Oberland. As he came around a
terrace in Basel, he saw them on the skyline and said, "Suddenly,
behold, beyond!" That mood is heightened with a feeling of awe
amounting to a kind of holy dread in Odell's account of his
futile attempt to find some trace of Mallory and Irvine just under
the summit of Mount Everest. As he turned back from their last

deserted camp he gave one parting glance at the summit of the mountain. "I glanced up at the mighty summit above me. . . . What right had we to venture thus far into the holy presence of the Supreme Goddess, Mother of the Mountain Snows. Had we violated it, was I now violating it? Had we approached her with due reverence and singleness of heart and purpose?" The sea prompts the same attitude in any thoughtful person. Passengers in the smoking room of a "ram-you-damn-you-liner" talk about this, their fifteenth "crossing the pond." That is not the temper of a sailor. I once asked a Cunard captain whether he liked the sea. He said, "That is not a question that it has ever occurred to me to ask myself. I don't know whether I like the sea or not. I only know that I respect it."

Carlyle in a neglected and all but forgotten work says, "Worship of a Hero is transcendent admiration of a Great Man. . . . Hero worship, heartfelt prostrate admiration, submission, burning, boundless, for a noblest godlike Form of Man—is not that the germ of Christianity itself?" If, as he goes on to say, hero worship was already going out of fashion in his day it has gone even more out of fashion in our day. "Show our critics a great man, they begin to what they call 'account' for him; not to worship him, but to take the dimensions of him." What was true then is doubly true now. Nevertheless, a recent companion of Albert Schweitzer, on his hurried trip to America in the summer of 1949, commented on the fact that our hard-boiled reporters and cameramen were, somehow, left deflated, humbled, and almost worshipful in the presence of Schweitzer. They instinctively realized that he was a "Great Man."

We accord the term "sacred" to the object of our worship. The wholly secular and perfectly irreligious man is the man for whom there are no sanctities in life and the world. He is the man who can make light of that of which many of the rest of us make much. True, our private sanctities vary greatly. What is sacred for one man is not necessarily sacred to another man; conversely his sanctities may not be mine. As a matter of common courtesy we ought to respect one another's sanctities, not violate them. Hence the warrant for Dean Inge's remark that a gentleman is a person who is never unintentionally rude.

Thus, for instance, a college is justified in requiring its students to respect its tradition. The word "sacred" is perhaps too strong to be used in this connection. But the connotation of any lesser word looks in that direction. Harvard, for instance, is conspicuously wanting in detailed rules governing the conduct of its students. But there is one general rule which is announced at the outset of the freshman year and enforced thereafter. Whatever a student does he may not bring the good name of the College into disrepute. If he does so, no excuses are accepted and out he goes. This is understood by all concerned.

One of our difficulties in a modern academic community is that we are dealing with a generation of young people who have little feeling for the "sacred." The trouble goes back more often than otherwise to their homes, where few sanctities were observed or expected. But it arises in equal part from a queer hiding instinct in modern youth, which prompts it to affect poses of sophistication and the like. Modern youth is by no means as hardboiled or insensitive as it would like us to believe, yet it is difficult to persuade youth of other than the conventionally pious church type to let us see its secret places. The temper of the times encourages them in these studied reticences. What Josiah Royce said over fifty years ago is even more true today. "We become more knowing, more clever, more critical, more wary, more sceptical, but we seemingly do not grow more profound or more reverent. We find much in the world that engages our curious attention; we find little that is sublime. Our world becomes clearer; a brilliant, hard, mid-morning light shines upon everything; but this light does not seem to us any longer divine. The deeper beauty of the universe fades out; only facts and problems are left."

Our basic problem, then, is that of the studied secularity of youth, what the Bible calls "profaneness." In some cases this secularity is the truth of the student; in many more instances it is a sort of psychological protective device, or chameleonlike tendency to conform to the pattern of an environing society, for the sake of being considered emancipated and popular. With any given individual the initial task is to discover what his sanctities really are and to proceed from them. A genuine feeling for the sacred can always be enlarged in its compass and horizons.

For the purposes of this paper I shall have to confine myself to the privately endowed, nonecclesiastical institution. The church college has, and on its own premises must have, its formal religious observances which it requires of its students. Its business is to perpetuate a single ecclesiastical and theological tradition. No one can quarrel with such an institution if it imposes its traditional sanctities on its students. It was brought into being to do just that.

The tax-supported institution stands at the other end of the line. It is theoretically prohibited from most formal habitual religious acts because of our American separation of church and state. It is true that in states which have a more or less homogeneous type of citizen, a minimum of religious usages is allowed. Indeed, in recent years, courses on religion have been on the increase, rather than the decrease, in our state universities. At this point the trend in tax-supported institutions of higher learning is the reverse of that in the grade schools, where a prudential timidity is deleting even the most neutral or catholic religious act—let us say the recitation of the Lord's Prayer. Why a state university should be quietly expanding in this whole area, while the lower schools are becoming more and more cautious is one of the interesting cultural and political riddles of the moment.

Meanwhile the topic, as proposed to me, carried a subtitle "celebration of community and educational values." How far can the tax-supported state university and the privately endowed institution find occasions for such acts of celebration? The tax-supported institution might, for instance, stage corporate celebrations of the fact of the state itself. We have not come to that as yet in this country, but the menace of political totalitarianism the world over does not put such acts beyond the realm of remote possibility. The practice of requiring loyalty pledges, already in force in many places, might be worked up in some communal ritual, an elaborated form of the salute to the flag.

Once again the observance of a "Founder's Day," already kept in many colleges and universities, might be developed as a sort of ancestor worship in Anglo-Saxon form. Obeisance to tradition has usually been a part of most religions with a feeling for history.

Or take our athletics with their vast stadiums and bands and cheering sections. In such a setting, a football game between two major institutions is something far more than a matter of physical combat. It is a tribal ritual. Its affinities are with the Maypole dance and the like. Most of us go to it, if we do go, for the sake of the ritual itself, not the game and the score. Thus, I remember a game played in the Harvard stadium on an Armistice Day. Between halves the crowd stood uncovered and in silence while a bugler blew taps. It was a very moving moment. I ventured to say shortly thereafter at a meeting held at Princeton to discuss religion in the colleges that that experience was one of a genuine social mysticism which bordered on the realm of religion. We had been guaranteed freedom of speech apart from reporters. In this instance someone leaked and the next day I was quoted in the New York papers as having said that football was the only religion left in the American college! Those reports became in turn the occasion for more than one Roman Catholic journal to point out how secularized American Protestantism had become when a dean of one of its oldest divinity schools could make such a silly statement.

One might in imagination multiply acts of this sort in which the entire academic community is required to share by compulsion or is willing to share voluntarily. How far can such transactions be called acts of worship in the religious sense of the word? My answer would be that they often have the quality of religion and of worship, but that they remain primitive religions, tribal religions like racism, or ruler worship. That silence in the stadium on Armistice Day, broken by the horn call, came as near anything of its kind I have ever known to being a communal act of worship in a purely humanist form, since it contemplated all the world's dead in wars. But for those who conceive of religion as a matter of humanism-plus, it could not fully express what is normally expected of a religion.

The danger of construing the religion of a college primarily in these terms and multiplying occasions for its observance in these ways is dual: (a) that such worship shall be too local and parochial, (b) that it give further occasion for the charge of subtle secularity so often brought against all forms of our American religious life. Emerson once said that the whole gods arrive when half gods go. We Americans are in danger of worshiping the half gods and stopping short of those clear intimations of a whole God experienced in the terms of indubitable spiritual universals. Therefore, I doubt if we can feel that we have solved our problem by multiplying the sort of observances which I have cited.

I find more hints of communal religion in certain other types of our institutional activities. I think, for instance, of our glee clubs. Their musical standards have been raised out of all recognition in recent years, since the days of the "Bulldog on the Bank," or "Darling Clementine." Today it is beneath the self-respect of any decent institution not to use the very best choral music available. I know more than one college graduate who has said that singing in a chapel choir or a glee club has been his most rewarding academic experience. The same might be said of

college orchestras, or of concerts of chamber music by profession-
als, which are always crowded out as soon as the doors are opened.
The sober passion for good music throughout our country as a
whole, and in our colleges in particular, is one of the most heart-
ening cultural signs of the times in a day when the skies are too
often heavily overcast.

Music, so construed and rendered or shared in and heard, is
universal in its appeal and connotation. It is not parochial. When
Koussevitzky suggested that the sessions of the United Nations
might well be prefaced by a symphony concert, at which Bach
or Haydn or Mozart could be played, he was in a truly religious
sense filling a gap created by the prohibition of opening prayers,
required by the official atheism of certain of the "united" (sic)
nations. In any case the boundaries of music are far wider than
those of a founder's memory, a stadium ritual, or a patriotic
celebration.

One must, I think, believe in the inarticulate religion of the
average man, for which the Soldier in Arms of World War I
pleaded so boldly before his death in battle. Neo-orthodoxy
which is much the theological fashion in many of our theological
schools does not represent the temper of our undergraduate colleges. They are still incorruptibly liberal by heritage and usage.
Cardinal Newman once said that nothing is easier than to use
the name of God and mean nothing by it. That is the facile vice
of too many conventionally orthodox persons. There may well
be clearer intimations of God—the God of all beauty—in a concert of chamber music than in many a formal ecclesiastical service. Therefore, in the name of communal religious observances
all such occasions should be encouraged and supported.

The same case might be made for the study of poetry or read-
ings by the modern poets of their own verse. I say this because I
happen to owe my own first clear personal concern for religion
as a firsthand affair not to a dreary course on Christian Evidences
which as an undergraduate in a church college I was compelled

to attend, but to a class in nineteenth-century English poetry—Browning in particular, who is now alas all but forgotten.

That bit of autobiographical reminiscence raises the whole problem of the department of religion in a faculty and the transactions of a classroom. It is understood by all concerned that the classroom should not be used as a thinly disguised setting for a revival meeting. However strong the lecturer's private religious convictions and his native desire to convert students to the terms of his own faith may be, he must resist that insidious temptation. He is under bonds to be dispassionate, to be fair to persons of other faiths or of no faith. The necessary discipline in fair-mindedness is good for the lecturer himself, and does much to win the respect and confidence of students. In the liberal arts colleges, as we know them, anything like proselytism is forbidden in the classroom. Important as the increasing number of courses in the field or the department of religion may be, they are not the occasion or the vehicle for communal acts of worship. One of our present dangers is that we shall regard courses in the Bible, in the history or philosophy of religion, as satisfying our academic responsibility or opportunity in the field. The main office of such courses is the imparting of accurate information as to the facts. The lecture room and the lecture hour are not, primarily, expressions of the religious life of the students themselves.

There is much to be said for the formal, and perhaps even perfunctory, recognition of religion on ceremonial occasions in our academic life. I have in mind a matriculation service for freshmen, or the conventional invocation and benediction at a commencement exercise. These items on a commencement program are so familiar to us that they pass unnoticed. But visitors from European universities, even those which have a formal religious heritage or connection, often comment with interest on the fact that we in America give a formal recognition to religion at such times, when usages in the Old World require no such observance.

A college or university might well consider the propriety and the long range wisdom of compiling and editing for such occasions some modest liturgical material of its own. A "college prayer" or "university prayer" to be used at such times gives continuity to the ongoing life of the community. As Wordsworth says of his own experience, it binds the days of the society each to each "in natural piety."

The same might be said of the occasional religious services held in a college chapel, the marriages and the funerals. A college pastor will do well to have a booklet containing the order of wedding service which he uses. Such a booklet might carry in its final pages a blank form, to be filled in, which can serve as the certificate of marriage which the minister always issues to the young couple. At the end of the service he gives them the very "prayer book" from which they were married. Thus, my wife still has the Church of England prayer book used at our wedding, carrying on its title page the legend *"ex hoc libro nupta,* B. H. Streeter." That book means far more to us than the run-of-the-mill certificate bought at an ecclesiastical bookstore.

So, also, of the funeral service. Those of my readers who are now college pastors, but have been parish ministers, will know what I mean when I say that a college is a limited cross section of human experience in its entirety. Birth and bread-labor and death lie outside its boundaries. In particular death comes as an unwelcome, unfamiliar, and almost unintelligible intruder into a community where youth and health are accepted as the norm. The occasional tragic death of a popular undergraduate sobers the community for the moment, but the shock and the grief are short lived. More often than otherwise the formal funeral is held, not at the college, but in the student's home town.

It is otherwise, however, with the death of some member of the faculty, whose funeral is held in the college chapel. Once again, faculty members tend to regard the death of even one of their elder statesmen as an interruption of normal life, something lying outside or beyond their several "fields." As a matter of common decency and respect they feel bound to turn up at the funeral. If they are emancipated persons they profess to deplore the apparatus of the mortician, the paraphernalia of paraded grief. The custom of holding a memorial service, a week or so after a private funeral, is increasing. That was done, in our own community, a week after the death of Alfred North Whitehead. Whatever form such an observance takes, whether a funeral itself or a subsequent memorial service, the occasion is one which invites those longer and more sober second thoughts about human life in its entirety, which can usually be postponed in the daily hurry and worry of lectures, tutorials, laboratories, and blue books.

May I be forgiven a personal word at this point. I have been for twenty years "Chairman of the Board of Preachers" in our University, i.e. college pastor. Some of the funerals held in the University Church have been among the most moving religious rites which we have had. I think in particular of the funeral of A. Lawrence Lowell. He was full of years, his wife was gone, he left no children. The mourners were at best once-removed. Meanwhile the whole community gathered in a crowded church to pay its sincere respect and debt of gratitude to a man who had given his life to the University. "Nothing was here for tears . . . nothing but well and fair." The service was simple, brief, and rather austere. To this day I still hear reminiscent comments upon the effect of that service, not merely upon the chronic churchgoer, but upon those who, apart from such occasions, take little interest in religion and never set foot inside a church. Out of that service, which represented a long process of nonliturgical trial and error, came an order of service for the burial of the dead, which has been printed and is now uniformly used at all University funerals. Over the years the community has become accustomed to this service, accepts it and shares in it as our own intimate and distinctive act. In short, in all these occasional services there is much to be said for formulating a tried and proven order of worship, instead of leaving such occasions to the "inspiration of the moment" or the vagaries of a diffuse, non-liturgical usage.

Which brings me to the college chapel itself. The subject is difficult, elusive, and never satisfactorily solved. The simplest thing for me to do is to record, dogmatically, my own reflections on twenty years' experience in this connection.

(A) There is much to be said for a building which is instantly recognized as a church. Services held in an assembly hall are not the same thing as services held in a building which can be identified as a church, by virtue of its architecture, interior arrangement and the like. The patent physical fact that an institution thinks it worth while to build and maintain a chapel is an initial vote of public confidence in the importance of religion and the propriety of acts of corporate worship.

(B) As far as possible this building should be reserved for religious services. The idea of religion requires, somehow or other, a concession of the element of "otherness." The church which is merely a pious rubber stamp of ecclesiastical approval set upon the secular ideas and interests of the everyday world has sacrificed part of its proper appeal to that world.

(C) If possible the fabric of the church should have a larger auditorium for regular services, and a smaller choir area or ante-chapel, self-contained architecturally, for services which gather fewer worshipers. This ought to be something more than a bleak room in a basement.

(D) There is little or nothing to be said for the perpetuation of compulsory chapel. Compulsory chapel may well be required in private secondary schools, where life is much more regimented than it is at the college and university level. At this higher level compulsory chapel is an inaccurate transcript of what life is to be like when the student gets out into the world. The custom which still survives in some institutions of requiring chapel attendance of lower classmen but of exempting them in their junior and senior years has always seemed to me an unhappy compromise. It makes nonattendance a premium to be achieved after the first two years.

(E) If the institution is located in a considerable community, with near-by denominational churches which have on their staffs "student pastors" particularly assigned to the care of their own constituencies in the institution, a good deal of pressure will be put on students to attend their own denominational churches, lest they "lose their religion" in the supposedly godless college or university which they are attending. To this extent such parish churches with their active student pastors will cut rather heavily into the attendance at the college chapel. The morning congregation there will by no means be the measure of the churchgoing of the student body as a whole. In general the institution will probably be well advised to accept this situation and co-operate with the local churches. But it might be pointed out from time to time that attendance at a denominational church, with consequent absence from the college chapel, deprives the student of the opportunity of meeting and worshiping with students of other denominations as well as of hearing preachers of denominations other than his own. At their best our American college chapels are doing, perhaps unwittingly, a pioneer job in the ecumenical field.

(F) Some single person—a resident professor or a full-time chaplain—should be in charge of the college chapel. He will be, as a matter of course, a member of his own denomination— Methodist, Episcopalian, Baptist, Presbyterian, etc. This inevitable fact will give rise to the suspicion that, unconsciously rather than consciously perhaps, he may be proselytizing for his own brand of Protestantism. An institution can safeguard itself at this point by setting up a "chapter" of visiting preachers, of which the local man can be "dean," which shall represent the major denominations in the student enrollment. Members of this "chapter" (or "board of preachers"), should receive formal appointment by the institution, and their names included as officials of the institution in the annual catalogue. The local chaplain will counsel with them on matters of general chapel policies and programs. If possible, a member of such a "chapter" should serve for a period of three or four years, and should be a visiting preacher at least twice in each academic year. Some arrangement of this sort publicly defends the stake of the major denominations in the conduct of the official religious life of the institution, and saves the institution from the charge of being too sectarian in the person of the resident chaplain.

(G) The most difficult problems of chapel administration arise from the warm-hearted and generous concern of the students for "inter-faith" ventures. At this point our college students are well in advance of the rank and file of church members in the wider world. Every encouragement should be given to their genuine catholicity of mind and heart. The future lies with them rather than with the stubborn sectarians in our still divided churches.

On the other hand, no single over-all order of public worship exists which can serve students coming from widely divergent types of church. The contrast between the liturgical and the nonliturgical churches is a case in point. Students with a liturgical tradition behind them do not understand easily a nonliturgical "free" service. Contrariwise, students from the nonliturgical churches do not find themselves at home in a liturgical service.

The situation becomes more complicated when an effort is made to include not merely the diversified Protestants, but—as in some instances—Catholics and Jews as well. We might as well face the fact that Roman Catholic students in our arts colleges will not be encouraged by their priests to attend college chapel, and more often than otherwise will be discouraged from attending, if not forbidden to do so. Given the present stiffening attitude of official Catholicism in such matters, we might as well accept this situation. Much as we should welcome Catholics at our chapel services, it will be only the occasional venturesome Catholic student who will come.

This reduces the problem to that of some service geared to Protestants and Jews. Once again, the orthodox Jewish student is not likely to come to a Protestant church. It is a fair question how far the conservative Jew will come. The problem is therefore further reduced to the liberal Jews and the several Protestant groups. There does not exist as yet any order of worship which can effectively bracket both these groups. There are whole areas of the New Testament which are culturally unknown and theologically unacceptable to even the most liberal Jew. Distinctively Christian hymns, even as nontheological as "O Master, let me walk with thee," go beyond anything a Jew can sing with good faith. Yet such hymns are second nature to the Christian, and dear to him.

There are in existence today pioneer groups of Protestants, Catholics, and Jews, meeting for friendly discussion in a quest for convictions common to all. Much hopeful work is being done in this area. But none of these movements, as far as I know, has ever ventured to draft an over-all order for public worship which has achieved anything like wide acceptance and use. We shall have to know one another much better than we now do before we can arrive at such an agreement, however devoutly our eager hearts may desire it. More particularly the liberal rabbis who have from time to time come as visiting preachers to the University Church which I know best have insisted that we shall do well not to insist that our religions are identical, however much common ground we find in past history.

A service of worship is essentially a transaction in which we try to give simple and sincere expression to the religion we already have. In Browning's words it is an attempt to "find a

way for the imprisoned splendor to escape." This does not mean
that a good service of worship is rigidly tailored to the measure
of any one of us at any given moment. Like all works of art it
should attempt, in Bernard Berenson's terms, to make us feel
with an intensity of 4 some truth or beauty which previously
we had felt only with an intensity of 2. There must be in the
worshiper, therefore, thoughts and feelings which call for this
act of "expression." If a chapel service drifts off into the areas
of a public forum for the discussion of controversial issues, or a
classroom in which a lecturer is inducting his students into some
intellectually unknown land, the quality of the act of public
worship will be lost. Indeed, such college chapels as have moved
in this direction have usually ended by emptying the pews.
"Desperate remedies" for a difficult chapel situation, by way of
the lecture-forum device, may give a chapel service a shot-in-
the-arm, but the effects are short lived and in the long run self-
defeating.

Such would-be, all-over orders of worship as I have seen, intended to compass Protestant and Jew—and the Catholic as
far as he ventures to attend—have had to be so theologically
censored that they have lost much of their spontaneity and
betray their manufactured forms. In so far as I have talked with
liberal Jewish students about these ventures they seem more
interested in defending the principle of such a service than in
supporting it by regular attendance. One such Jewess told me
that she would fight for the abstract idea of a college chapel so
conceived and conducted, but that she had no idea of coming
to it regularly. There are, of course, a vast number of persons
who think that churches are on the whole a good thing, even
though they do not go to them. But such persons are very little
practical help in actually keeping churches going.

I see nothing for it, therefore, for an institution predominantly
Protestant in its student membership, but to maintain as neutral
and comprehensive a Protestant service as it can devise. Even

such a service will be unsatisfactory to a student with strong denominational ties and traditions, but patently in a nonecclesiastical institution, the form of public worship cannot be determined by the usage of any single denomination, to the neglect or exclusion of students belonging to other denominations. In short, if students are to attend chapel at all, they must feel as nearly at home there as is possible under the circumstances.

(H) These reflections give rise to a still further matter. The chapel service ought to be an integral part of the whole educational program. But the service cannot be construed as one more lecture hour in which information is being imparted. Hence the necessity of gearing our orders and forms of worship to the churches from which our students come and to which they ought to return. One of the dangers of a successful college chapel is that it may be, in a wholly proper sense of the word, so successful that it unfits its student congregation for wholehearted membership in parish churches when they leave college. To put it on no other ground the music will certainly be better than that which they will find in the average parish church. Listening to visiting preachers, often among the most distinguished in the land, they become at a later time impatient with the day-in and day-out preaching of some local minister. We ought not to conceive of our chapel services as something so unique that they are apart from the church life of the country at large.

This problem is often first met in the hymnal used in the college chapel. Of all the changes in the taste of the American people that in the field of music has been the most considerable. The college chapel has outgrown our sentimental affection for the old-time gospel hymn. It has indeed censored most of the denominational hymnals, both musically and theologically, and has forbidden much of the music that was written during the nineteenth century—what Professor George Foot Moore used to call "the vanilla flavored hymns of Barnby." Once you have become disciplined and accustomed to music both older and newer, which is more austere and less sentimental, you realize that you have lost your taste for vanilla flavored tunes. For instance, two of the loveliest hymns we know are "Dear Lord and Father of Mankind," and "O Love That Will Not Let Me Go." But most college organists and choir directors whom I know will no longer allow the familiar tunes to which those hymns have hitherto been sung. The tunes to which they have been newly set seem by no means inevitable and are often unsingable by a congregation. They become therefore one more anthem by the choir. Again, I come across hymns and tunes in many of our college hymnals which have been arbitrarily shuffled and dealt again in a new combination. I always feel, in the presence of such a book, as though I had gone out to a dinner party to find familiar friends, divorced from long-time partners and re-married to other persons within the same social circle. It had seemed to me that they had been getting along pretty well on the old basis. Why these arbitrary remarriages of whim or convenience?

The hymnal used in the chapel to which I minister is, both musically and theologically, one of the most austere and anti-septic in the whole country. All our visiting preachers despair of it and disparage it. Yet it contains many lovely hymns not found in most of our conventional church hymnals. Furthermore, in certain instances the tunes which have been chosen to supplant those of vanilla flavor are, when one becomes used to them, undoubtedly more beautiful. But one has to live with the book over a period of years to know it and appreciate it.

The book does, however, present certain problems to the minister. When freshmen come to a matriculation service at the opening of the fall term, bewildered by the strange world they have entered, they ought to feel at home. They can be made most at home by the use of hymns which are familiar. At this point our book presents some difficulties. It is not always easy to find three hymns, appropriate for the occasion, with which incoming freshmen are familiar. The continuity of their life as churchgoers is by no means guaranteed through the hymnal. They may well need musical re-education, but a matriculation service is not the occasion for it. Nor indeed can that re-education be achieved through a succession of Sundays. It has taken me twenty-five years to discover the merits of the book and to make it a natural and easy medium for the expression of my own capacity for worship. I doubt if it can be done during the briefer four years of undergraduate life.

May I then comment on the sort of anthem now usually sung by the chapel choir? We no longer hear the familiar solos sung by an alto or a tenor, or the hackneyed anthems by the church quartet. That probably is just as well. They too were often over-flavored with vanilla; "Oh for the Wings of a Dove," "God Is a Spirit," *et al.* There is a distinction between sacred and secular music. One of the differences is this, secular music makes constant use of the half-tone step. Religious music is square toed and confines itself to the full-tone step. Thus, Delilah's seductive song to Samson, "Mon coeur s' ouvre à ta voix" slithers its way up and down the chromatic scale. The truth of the matter would seem to be that its connotations are, as they are intended to be in that instance, sensual. This device, so unashamedly employed in the traditional gospel hymn—cf. "Some Day the Silver Cord Will Break"—and often found in musically more respectable hymnals, introduces a false sentimentality into the situation.

In any case the reaction against too saccharine and sensual music has driven most of our modern choir directors back to the austere and impersonal church music of a much earlier time, to Byrd and Purcell, to the music of the Greek Church and ultimately to ancient Catholic settings for the Mass. Gregorian plain song for the Psalms and Canticles when it is well done, is undoubtedly affecting and effective. It gives the mysterious hint of "otherness" which one needs. But after a long discipline as a listener at the hands of austere choirmasters I am still personally left somewhat unconverted. The music is indubitably lovely. But the choirmaster seems to me to select his anthems solely with a view to the music itself, and with little or no regard for the words. The text is usually Latin. It is hard enough to understand the words of any anthem; it is doubly difficult in the case of Latin excerpts from the Mass. One gets a word or two here or there, but unless one is familiar with the Missal, the words pass unidentified, or, if identified, too often seem rather irrelevant. Thus I remember our first daily chapel some years ago, when we gathered on a lovely late September day, filled with the hopes and enthusiasms begotten by the prospect of the opening college year. The choir welcomed us with a *Miserere*, which seemed to me unnecessarily inappropriate for that particular occasion.

Furthermore, this material from the Missal makes use of many religious ideas which, from the Protestant standpoint, are no longer credible. It is often said that the creeds were "meant to be sung," not recited, and that words sung need not be subjected to the scrutiny of a sensitive conscience. Even those creeds which have been preserved in many Protestant churches lose some of their sobriety when overelaborated as anthems. Thus Dean Inge says, "They turned the Nicene Creed into an anthem; before the end I had ceased to believe anything." Our own choir once sang as an anthem a Latin hymn to the Virgin. The visiting preacher for the day, a distinguished Scottish Presbyterian, Dr. Johnston Ross, announced that if they intended to do that sort of thing again he would never come back to us. The Dean and the Doctor may have been unnecessarily fussy and atrabilious. But I have to admit that, while I find much of the ancient music for the Mass strangely moving, it never seems to me to fit easily into a Protestant service cast otherwise in the vernacular.

The occasion for the antivanilla revolt was and remains a sound one. But the familiar solution, in the form of a retreat to medieval modes and Latin texts, though probably the simplest and most obvious at hand, sometimes seems too easy a solution of this whole problem. One has the suspicion that the choice of much of this music is prompted in part by a pedagogic attempt to improve our musical taste. That improvement must take place gradually; it is never a sudden conversion. In any case, when the pedagogic attempt to inform and improve us supersedes the endeavor to find fitting vehicles to express what we already think and feel, the nature of the resulting act of worship is subtly altered. By going to a church which has good music my taste may be developed in the course of time, but I do not go to church in the first instance to have it developed, even though such development may ultimately ensue. All this reminds me of a girl's school where I occasionally minister. The school prides itself upon its French. Therefore the Lord's Prayer is always recited in French. Here again the pedagogic, perhaps slightly exhibitionistic nature of the transaction is felt. The act is rather artificial. One should say one's prayers in the vernacular, and not use his prayers as a device for familiarizing himself further with a foreign language.

(I) Finally, there is the attitude of the faculty toward this whole situation.

The average faculty in an arts college has on it a good many members who are candidly anticlerical. They are usually persons who were brought up in childhood and in youth in some conservative and ultra-orthodox sect from which they have escaped and can now happily call their souls their own. Their mistaken intimations as to what the Christian religion is derives from these unhappy "recollections of early childhood." They do not propose to let any church ever get its lasso around their necks again. So long as they do not indulge in the classroom in rather sophomoric dismissal of all religion as an outmoded fetish, we have no quarrel with them. They must let live as well as live; there must be at least a gentlemanly recognition of the fact that to other persons religion may still be real. But for the purposes of the public religious life of the institution such faculty members must be written off as a dead loss.

There is, however, another group on the faculty which professes and practices religion. Even this group is by no means uniform in its attendance at a college chapel. The "faculty section" in such of the many chapels which I know well is seldom overcrowded. The truth is that many professors prefer to do their churchgoing in a local parish church. There are good reasons for their so doing. To put it on no other ground, they live six days of the week in a uniformly undergraduate atmosphere. There are many human concerns which lie outside those which occupy the four eager years of youth from let us say the age of seventeen to twenty-one. An older man is not to be criticized if he finds some relief, on a Sunday, in seeking a different social milieu. Human life cannot be exhausted by or limited to the concerns of the undergraduate generation. Therefore, if the faculty member wants to keep his touch with a wider world, he will probably make such contacts better in a parish church than in the college chapel.

Beyond all this, if he has a family, there is much to be said for his having a "church home" in the old-fashioned sense of the word, in which his children can grow up in the church school with their contemporaries. No college chapel, whatever provisions it may make for faculty children, can be quite the same thing. If, however, the college chapel makes in the case of churchgoing faculty members this entirely proper concession to local parish churches on Sundays, there is added occasion to invite the co-operation of the faculty in the conduct of Daily Prayers, if such services are held. Whatever his private religious faith the professor is unwilling to use his classroom as a place and occasion for witness to that faith. Indeed he ought not to do so. He should not put himself in the position of being charged with tacit theological or ecclesiastical propaganda. But in a definitely religious service like Daily Prayers he is the more free to speak his own mind intimately and candidly.

My own observation is that students are more interested to hear members of the faculty in such a setting than they are in listening to visiting preachers from the outside world. When President Conant or Provost Paul Buck, or, as for many years, Dean Roscoe Pound, or Professors Pitirim Sorokin and Kirtley Mather and Howard Jones are speakers for us, the student attendance is appreciably larger than on days when some visiting preacher comes to us, however noted he may be. Fortunately we have a list of some fifty such faculty members who co-operate with the chapel in this connection regularly and, apparently, gladly.

Yet in all these matters a chaplain has to reckon with the fact that an arts college is, vocationally, an educational institution and not a church in disguise. The faculty is right to encourage an adequate recognition of religion, as a major cultural fact in history and in contemporary society, through dispassionate presentation in the curriculum. It is further right to oppose all attempts to make the classroom the scene for veiled evangelism, whether Catholic, Protestant, Jewish, or Humanist. Nor can attendance at chapel be expected of the faculty as a part of their academic duty. If there is no compulsory chapel for students there certainly can be none for the senior members of the institution.

In this connection I always remember an incident told me by my brother-in-law, the late Professor Charles A. Bennett of Yale. The late Dean Charles R. Brown was at the time acting minister of the college church, which met in Battell Chapel. He conceived the bright idea of a larger service in another setting and moved the Sunday service from Battell to the great auditorium in Woolsey Hall. Having done so he urged faculty members, at one of their regular meetings, to come and sit in a circle of chairs which should be placed on the vast stage at

Woolsey Hall, to back up the lonely preacher at his desk at the front of the platform. The chairs were duly placed but for the most part were unclaimed and unfilled. A month later Dean Brown made a motion at faculty meeting that the faculty request the Yale Corporation for an appropriation to provide a semicircle of potted palms to fill the place where the faculty ought to be! He learned, as most of us have learned, that members of an arts faculty cannot be regimented for formal support of public acts of corporate worship.

Meanwhile, I venture to pass on a comment made to me by President Lowell, that it is, on the whole, as important to try to care for the religious life of the permanent senior members of the college as for the needs of the rapidly passing generations of undergraduates.

(J) Those who are responsible for the organization and conduct of the public worship of the institution, the trustees, the president, the chaplain and the like, will be constantly besieged by ecclesiastical pressure groups outside the institution. Such groups attempt to influence policies and in particular to obtain some kind of official recognition either in the pattern of worship or in the persons of those responsible for worship. These pressure groups are usually critical and unsympathetic. They intimate that the godless irreligion of the place might be cured by them if they were given a chance to control and conduct the acts of worship. The more orthodox and dogmatic of these groups dissent at the outset from anything like a liberal interpretation of religion.

If these pressure groups are granted formal recognition they will often gather students of their own types for sectarian acts of worship. In so doing they dissociate students from the community as a whole. It would be very easy to pass up the whole problem and hand over the conduct of worship to these divided bodies. The result is always an atomistic type of religious life in no way connected with or representative of "The Beloved

Community" in its entirety. Such a solution is an admission 'of failure in the presence of what is always a difficult problem in both theory and practice. On the whole it is better for the institution to insist on its own distinctive act of communal worship, even at the cost of the inevitable theological and cultural compromises involved in such a service. The curious fact is that such services in our larger universities—Yale, Princeton, Chicago, Stanford, Syracuse, Harvard—seem to be more effective than those in the small colleges. It may be a matter of mere numbers or a transcript of the acknowledged cosmopolitanism of the larger institution. It may be the architectural dignity and beauty of a building. It may be the effectiveness of a well-trained choir. But no one can say the college chapels in such institutions are "collapsing." They are as effective and successful as many of the other transactions going on in the institution as a whole.

(K) In short, the whole problem seems to me to come down to the willingness and intention of the institution to say "God" in so many words. If the institution is unwilling to say "God," imperfectly religious communal acts may be substituted for the public, corporate use of this word. The resultant act will always be, as I have intimated, a celebration of the half gods—one more phase of that subtle secularity of our churches which is probably the gravest fault in so much of our American religious life. In the classroom in philosophy God may be, as Professor Hocking has said, discussed as "he"; in an act of worship he is addressed as "Thou." If we give up trying to say "Thou," there is little gain, other than interesting speculation, in saying "he."

10

The Development of Religious and Moral Values

Howard Y. McClusky

MOST people, including most educators, need to be reminded that education for everybody and education about everything is a radical idea. Never before have so many people gone to school. Never before have so many different subjects been taught. We are finally having to face the consequences of our democratic faith that all people are educable and that all education is good. As a result, the cozy dimensions of earlier days are no longer sufficient to accommodate the burgeoning demand for instruction, and it is not surprising that many of our educational institutions operate in a state of chronic emergency.

It would be easy to diagnose the current state of higher education almost wholly in terms of the "growing pains hypothesis." It would not be a definitive appraisal, and would leave much relevant material untouched, but some reflection on its impact would remind us that an educational revolution such as we have witnessed in the last twenty-five years takes time to assimilate and that no person or group of persons knows enough yet to grasp its full significance.

In this period of expansion all levels of education have been critically examined. The examination of higher education has been particularly severe. In the course of an assignment from the American Educational Research Association, the writer[1] found over seventy-five substantial bibliographical items on general education which appeared in the period 1939-44. Since 1944 such efforts as the Harvard Report on General Education[2] and that of the President's Commission on Higher Education[3] have continued to fuel the academic fire. Out of this ferment have appeared certain recurrent criticisms, two of which are selected here for comment.

One concerns the evils of irresponsible specialization, and the other relates to a pedagogical amorality leading institutions of higher education away from a dedication to values transcending self-interest. The evils of irresponsible specialization include the fragmentation of knowledge, the contamination by the career motive of interest in pure learning, the insignificance of much scholarship, the devaluation of great teaching, and the neglect of seeing life steadily and seeing it whole. Some of the common errors of the higher amorality are a low view of man, an insensitivity to the overpowering beauty and mystery of life, a preoccupation with material creature comforts, and a cynical rationalization of self-interest as the dominating source of life incentives. The awareness, sometimes faint and sometimes sharp, of these twin groups of evils has thrown consternation into the battalions of the higher learning. Even the most neutral of the neutral and the most skeptical of the determinists have become alarmed at the prospect of the "superior scholarship" producing generations of uneducated experts whose major goal is to get ahead, or stated technically, whose life purpose is upward

[1] H. Y. McClusky, "General Education and Work Experience," *Review of Educational Research*, XIV (October, 1944), 289-300.

[2] A Report of the Harvard Committee. *General Education in a Free Society* (Cambridge: Harvard University Press, 1945).

[3] President's Commission on Higher Education. *Higher Education for American Democracy, A Report* (New York: Harper, 1948).

mobility in the class and occupational structure of American society.

This alarm is at once symptomatic and promising. It is the view of this discussion that, properly envisaged, the answer to this alarm is essentially a moral and religious one, and that implementation of the answer is a major responsibility of institutions of higher education.

It is proposed that the process of implementation should involve three kinds of overlapping effort. The first two are intramural in character and relate to the curriculum on the one hand, and to the processes of instruction and administration on the other hand. The third is extramural in character and would potentially affect all phases of higher education.

The curricular responsibility involves at least two elements: first, an approach to instruction that will distill out the religious implication of ALL subjects, and second, instruction in the subject of religion as an attractive and academically respectable option in the forum of higher education.

I. RELIGIOUS IMPLICATIONS IN THE CURRICULUM

Let us begin with what we will call the "religious distillate" of presumably secular subjects. To a teacher with imagination and broad sensitivity, each field of knowledge has its own treasure of moral and religious implication. It is beyond the scope of this chapter as well as the competence of the writer to detail the areas of religious relevance in the various curricular divisions of the higher learning. Fortunately, however, a number of highly competent scholars have recently been coming to grips with the religious perspectives of their respective disciplines. A reference to selected portions of their writings will be useful at this point.

As a representative of the physical sciences Einstein's views of the religious component of his field are worthy of attention. On one occasion he declared that the cosmic religious experience is the strongest and noblest mainspring of scientific research. . . . The most beautiful and profound emotion we can experience is the sensation of the mystical. It is the sower of all true science. He to whom this emotion is a stranger, who can no longer wonder and stand rapt in awe, is as good as dead. To know that what is impenetrable to us really exists, manifests itself as the highest wisdom and the most radiant beauty which our dull faculties can comprehend only in their most primitive forms—this knowledge, this feeling is at the center of true religiousness.[4]

Turning to the field of psychology our discussion is enriched by a recent penetrating interpretation of the role of religion in personal development. As Allport, one of the leaders of American psychology, explains,

Modern empirical psychology initially separated itself sharply from religion. "Psychology without a soul" became its badge of distinction and of pride. There was good reason. Too long had the understanding and cure of man's spirit been regarded solely as the province of religion and philosophy. In order to bring to bear the demonstrated merit of the scientific method and inductive thinking psychologists were forced to chart a new course. . . .

At the same time there is inherent absurdity in supposing that psychology and religion, both dealing with the outward reaching of man's mind, must be permanently and hopelessly at odds. . . . From many sides today comes the demand that religion and psychology busy themselves in finding a common ground for uniting their efforts for human welfare.

In seeking to trace the full course of religious development in the normally mature and productive personality, I am dealing with the psychology, not with the psychopathology of religion. The neurotic function of religious belief, its aid as an "escape from freedom," is indeed commonly encountered, so commonly that opponents of religion see only this function and declare it to dominate any life that harbors a religious sentiment. With this view I disagree. Many personalities attain a religious view of life without suffering arrested development and without self-deception. Indeed it is by virtue of their religious outlook upon life—

[4] Lincoln Barnett, *The Universe and Dr. Einstein* (New York: William Sloane Associates, 1948), pp. 105-6.

expanding as experience expands—that they are able to build and maintain a mature and well-integrated edifice of personality.[5]

From Professor Boulding comes a very revealing statement of religious perspectives in teaching college economics.

The danger in the economic abstraction lies in its very success. I am not attacking abstraction as such—it is absolutely necessary if the huge complexity of human life-experience is to be reduced to manageable terms. . . . But because of its coherence, its beauty and its success, its practitioners—especially those skilled in mathematics—are apt to forget that it is an abstraction, and that it is men and not commodities that are the ultimate social reality. A good example of both the necessity and the danger of economic abstraction is found in the study of labor: unless we understand clearly that labor is a commodity, in spite of all pious pronouncements to the contrary, we shall never understand the phenomena of industrial relations. But we shall also not understand industrial relations unless we realize that labor is much more than a commodity and that the labor-bargain involves a complex set of psychological, sociological, even theological relations out of which the commodity aspect is abstracted. . . .

It is at this point, I think, that the teacher whose acquaintance with religion is something more than second hand can be of great help to his students, not only as persons but also as economists. To seek God is to find man. To live deeply with the life of Jesus, as revealed in the Gospels, is to know the glory, wonder, folly, and depravity of man in his fullness. Unless the economist has something of this sense of the fullness of man he will be in constant danger of misusing his abstraction, particularly as applied to the interpretation of history and in developing an appraisal of economic policy.[6]

As a final example of the relation which religion may have to a presumably secular subject let us consider the field of history. In this instance we will draw on a recent discussion by Professor Harbison.

[5] Gordon W. Allport, *The Individual and His Religion* (New York: Macmillan, 1950), p. viii.

[6] Kenneth E. Boulding, *Religious Perspectives of College Teaching: In Economics* (New Haven: The Edward W. Hazen Foundation), pp. 21-22.

The Christian who is also a historian, then will be known neither by any fully rounded "philosophy of history" which is the necessary outcome of his Christian belief, nor by the amount of time he spends talking or writing about Christianity. He will be known by his *attitude toward history*, the quality of his concern about it, the sense of reverence and responsibility with which he approaches his subject.

The attitude of the Christian historian toward the past will be like that of the Christian toward his contemporary fellow beings. He may seldom mention the name of God, of Christ, or of the church, but in every remark he makes in the classroom and in every paragraph he writes in his study there will be a certain reverence and respect for his material, a certain feeling for human tragedy and human triumph in history which is closely parallel to the Christian's respect for human personality in general. . . . He will not bleach the moral color out of history by steeping it in corrosive skepticism. Nor on the other hand will he use history as a store house from which deceptively simple moral lessons may be drawn at random. . . .

He will know that to see any meaning at all in history is an act of faith, not a result of studying documents, but he will not dodge the question for that reason. He will be aware that every man in his beliefs belongs to some school or party or church, and he will not be afraid to admit that his own beliefs have their source in a church. . . .

He will not "know it all." He will neither sell his fellow human beings short, nor will he overrate them. Behind both the personal decisions and the vast impersonal forces of history he will see an inscrutable purpose. He will look for the working of God both in the whirlwinds and in the still small voices of history. He will give a sense of pondering and wondering more than of either dogmatizing or doubting. ". . . And if God's motives are hid, are they therefore unjust?"[7]

Statements for other fields of knowledge could be presented. But the excerpts from the physical scientist, the psychologist, the economist, and the historian are enough to establish the point that the main stream of the substantive program of the higher learning may be immeasurably enriched when it is illuminated by the persistent relevance of religion.

The effectiveness of establishing relevance depends on the

[7] E. Harris Harbison, *Religious Perspectives of College Teaching: In History* (New Haven: The Edward W. Hazen Foundation), pp. 26-28.

skill of the instructor in teaching for transfer of training. That is to say, a subject may be replete with religious implication, but we cannot depend on implication automatically besieging the perception of the student without some assistance from one who has been along the same or a related intellectual path before. This calls for imagination and a deep concern for communication.

But in sifting out the religious implications of presumably secular subjects the teacher should be cautioned against forcing a religious interpretation on nonreligious material, and he should be equally careful not to use the search for religious implication as a rationalization for moral pontification. At the same time, however, the caution against the preceding abuses should not be regarded as an invitation to religious intimidation.

It is suggested that the teacher keep his subject in modest perspective and that he guide his instruction by the topical and theoretical limits of his orbit. It is also proposed that he remind himself of the boundaries of his subject and the major postulates and methods on which it is based. By knowing what a subject purports to do and by remembering what it does not do, by constant alertness to the provisional character of its major assumptions, he could avoid much intellectual naïveté and academic arrogance. Thus, he may prevent much of the damage of secularism in higher education which arises from the presumptuousness of many unwarranted academic excursions and a limited view of the whole field of reality of which the subject concerned is only a part.

II. INSTRUCTION IN RELIGION

So much for the religious value of nonreligious subjects. Now let us review the responsibility of higher education for systematic instruction in the subject matter of religion.

In order to establish our case, we will argue for instruction in religion at the point of greatest dispute, namely, in tax-supported institutions, on the theory that if the case can be made there, it can be much more easily made with respect to institutions dependent on private support. In this connection, we propose to draw heavily on a recent unpublished report of a committee of the College of Literature, Science, and the Arts at the University of Michigan appointed to deal with this problem.

We may begin by asking whether any course in or on religions can or should be given by the College of Literature, Science, and the Arts. It seems clear that it is no business of a state university to give courses in which any sectarian point of view is inculcated or dogmatically stated as the truth—even if other courses in other sectarian points of view are also presented. But on two sides it is argued that no courses dealing with religion in any but an indirect or incidental way may be given or officially sanctioned by a state-supported school. Certain groups take the position that their religious point of view is the truth, and that, since the university cannot legitimately present that view as the truth, it should refrain from concerning itself with religion at all. This, of course, is a point of view which no school, other than those of the groups in question, need consider as a basis for determining its policy, except on grounds of expediency. Other groups, some religious and some non-religious, argue that the democratic state has the duty of perfect neutrality in the sphere of religion, and therefore its schools cannot legally or constitutionally offer courses in religion. A strong case can be made for this position on the ground that the democratic state stands for complete freedom of conscience, both for believers in the various faiths and for unbelievers.

In reply it may be said that the founders of our nation and of our state universities certainly did not intend that the principle of religious freedom should be construed as entailing indifference to religion on the part of the state. Witness the article in the Northwest Ordinance: "Religion, morality and knowledge, being necessary to good government and the happiness of mankind, schools and the means of education shall forever be encouraged. . . ."

But the main point to be made is that a state of perfect neutrality of the kind involved in the above position is impossible in the field of religion. Just as an act of omission is often as much a crime as one of commission, so inattention to religion is as much an act against religion as some more positive deed. To use William James' terms, not to offer any course in religion is to help it become a dead option, not to remain a live one. More than that, it is to encourage a negative resolution of the option between religion and irreligion, and so to support the "sect" of those who are against religion. As has been well said,

"In a sense mankind is incurably religious; every person is basically committed to some all controlling person, ideal or principle. . . . In this sense modernism, liberalism, secularism, communism, naturalism, scientism, and even atheism, are forms of religion as well as Judaism, Christianity, Mohammedanism. There is no religious vacuum. Where true religion is discarded or ignored, idolatry . . . in some form fills the void. The absence of formal courses in religion does not spell a comfortable neutrality. It rather implies an abdication, a surrender to the religion of secularism, a way of life which denies the relevancy of religion to other categories of life."[8]

For the university the conclusion must be that the College must give some respectful attention to the study of religion if its neutrality is not to be a malevolent neutrality. . . .

If these who are opposed to religion could fairly maintain that in all its forms it has been shown to be false, or if the proponents of one religious faith could make this claim with regard to all other creeds, then the argument just given might be said to have little weight. But this is not the case. Some articles in some religious creeds may possibly have been disproved by scholarship and science, but the essential features of many remain unrefuted, as is shown by the number of competently trained thinkers who still subscribe to them.

However, even if the main forms of religious faith could be said today to have been entirely discredited, it would still be true that they have been vital elements in our culture and development, and it would still be important that we be given an opportunity to study them, at least as important as it is to study the history of science, political and economic institutions, or literature. This justification is all the more cogent if religion is still, as we have argued, a live issue.[9]

It is not in the province of this discussion to detail the topical outline of the curriculum suggested by the preceding argument.

[8] L. J. Flokstra, *The Calvin Forum*, June-July, 1948, p. 233.
[9] *Report of the Committee on Religion.* College of Literature, Science and the Arts, University of Michigan, Ann Arbor, Mich. An unpublished manuscript.

Such details are available in a number of places.[10] Moreover, it is not proper at this juncture to propose the administrative machinery required for putting a curriculum on religion into operation. The weighing of such issues as the relative merits of a departmental versus an interdepartmental organization is more appropriate for another context.

Some attention, however, should be given to the teacher, who is after all the key factor in a program of instruction in religious subjects. It is obvious in this connection that, in training and academic competence, he should be the peer of his colleagues in other departments. Any dilution of standards would defeat the object of instruction in this field.

Furthermore, it is axiomatic that courses in religion should be based on sound scholarship and should not become a vehicle for the special pleading of organized groups and institutions. On the other hand, it should be frankly realized that courses in religion could, in effect, be antireligious in outcome in the hands of some instructors. Exposure to the subject matter of religion is by no means a guarantee of an affirmative result.

It is proposed, therefore, as a minimum that the teacher be able to present the religious values of his courses with respect, if not belief, and as a desirable optimum it would be hoped that in many cases he would be sympathetic with religion not only in the sense of "understanding it as a social phenomenon but in the sense of appreciating its values and of believing in an essentially religious conception of the world."[11]

In either case, he should be a scholar first and (if at all) a disciple second, but if he should have a genuinely affirmative experience of spiritual values this fact should be welcomed as an important asset for instruction in religion.

[10] The curricula of Princeton and Yale universities are illustrative. The full report of the Committee of the College of Literature, Science and the Arts at the University of Michigan is also useful, as well as the files of the National Council on Religion in Higher Education, 400 Prospect Street, New Haven, Conn.

[11] *Report of the Committee on Religion*, p. 4.

III. Instruction, Administration and Personal Values

Turning now to the second phase of our discussion, it may mystify some to learn and disturb others to concede that moral and religious values are involved in processes of instruction and administration as well as in the curriculum of higher education. In making this point it would be easy to become distracted by a comparison of the relative merits of substantive and methodological considerations in education. But such a comparison is an unprofitable issue because substance and method are both important and basically inseparable in the educative process. Moreover, it is a trap of irrelevance since the supreme concern of education is the person for whom substance, method, and even administration are intended. In other words, the student is at once the object and a means of education. This is the basic fact from which the moral and religious values of the instructional and administrative processes are derived.

It is the neglect of the valued and valuing person as the object and means of education that has led the higher learning to tolerate a number of programmatic and procedural defects which from the viewpoint of this discussion are immoral. A brief analysis of two of these defects will suffice to elaborate the point. One relates to the area of instructional method and the other concerns the field of administrative procedure.

To begin with method, education has something to do with teaching and good teaching among other things involves lucid intercommunication. Evidence for the breakdown of higher education at this juncture is the mistake commonly made by the higher learning of regarding exposure or confrontation as the equivalent of communication.

Now communication consists at least of exposure, attention, understanding, as a minimum, and acceptance and incorporation into a system of belief and behavior as an optimum. For example, a teacher may lecture but his pupil may not hear, a pupil may hear but he may not understand, he may understand but he may not accept what he understands, he may accept what he understands but he may not modify his beliefs, he may modify his beliefs but he may not change his behavior. Mere exposure is clearly not the equivalent of communication. And confidence in their equivalence reflects either an incompetent pedagogy or an irresponsible stewardship of knowledge.

A neglect of the valued person as the object and a means of education has led to a serious defect in administrative procedures. For example, it is a common assumption that all aspects of the management of the educational situation are the responsibility exclusively of the administrative officers. This assumption in turn implies that the student is either incapable of, or should be unrelated to, educational administration. Whatever its implication, the assumption constitutes a clear depreciation of the student's ability and violation of his responsibility for contributing to his own management.

A number of subtle evils flow from this condition. One is the loss of educational growth that comes from sharing in the process of management. Another is a reduction in the effectiveness of administration that properly emerges from widespread involvement. A third is the enormous burden of management which administration is compelled to assume. A fourth is the habit of irresponsibility acquired by the student because he has no part in management. And a fifth is the attitude of scapegoating which a student thrusts on the administration as a consequence of this habit of irresponsibility.

These evils are clearly inherent in the student-administrative dichotomy in educational management. The serious character of the neglect of the valued person as a means of education is accented when one considers the hope for more responsible instructional and administrative pedagogy contained in recent advances in the field of applied dynamic and social psychology.

Thanks to fresh insight in group dynamics and related fields, new substance is given to the way in which the valued and valuing person may contribute to the process of his own instruction and educational management.

One source of insight is a service approach to the problem of leadership. According to this view, it is not necessary for a leader to assert his authority in order to compel obedience and defend his status. Rather the leader secures his jurisdiction by service to the group. In this capacity he may engage in a number of functions. First, he may take a major responsibility for setting a desirable feeling tone for personal relations within a group. Second, he may give much attention to helping members of the group learn skills of co-operation. And third, he may devote much effort to the cultivation of leadership ability in others.

This kind of thinking leads us to a participative view of group membership. The old concept of followership which implies an undiscriminating doglike servility to the bark of the leader is no longer adequate.

Participative membership calls for a differentiation of tasks sufficiently diversified to allow all members to make a genuine contribution to group welfare. Some of these tasks may involve an assumption of many leadership responsibilities. Other tasks may require a fluctuation of roles from situation to situation and from time to time thus avoiding the inhibitive stereotype resulting from unvarying specialization. The total effect of this approach is to give the individual member a greater sense of status, release the full power of his personality, and increase the productivity of the group.

The service approach to leadership and the participative view of membership are alike in stressing the worth of the individual in the process of educational growth. It requires little imagination to grasp what transformations an application of these concepts would make in pedagogical practice. The repressive, impervious dictator-type teacher and administrator would give way to the adaptive leader who is skillful in the interpretation and satisfaction of individual and group sensibilities. The supine, scapegoating student and teacher would yield to the responsible seeker for unique roles in group production. In both cases, the practice of education would become a highly moral affair because the status of the student would achieve the transcendent importance which his value as the object and means of instruction requires.

IV. Extramural Aspects

The extramural component of this argument is capable of indefinite expansion. There is space for only two points. The first deals with the impact of certain extramural factors on intramural policy, and the second is concerned with the responsibility of institutions of higher learning to the larger community of which they are a part.

In elaborating the first of these points, it is proposed that as far as possible the inequalities of our society that are hostile to the great premises of Christianity should have no influence on the administrative policies of higher education. Reference is made to the doctrines of the brotherhood of man and the sacredness of personality which are the ethical basis for the American faith in the principle of the equality of educational opportunity.

Stimulated by the Lynds'[12] two studies of Middletown, a series of investigations have recently appeared, throwing much light on the class structure of American society. Data clarifying the full implications of these studies for education are just now becoming available. They indicate that the status system of the American community is too much reflected in our practice of education, and that of all levels, institutions of higher learning are the worst offenders.

The moral implications of these data for higher education are clear. Higher education should not only not perpetuate (cer-

[12] Robert S. and Helen M. Lynd, *Middletown: A Study in Contemporary American Culture* (New York: Harcourt, 1929).

Robert S. and Helen M. Lynd, *Middletown in Transition* (New York: Harcourt, 1937).

tainly not accentuate) the moral irrelevancies of the American status system but should do all in its power to eradicate them. We are so much a part of our culture that we often fail to realize how imperceptible the slow stain of this poison is. Too often we let the accidents of color, ethnicity, religious affiliation, and economic condition determine the composition of our student body, and much more often we allow these same accidents of birth and familial propinquity to determine the selection of our faculties and administration, and much more often these factors, wholly fortuitous, determine the complexion of our governing boards of trustees, regents, etc.

A personable, healthy young man with an I.Q. of 130, son of a poor Negro farmer, has about one chance in ten of securing a higher education commensurate with his abilities, a comparable young man, son of a poor white farmer, has about two chances in ten, while a young man of equal ability from a well-to-do white, gentile urban family has about ten chances in ten. The probability of a Jewish youth from the Atlantic seaboard entering many professional schools is probably one fifth as great as the chances of a gentile youth of similar circumstances.[13] And even more remote are the probabilities that a Negro will become head of the department of history, still more remote, a Jew becoming president, and even more unlikely that a member of the CIO will become chairman of the board of trustees of many institutions of higher education which we could mention.

The implications of the general point of which the above instances are illustrative, ramify in innumerable and surprising directions. It is enough here to insist that institutions of higher learning should not violate basic moral values by accepting the inequalities of the American status system which are inimical to the high purpose of education.

[13] These comparisons are only rough approximations inferred from data secured from a variety of sources. They should in no way be regarded as precise statements of quantitative relationships. They are presented only to illustrate the presence of a crude hierarchy of educational opportunity.

The second point is more extramural in the traditional sense of that term. It may be considered in two categories, one relating to the natural community as the setting for instruction which may originate intramurally, and the other concerning the responsibility of institutions of higher education for including the adult population within the clientele of its program.

One reason for the innocuousness of so much intramural instruction is its extramural irrelevance. One argument for democratizing the college as a subculture is that experience in the subculture is capable of significant transfer to the larger culture of which it is a part. This point suggests Hocking's[14] principle of alternation, which in practice would involve a process of intra- and extramural shuttling. There must be reflection at the undisturbed academic center, but there must also be experience with the living and suffering community. Especially in the field of religion and moral values, literary statements and systematic formulations often fall flat when confronted with real experience in a typical community.

Again, if the higher learning has a moral and spiritual obligation to society we cannot confine our instruction to youth. Such exclusive dependence on a product whose full social impact is inevitably delayed, too greatly dilutes the power of higher learning and high religion. If our responsibility to society is a major concern, we must constantly remind ourselves that the power segment of our population is composed of adults. They vote, manage, operate; they have economic, political, and social power. Admittedly adult education is a task for many agencies, but higher education should carry its share of the general responsibility and especially in the field of religion and morality. For it is here that adults have great need for a spiritual clarification and renewal which institutions of higher education are best equipped to give.

[14] William E. Hocking, *The Meaning of God in Human Experience* (New Haven: Yale University Press, 1912), pp. 405-27.

In conclusion, what constitutes the major role of higher education in society? It is not political and economic in the literal sense of those terms. Colleges and universities can swing few elections. They produce and distribute few goods; they are certainly not centers of finance. The members of their staffs are so rarely elected to political office (though this is changing slowly) that such an event is still cause for excitement. No, the power of higher education lies in its almost exclusive influence on and control (direct and indirect) of the intellectual and spiritual climate of the nation. It can be said without danger of exaggeration that that ideology which captures the higher education of a nation will ultimately determine its mind and soul. If we want a nation nonreligious, if not antireligious, in intellectual and spiritual outlook, we can achieve this end by presenting higher education in a religious vacuum, but if we wish religion to make its contribution to the life and culture of a people, it must have its place in the higher learning.

II

Academic Freedom

MILDRED McAFEE HORTON

FREEDOM is tolerable when men are secure. Nearly two hundred years ago William Smith of the College at Philadelphia said, "Liberty is the most dangerous of all weapons in the hands of those who know not the use and value of it."[1] Whether used with skill or without, it is always fraught with danger, for the freedom to make choices and to engage in activities always involves the possibility of making unpopular choices and engaging in activities subversive to some other person's interests.

Academic freedom, like every other kind, is possible in a society which feels itself fundamentally secure but freedoms of every kind are curtailed under conditions where their possible misuse threatens the existence of the regime which has the power to grant or to limit them.

There is an inescapable logic in the restrictions imposed on the colleges and universities of China as the Peoples' Government begins to consolidate its position. In the first flush of enthusiasm for the new regime there was such universal approbation of the government that its officers could afford to be generous to the point of allowing virtually unlimited freedom to institutions of

[1] Howard K. Beale, A History of Freedom of Teaching in American Schools (New York: Scribner's, 1941), p. 32, quoted from James P. Wickersham, A History of Education in Pennsylvania (Lancaster, Pa.: Inquirer, 1886), pp. 66-67.

higher learning—even those with major financial support from the west. It is to be expected that if opposition develops anywhere and the problems of governmental control become more acute, the universities will be restrained from teaching in any way which could serve to inspire subversive elements in the population. Nor do we need to go to China for illustrations of this tendency. When any society begins to fear that it must cope with serious adversaries, that society tightens its restrictions and limits the freedom of potentially dangerous elements within it.

I. Academic Freedom—An Easy Target

In the kind of situation which makes it seem reasonable to limit freedom for the sake of protecting it the academicians are highly vulnerable to attack.

In the first place, academic institutions deal with youth. Misleading them jeopardizes the future as well as the present. We are told that truth is strong meat. "When young people are old enough to evaluate truth wisely they can be exposed to it. As young people they should be protected from mistaken judgments," and any judgment is considered mistaken which seems to undermine the tottering structure of a society which feels insecure.

In the second place, professors are articulate by nature and what they say in their freedom has a forum which makes it conspicuous. They talk a lot and what they say is quoted—and misquoted. Professorial dicta have a peculiar disadvantage in that they almost always presume a context which is not available to the casual listener who hears a concluding, or transitional, sentence without its surrounding qualifications. The professor, conspicuous by his very function, is, therefore, highly susceptible to being misunderstood.

Furthermore, in our American scene the professor is a tempting butt of criticism in any case. Howard K. Beale makes an interesting observation about the tendency to discredit higher education as early as the days of Andrew Jackson. He says,

> . . . Higher education was neither attainable nor useful to the ordinary American of Jackson's day. Nor did this ordinary American desire it. In fact, frontier experience had made him contemptuous of too much learning. Other qualities had served better in frontier life. Yet true democracy could brook no inequalities. Therefore it convinced itself that education was not a mark of superiority. So deep did this distrust of education sink into the soul of America that to this day most men do not regard as better than anyone else's the opinion of a highly educated person, unless, perhaps, that person's education is technical or practical, so that the lingering frontier consciousness is able to appreciate it.[2]

When a society is panicky it wants to attack somebody, and "unrealistic" professors, disturbing youth with crazy notions, seem to be good targets.

The effort to control academic utterances in the interest of security for the larger society is accentuated to the degree that academic institutions are conceived to be agents of government. If the state employs teachers to do society's work, clearly the state does not expect them to undermine its very existence. That is both common sense and an elementary principle of employment. Sabotage is not an act of loyalty to any employer. Our state universities are often considered to be mere agents of the state. Are their employees not paid by the taxpayers? What right have they to say or do things not approved by those taxpayers?

When the state is secure, sure of itself, unafraid to teach its citizens to seek and use the truth, wherever it may lead, then the university can be truly free. When other interests of the state overpower its concern for the truth which makes men free to criticize, to suggest changes, to challenge shaky presuppositions, then let the university watch its step.

When academic institutions are virtually taken over by gov-

[2] Beale, *op. cit.*, pp. 76-77.

ernment projects in time of crisis, it is hard to avoid the implication that they are tools of government. A New York newspaper once quoted a rather plaintive comment by an educator who said that schools wouldn't mind being taken over for rationing purposes but he did wish the government instructions about rationing could be simplified.[3]

The use of universities by government seems to make sense when the alternative is the establishment of great government laboratories to duplicate what the universities already have. Moreover, the supply of scientists and other scholars is sufficiently limited so that when the government needs them it must either kill the universities by draining off all professorial talent in certain technical fields or let the scholars stay at home and work with adequate resources on problems which are directly "in their line." The threat to academic freedom under these critical circumstances is not primarily in any overt control to force the professors to reach certain conclusions. The threat comes first in the limitation of the area within which the university is free to encourage its scholars to work and, sometimes, in the limitation on those scholars of the exchange of information with other scholars. Top-secret security is not conducive to first-rate scholarship. Even more threatening to academic freedom is the impression on the public mind that the university is not a free agency for the search for truth, but is an agency of government.

Critics of the ROTC are disturbed by its militarizing and regimenting influence on the minds of youth. They also object to censorship by the occasional 100 per cent militarist officer whose residence on a college campus tempts him to interfere in normal academic life. These risks are less alarming than the identification of the university as an agent of government in its least educational aspect. It is a convenience to government officials to go to the places where selected young people are

[3] *New York Times*, July 28, 1950.

already assembled and to provide training under conditions which call forth a minimum of parental objection to the interruption of the normal education of youth. Many people familiar with military training recognize much of value in it and are not afraid that its regimentation a few hours a week will overpopularize mental regimentation. And most commanding officers stick to their own business. But military training and university education are diametrically opposed in principle and technique. The more the university is conceived as an agent for the accomplishment of noneducational functions of government, the more vulnerable is its claim to academic freedom.

Dependence of universities and colleges on government funds for any purpose is feared by many of them not because they suspect government officials of intending to censor their activities but because receipt of funds does put an obligation on the recipient. Failure to conform to current government practices and policies makes of the university an unfaithful servant, liable to legitimate criticism. The agent is not morally free to violate the terms of the agreement.

The problem of loyalty to an employer applies as truly to private philanthropy as it does to government subsidy. One of the grave problems of today's high cost of operating private colleges and universities is the extent to which special interests of donors become a matter of attention in college organization. Many an administrator has had reason to wish that prospective donors would be as interested in the basic objective of the institution as in some theory of their own whose demonstration they are willing to subsidize.

II. ACADEMIC FREEDOM—ITS NATURE AND IMPORTANCE

When freedoms begin to be curtailed in an insecure society, it is easy, for all reasons which have just been noted, to begin to limit the freedom of scholars in their scholarly function. Scholars and their defenders insist that for the welfare of society the very last freedom which should be jeopardized should be that of the scholar. Most of them would hesitate to share that last spot even with religious freedom. The argument is that restraint on the freedom of the scholar is restraint on the search for truth and that understanding of truth is of practical importance to society. Of course the scholar claims his civil rights, feeling that no occupation should deprive any law-abiding citizen of his self-evident right to "life, liberty, and the pursuit of happiness" as safeguarded in the bill of rights. But he claims more than that. He claims a contract protection in his job so that he cannot be dismissed "without cause." This matter of tenure is perplexing to a good many people outside the academic world and to a few close to it. Most boards of trustees include at least a few "hard-headed" businessmen who find it very hard to understand why a man who is a teacher should, in the name of academic freedom, hold his job when trustees don't like what he has said in a political campaign or when he has participated in a strike in a company town.

Men socially enough concerned to be university or college trustees are apt to be benevolent. As kindly gentlemen they know that every company carries employees who have been with it a good many years even though those employees are not as useful as others they might find. But that seems to be something quite different from academic tenure. The benevolent employer retains the relatively inefficient employee not because it is the employee's right but because the employer is generous. The employee is expected to appreciate it, not to count upon it. Tenure is something else again! It is considered in academic circles as a right, not a privilege. There is not a good college in the land which has not sometime carried somebody it would have dispensed with willingly because its authorities recognize a moral obligation to maintain tenure agreements.

Such agreements differ, too, from trade union employment rights with which trustees are usually familiar. The teacher must have a decent standard of living to be truly free and wise men have urged them, therefore, to join forces with other laborers who organize to maintain a decent standard. The tragedy of labor union procedures today is that they are almost always the tactics of war, carried out in an atmosphere of belligerency between labor and management. The searcher for truth is in a stronger position when he can be outside factional divisions. Tenure protects the servant of the public welfare from attacks from any source and therefore seems more appropriate for the scholar than does a self-protective union contract.

Try to explain tenure agreements to critical undergraduates who have been bored in the classroom of a teacher whose spark has dimmed or whose promise—on the basis of which tenure was assured—has not been fulfilled! The only way tenure makes sense is in terms of the freedom it provides for the accomplishment of the basic purpose of the institution. To carry a few misfits is a relatively cheap price to pay for the achievement of those real teachers and scholars whose professional security releases them from inhibition in their pursuit of truth and its transmission to their students and the rest of the world.

The reason the freedom of the scholar must be assured is that he is engaged in an occupation where his freedom of mind is an essential tool for the accomplishment of a socially essential end; namely, the discovery and dissemination of truth and the training of younger students to continue in that activity in the next generation.

There would be relatively little difficulty in connection with the search for truth if truth were found in its ultimate form at any one stage. Our trouble is that it is discovered a bit at a time and before it is proved there may be any number of false hypotheses to be tested as though they were true. Moreover, truth on any subject has many angles. Expressed for one audience with certain presuppositions it will have certain emphases; stated under other auspices it calls for different emphases. The listener in the wrong audience finds truth terrifyingly confusing. Furthermore, attacks on tentative convictions have an almost irresistible tendency to strengthen them. What is advanced as a hypothesis becomes a dogmatically held axiom in the course of debate. The course of discovering and expounding truth is not smooth.

Truth is not simple in its implications. The same premise can result in astonishingly diverse conclusions. When the premise is theoretical and the conclusions result in action, the scope for diversity is exceptionally large. Many a scholar in his classroom or study can expound a general principle to which little or no exception is found. Let him be free to act on the implications of that principle and he runs the risk of offending people who cannot believe that a principle in which they believe could produce action so radically different from their own.

New insights into truth must be publicized if they are to be tested against other people's insights. Parenthetically, this is the great justification for pressure on scholars to do some writing and publishing. The stimulating teacher who associates only with the less mature minds of undergraduates avoids the searching criticism of his contemporaries and seniors. He needs to subject his own thinking to the mature scrutiny of colleagues in the field of his own competence.

The scholar who is not immune from the slander of people who are afraid of his insights is subjected to appalling pressure to see and say only what is acceptable: the tried, the trusted, the trite—unprovocative—truism. Let Owen Lattimore say this with the forcefulness of one who has endured "Ordeal by Slander." Referring to problems of American policy in China he says,

> In the future we are not going to be able to deal any better or any more promptly with such problems as these unless the people in America who study and write about them can safely engage in public debate without the threat of persecution for those who hold minority opinions. Our experts must be allowed to translate, publish, and discuss the

writings of Russian, Chinese, and other Communists. They must be allowed to recognize that, regardless of whether the theories of these Communists are right or wrong, they are the theories that shape the lives of hundreds of millions of people under Communist rule. To that extent they are not only theories but political actualities, and must be dealt with as such. . . . Research must not be bounded by any kind of political doctrine. When the presentation of unpalatable knowledge becomes dangerous to the individual, the state itself is endangered.[4]

In a democracy, the independent thinker is indispensable both to the planning of a successful foreign policy and to the maintenance of our democratic traditions. There is no way to maintain his independence and make it available to the service of the nation except by defending the freedom of inquiry and opinion of one and all. This does not mean that Communists who actually organize for subversive purposes should not feel the weight of the law, or fascists, or Ku Kluxers who organize to intimidate any section of our society, or lobbyists for any foreign power, whether or not they receive pay from a foreign source, if they resort to vilification and intimidation of their fellow citizens in the interests of a foreign power. But action for subversive purposes should be kept separate, in our minds as well as in our laws, from freedom of opinion. The freedom of the majority is only safe if the freedom of the minority—any minority—is protected.[5]

A scholar is not truly free if he is not free to challenge the presuppositions of fellow scientists, of a dominant political group, or of the adherents of any tradition, if any of them seem to be at variance with the truth. Unwillingness to reckon with the data which refute his tentative conclusions is the mark of the dogmatist, not the scholar. No scholar in a free society would stifle Lychenko's right to expound his theories of genetics; students of modern science should doubtless study his theory enough to know what his argument is. Scientists' objection to Velikovsky's volume is not that he has no right to reach or state his conclusions but that they think his book distorts the facts on the basis of which other scholars reach different conclusions. The tragedy of

[4] Owen Lattimore, *Ordeal by Slander* (Boston: Little, Brown, 1950), pp. 228-29.
[5] *Ibid.*, p. 234.

a society which forces its scientists to reach certain conclusions, regardless of the facts as they see them, is that it deprives itself of the stimulus of criticism by means of which scholars come to increasingly clear understanding of situations which are controllable not by will of the scientists but by the nature of the universe.

Free men know that the minority may have the true insight. The importance of truth grows out of a basic conviction that in an orderly universe truth has a power which untruth—intentional or unintentional—cannot have. False interpretations of existing conditions lead to ineffectual handling of those conditions. Truth is not merely a scholar's delight. It is an essential tool for the accomplishment of society's purposes. This presumes a standard of rightness separate from the ideas or programs of any group, however powerful this may seem to be at any given moment.

The president of a Christian university in a Moslem country used to introduce visitors to what he called his evangelistic room. Expecting a chapel, his callers were startled to be shown into a chemistry laboratory. The evangelism consisted of assuring students that there are natural laws which can be counted upon to operate under given conditions; life is not controlled by a god of whim and of unpredictable irresponsibility. A universe of law, of order, of truth, is worth examining, worth knowing, for such a universe rewards truth and punishes untruth.

This kind of argument justifies freedom for the scholar or for anyone who expounds the truth as he sees it. His statement is worth hearing, for it may reveal real truth. And truth matters.

III. ACADEMIC FREEDOM—THREATS TO ITS EXISTENCE

We have seen that when a society feels itself insecure, it becomes nervous about the liberty of its teachers. From outside the academic institution efforts are made to safeguard the values which society or some part of society feels to be threatened. It is easy to mock or rage at the politician, the businessman, the crusader who tries to invoke legal or social pressures to force schools and colleges to conform to his idea of what is "safe." It is not so easy to thwart his efforts when the contagion of insecurity spreads. His efforts to prescribe the limits of the curriculum, the character of the personnel administering that curriculum, or the procedures within the institution rouse sympathetic response on the part of people sharing a deep fear that important values are threatened. Refusal to support institutions whose programs are "dangerous" makes potential donors potent factors in the struggle for academic freedom.

Reawakening interest in the relationship of religion and education has introduced a different type of restraint on academic freedom, the use of church facilities to broadcast criticism of certain colleges as threats to youth. Adverse publicity, warning parents to discourage students from entering, becomes a potent weapon in the hands of those who would force certain policies on academic institutions. Demands for the discipline or dismissal of individuals, faculty members, or students, are to be expected from people who are more concerned with conclusions with which they agree than with the atmosphere of freedom which can tolerate conclusions with which they disagree. Donors, motivated by religious conviction, require creedal commitments or impose conditions on appointees which threaten full freedom—though the danger can be averted by scholars of sincerity.

These are the self-evident symptoms of restraints on academic freedom but it should be noted that such attacks from outside are often matched by conditions inside academic institutions which are almost equally disastrous to true freedom to search for truth.

Anything which limits the opportunity to find truth is a limitation on academic freedom. From this point of view the teacher who allows his professional skills to grow rusty so that he no longer has the incisiveness of mind to cut into problems nor the synthetic skill to solve them is a foe to academic freedom. Tenure agreements can be serious threats to academic freedom when they are used to protect mediocrity. There should be a clear-cut line of demarcation between the protection of a teacher's right to proclaim the truth as he sees it and the protection of his job whether or not he does the job well. Anyone who follows with the care they deserve the reports of the American Association of University Professors on violations of academic freedom will know that this distinction is not always clear. Indeed it is clear that most of the instances of persecution involve difficult personalities—either in persecuted or in persecutor. Whenever the nonco-operative, irascible person hides behind his right to academic freedom to protect himself from the consequences of his nonco-operation or irascibility, he strikes a blow at academic freedom. The quip that the best way for a mediocre person to achieve academic recognition is to be radical has a barb in it for academic freedom.

Trustees menace academic freedom as much when they tolerate the appointment of people with no intellectual distinction as they do when they try to dictate what shall be said in classrooms. Moreover, trustees who think they provide academic freedom because they allow anyone to express his opinion are yet limiting that freedom seriously when they provide inadequate tools for the scholar. It is only as good scholars do their job well that they justify their claim to the special protection which is granted them in the name of academic freedom.

IV. Academic Freedom—Its Preservation

For years the American Civil Liberties Union has been advocating the organization of teachers' organizations to insure freedom of teaching. However valuable such activities may be, the defense of academic freedom is far more important than the mere defense of the civil right of an individual to express himself. It is not teachers alone who are called upon to insist on their freedom. Indeed, they may be less effectual in demanding rights than are others who have no personal ax to grind.

The university as a whole has a stake in the struggle for academic freedom. It is of the utmost importance that institutions of higher education clarify their function in modern society. Many influences are at work to put colleges and universities into the category of agents of government to enforce the *status quo* rather than that of searchers for truth. In line with a great tradition, educational institutions want to be known as concerned for social welfare. Our colleges have been marked throughout their history as institutions concerned with making good citizens as well as good scholars. Indeed, responsible scholars have been leaders in service to the organized life of their communities. It is important, however, for taxpayer, donor, parent, and graduate to understand the difference between rendering voluntary service as scholars and rendering service as "hired help." The university is a member of the society of which government is the official organ but it is a member which may find itself in the position of being "his majesty's loyal opposition." The university is outside government—supported by taxes for that purpose—aiding and abetting government where it can conscientiously do so, criticizing where it feels it should. It needs to be understood by the public as a place where the search for truth is going on; a place which can be trusted to be sincere in that search; a group of people genuinely concerned about truth as an important end of its activity. This interpretation of the university needs to be made in a society accustomed to spoon-feeding through advertising techniques. The university cannot be immune from comparison with other institutions whose wares are being made available to a public which expects to be "sold" before it is convinced. This is the reason for the existence of public relations programs. These are sometimes resented by scholars as violating the sanctity of academic activity, but the

modern teacher truly needs them to convince the modern public
that what he is doing should be preserved at all costs.

A teacher in a liberal arts college recently told a group of
graduates that a college is like an organism in which the faculty
are essential organs while the administrators are mere auxiliary
aids. It is debatable whether eyes and ears and mouths are
"essential organs" or not, but administrative officers who look
and listen to public reactions and then talk fast and often about
the significance of what the college is undertaking to do are
performing a most important function. It is time for faculty
members and administrative officers and alumni and trustees
and students and all the other elements in the academic scene to
stop thinking in terms of who is most important in an enterprise
that involves them all. The more unified the entire institution is,
the more clearly its role can be established. In this connection it
is fair to say that departmental segregation in academic institutions is a threat to academic freedom since all parts suffer from
misunderstandings engendered by any of them.

The role of the administrator in any kind of organization is
an interesting subject in itself. Think of all the national organizations, political, religious, educational, social—any kind. Is it
not true that there is apt to exist tension between "headquarters"
and "the field"? It is the kind of tension which develops with
singular ease on academic campuses between "administration"
and "faculty." Singular, because they are essential partners in
a total enterprise. That which represents the whole is apt to be
resented by the part since the part, seen in the light of the whole,
always looks different from the part (or the whole) seen from
the vantage point of the part! In academic communities the role
of the president or deans or public relations vice president is a
paradoxical one. It involves prestige of a high order—ordinarily
higher off the campus than on it—but it frequently involves the
assumption on the part of other elements in the academic community that the administrative officers are "outsiders," threats to

academic freedom, from whom teachers must be protected. If academic freedom is to be preserved it is important that the university or college should be united in asserting the importance of the search for truth, recognizing that "the members are many but the body is one."

Academicians find it easy to be bored by personnel programs and to suspect a conflict of interest between themselves and physicians, deans of men and women, heads of dormitories, student counselors who seem to "pamper" the young and spend hours interpreting them to their parents. There are fair and difficult questions to raise about the speed with which young Americans should be encouraged to move into maturity. They may, indeed, be pampered too much, but there is little doubt that activities which assure parents that academic institutions are concerned about the personal well-being of their children are assets to the reputation of the institution. Being assured that university authorities care about Susie's health and morals, critics are more amenable to the suggestion that her introduction to truth of a potentially disruptive sort is not really subversive. Welfare services, in other words, are actually contributory to academic freedom as means for winning friends and influencing people to trust the university.

The university must not betray that trust by fooling people into thinking that nothing is being taught which is different from the "going belief" at a given moment. It must use its trusted position to reassure public citizens that its critical activities are not only legitimate but socially valuable.

Institutions do not inspire confidence any more than individuals do by secretiveness or aloofness from the main stream of human experience. It does not hurt to have enough town-gown personal friendships so that town refuses to believe that gown is subversive. Life in an academic community so isolated that it touches the nonacademic world only as though that were a necessary evil is not conducive to academic freedom in a crisis.

Professor X who shows himself to be a good neighbor, concerning himself in those aspects of community life which make life easier for all the neighborhood, can be trusted to handle even the dynamite of truth. Professor Y, absent-mindedly ignoring his neighbors and making paths on their lawns as he strides to and fro from home to class, is suspected more easily!

But academic freedom is not preserved by general good will toward an institution. However effectively a particular college interprets itself to the public, the chances are great that in the days ahead there will be need for individual martyrs in the cause of academic freedom.

The role of the true martyr is never a pleasant one. It requires courage of a high order and only the brave can be counted upon to play it effectively. Fortunately, relatively few are called to be martyrs. However, in days of tension almost everyone faces the problem of choosing whether or not to repudiate or defend some victim of the attack on freedom. The jittery public is ever-unsympathetic to martyrdom. Believers in freedom for the search of truth must undertake to defend genuine victims of suppression. In that task they need to be assured that they are not defending mere frustrated seekers of the limelight.

Heaven defend colleges and every other social institution from self-made martyrs, the people who create situations in which they can give themselves pleasure by playing the martyr's role. Such pathological people we shall long have with us; the only point of mentioning them here is that they complicate the problem for people who have to decide whether or not to support martyrs in their suffering. It is probably better, however, to defend a dozen self-seekers lest we fail to protect one bona fide seeker for truth, but the cause of academic freedom is not advanced perceptibly when it is attached to the cause of personal license rather than the liberty of truth.

One constructive way to defend martyrs is to prevent the creation of situations which produce them. Chief among such situations are those created by the passage of unrighteous laws. Friends of academic freedom can serve it by combating the passage of legislation which requires conscientious violation.

Within college communities, restrictions on student activities imposed either by faculty, administrative, trustee, alumni, or student authorities need to be studied in the light of their effect on the encouragement of the pursuit of truth. Government by law, prohibiting young people from exposure to dangerous doctrine, is apt to be futile. Situations in which it is tempting to avoid risk by prohibition often provide opportunity for the best kind of realistic education. The scholar's method of considering all sides of controversial issues is probably sounder practice than the authoritarian's refusal to admit a notorious object of curiosity to a public platform. And the scholar's technique minimizes the number of undergraduate rebels for conscience' sake. (And it may also require a lot of explanation by the president to the local newspaper!)

But the laws which complicate academic freedom most are not those within the direct control of a college faculty. They are the laws introduced into state legislatures, often very plausible-sounding laws. Patriotism by legislation has had many advocates during the recent years of threat to our way of life. What harm could there be to anyone in requiring him to salute the flag? Why not require an oath of allegiance and of loyalty of teachers lest they be tempted to use their unique position in schools to mislead the young? After all, why should any loyal person object to affirming loyalty to his native land? If he affirms it falsely he can be convicted of perjury—and perjury is easier to handle in law than is mere disloyalty. In anxious periods of national life these questions sometime give rise to hasty legislation. Let advocates of academic freedom examine such proposed legislation well in order to be sure that under the stress of momentary anxiety they do not create the conditions within which they or their colleagues must be called upon to be martyrs.

The American Civil Liberties Union has long since gone on record as opposed to loyalty oaths for teachers and its summary of arguments is as brief a way of stating the position of anti-loyalty oath adherents as any:

1. It is an unjustified reflection upon the loyalty of the teaching profession to require it to take a special form of oath not taken by other public servants.

2. Such oaths can accomplish nothing in practice by separating the loyal from the disloyal among teachers.

3. The tendency represented by taking such an oath is dangerous to democratic education by suppressing discussion of vital changes and reforms in our political and economic institutions. It strikes at freedom of thought and belief among teachers.

4. No condition in education now exists to warrant the imposition of such oaths on teachers. . . . Their loyalty throughout the history of the public school system has never been questioned.

5. Definitions of loyalty differ; imposing the oath would open the door to pressure for conformity to the notions of whatever forces happen to control a local school system.

6. Commitment to a prescribed oath would encourage espionage among school teachers, parents, and even pupils to magnify any critical utterance into "disloyalty."[6]

These formulations made in 1933 sound modern today but the issue now is, of course, in terms of membership in the Communist party. Shall we have laws requiring teachers to testify that they are not and have not been members of a group which is recognized as fundamentally opposed to the principle of academic freedom? The Council of the University of Chicago Senate went on record in October of 1949 in a statement on academic freedom which included the following paragraphs:

A widely accepted statement in favor of excluding Communists from membership in university faculties rests on the premise that all Communists adhere to a set of rigid dogmas and are required to accept political direction of their intellectual and practical activities. The argu-

[6] David Bunting, *Liberty and Learning* (Washington, D. C.: American Council on Public Affairs, 1942), p. 47.

ment is then advanced that since Communists do not possess intellectual freedom, their exclusion from university faculties does not impair freedom but in fact preserves and furthers it.

The answer to this argument consists in questioning the premise on which it is based. Any such conclusive presumption about a group when applied to individuals without investigation of their individual competence, freedom, and integrity is a violation of academic freedom that is both unnecessary and unwise. If a particular Communist meets in fact the requirements for membership in a university faculty, he should not be excluded from this kind of community on the grounds of political affiliation.

Furthermore, the proposals which have been made cannot accomplish the results their proponents have in view. Once such proposals have been adopted, those Communists who do accept political direction of their intellectual activities, and who are seeking university employment, will avoid formal affiliations with the Party and will conduct their activities underground. If they are disloyal to this country, they will not shrink from perjury. Therefore, it is likely that elaborate investigations into the loyalty of university faculties will be held. The evidence ceases to be proof of membership in the Communist Party. It becomes evidence of associations and the espousal of ideas that the reviewing committee might take as sympathy for Communist views. An atmosphere of intellectual freedom cannot be preserved if men of integrity and competence are to be subjected to punishment or loyalty proceedings because of the ideas they hold.

Universities cannot yield to pressure that a particular minority group be excluded from the academic community. The road suggested by such proposals is that which in the past has led to the exclusion of scientists, Catholics, Jews, and indeed all groups that may, at a particular time and place, be unpopular with the majority. It is convenient and easy to have an automatic method of excluding members of unpopular groups from university faculties; but academic freedom is too important a matter to be subordinated to convenience and ease of administration.

. . . The answer to wrong ideas is not to be found in suppression but in their examination by free minds guided by competence and integrity.

It might almost be argued that the confession of membership in the Communist party in a time of tension would be all the safeguard needed to protect the university from the danger of

Communist influence. Being "on guard" against indoctrination would seem to be a healthy antidote. It is the person of sufficient lack of integrity to refuse to admit his affiliations who would seem to make himself immediately suspect in an intellectually sensitive community.

Proponents of academic freedom must be active in a less explicit sphere than the legislative. Reports from China tell us that long before regulations were passed about higher education, professors were hesitant to express ideas critical of the new regime. The atmosphere of public opinion is more potent than any laws. The insidious fear of being accused of disloyalty dampens anybody's ardor in the search for truth.

For years Americans have pointed with dismay to the insistence by the Russian government upon statements of loyalty in irrelevant places. Why should artists, novelists, scientists, waste their time in their works of art and learning to protest their loyalty to a political group? Where was their freedom? But let any reader of this book ask himself how often he has felt impelled to explain that what he has just said or was about to say did not mean that he was a "Red." One hundred and fifteen years ago de Tocqueville observed the power of majority opinion in a country which credits the majority with final authority:

In America the majority raises very formidable barriers to the liberty of opinion: within these barriers an author may write whatever he pleases, but he will repent it if he ever step beyond them. Not that he is exposed to the terrors of an auto-da-fé, but he is tormented by the slights and persecutions of daily obloquy. His political career is closed forever, since he has offended the only authority which is able to promote his success. Every sort of compensation, even that of celebrity, is refused to him. Before he published his opinions he imagined that he held them in common with many others; but no sooner has he declared them openly than he is loudly censured by his overbearing opponents, whilst those who think without having the courage to speak, like him, abandon him in silence. He yields at length, oppressed by the daily efforts he has been making, and he subsides into silence, as if he was tormented by remorse for having spoken the truth.[7]

Howard Beale in commenting on that passage adds,

Many of the conditions that created the intolerance of democratic America have passed, but the attitudes of mind created by them have become the mental stereotypes of descendant generations.[8]

The creation of public opinion in favor of the search for truth is the responsibility of proponents of academic freedom and it has all the difficulties of the creation of any other kind of public opinion. It requires willingness to take trouble to rise in defense of people and ideas in small groups, in large groups. It involves argument, persuasion, patient interpretation and occasional outbursts of righteous wrath. It involves understanding the forces creating the sentiment opposed to the public opinion we desire to see created.

V. Academic Freedom—Its Sure Foundation

We cannot hope for academic freedom in an insecure society. We cannot hope for security so long as the conviction prevails that change is dangerous; that we have an inflexible, unalterable set of practices which, being endangered, endanger all that we hold dear. The true assurance of academic freedom is a fundamental inner security which makes for an adventuresome spirit. This can never be derived from possession of atomic bombs. It cannot derive from assurance that free enterprise is ultimately stronger than a temporarily efficient dictatorship. It cannot derive from the conviction that democracy is the best policy, nor that Russia will eventually be "kept in her place" by an Atlantic and/or Pacific Pact.

This is the point at which the possibility of academic freedom rests fundamentally on a religious insight, an insight which is

[7] Alexis de Tocqueville, *Democracy in America* (rev. ed., New York: Appleton, 1899), I, 267-68, quoted from Beale, *op. cit.*, p. 81.
[8] *Ibid.*

theistic and Christian. The theist who looks at history in the light of eternity; who sees relative standards in the light of God's absolutes—such a person (or society) has an objectivity which can create fundamental security. He knows the stars in their courses fight for the same truth for which he himself contends. Beyond the divisions in time and space as we know them there is a unity which can ultimately resolve the differences. One world can really be one world if there is really one God. To a believer in such a God such a world is worth working for in confidence even when immediate issues look insoluble.

Within the framework of a universe ordered by a God who values personality there is room for vast divergencies in theory and practice. That nation can be secure which sees itself—and its competitors—in the framework of such a universe. A nation with faith in the ultimate security of its people can afford to be tolerant. A conviction that there is a God who sees the whole world and controls it ultimately can give power to a people who believe in him. Out of that sense of power comes tolerance for freedom in the search for truth.

This cannot be said without invoking memories of crusades, inquisitions, bigotry of all kinds. Surely there was no educational freedom in the American colonies when they were dominated by opinionated men of God who were sure they had direct communication with divine authority which made it their Christian duty to exterminate heretics! Surely they were not able to create a society with sufficient inner serenity to permit free men to live and teach in freedom. Sectarianism in the name of religion has blighted education at every level of age and experience. Any dogma which assures the believer that he has The Truth and The Whole Truth stifles the discovery of new truth. Religious faith which is exclusive in its scope, faith which makes the believer feel an exclusive responsibility for accomplishing God's purposes, faith which scares the believer by presenting him the danger of eternal punishment as a penalty for misunderstanding

God's will for him—such faith has endangered freedom through the ages. Such faith is in disrepute among scholars.

If men would be free they must have a faith, an inclusive, generous, assured belief that they are part of a God-controlled world society within which they can move freely. To cultivate such a faith is to make a more secure world and its achievement is something to be profoundly desired by men who would be free.

Proponents of academic freedom will do well to work toward an achievement of such spiritual insight as will offer abiding security to men and women faced with perplexity in a time of shifting values. This means that the search for truth in the areas of religion and philosophy is essential. Thus theologians and philosophers have profound responsibility for freedom for scholars in all fields. If there be no orderly universe in which truth is discoverable and in which personality is of ultimate worth there would be some reason for thwarting academic freedom as an unnecessary interference with the convenience of a dominant majority or minority in any given society. If the best efforts of men's minds come to that conclusion we should know it and stop struggling to defend the indefensible. However, there are people and groups of people whose faith gives them courage to adventure into an unpredictable future. This is a fact, an important fact, an all-important fact, so important that those who would be free, as these believers are free, would do well to examine and, haply, possess themselves of the same faith.

VI. Academic Freedom and Commitment

There was once a professor of philosophy who was said by his students to have a "mind so open it was open at both ends." His unwillingness to commit himself to anything lest new truth might ultimately make him change his mind minimized his influence and made even truth seem so ineffectual as to be undesirable.

A case might be made on paper for the assertion that academic freedom is limited as long as there are any convictions to which the thinker is willing to commit himself. In practice, however, no area of research is unlimited. The finiteness of human understanding leaves room in the search for truth for the delimitation of areas within which any man or institution chooses to work. The man who has found a faith for himself which can keep him steady and serene and unafraid makes a contribution to academic freedom which is harder for the unrooted man to make. The demonstration to students and the general public that this investigator into truth is a "well-adjusted" human being, secure and therefore adventuresome, gives credence to his conclusions. The scholar who uses his scholarship as a compensation for insecurity in his personal relations does less to create the atmosphere of security within which adventure is safe and tolerable. The professor, fighting conscientiously for academic freedom, helps his cause, according to this point of view, when he also identifies himself with such institutions as the church or synagogue which relate him to more than temporal security.

It would be absurd and unfair to deny that some of the most vigorous and effective advocates of academic freedom have been avowed humanists unwilling to concede for a moment that their insistence on freedom relates them to any cosmic principle or divine personality. So be it. For most of us atheism which provides man with "no invisible means of support" (as someone has defined it) is not enough to steady a society in confusion. Until there can be such steadiness the struggle for freedom must be made again and again and again as the inevitable terror of an insecure public makes it fear the truth which free scholars will seek and find.

Academic freedom must leave an individual free to commit himself to such truth as he believes. Is there such a thing as legitimate institutional commitment to anything but the prin-

ciple of freedom? The practical question in our American culture
is whether or not a college can identify itself as Christian and
at the same time claim to be an academically free institution.
Of course Christians who believe themselves to have appre-
hended a true understanding of the nature of God and the
universe see no incompatibility between their commitment and
freedom to express truth. But what of those who disagree with
the particular form of Christian conviction which is expressed
by the authorities of the institution? Surely they are not free, are
they, if they are required to accept without criticism the conclusions of the dominant powers that be? "You can't require
religion" has echoed through academic halls from coast to coast.

Minds are not stifled by exposure to certain favored doctrines
so long as they are permitted and encouraged to compare them
with any others which they choose to investigate. A teacher of
comparative religions once spoke in a faculty meeting in favor
of a required prerequisite of Old and New Testament study
saying that he found it difficult to teach comparative religions
until students had something to compare them with. Insistence
that students should experience certain forms of public worship,
that they should learn something about a religious tradition can
be a stultifying requirement if the practices of that tradition are
imposed as final truth, unsusceptible to criticism. On the other
hand, the creation of a community committed to a Christian
way of life—however that is defined—seems to be a legitimate
setting within which the search for truth can be encouraged.
Nobody denies the "right" of college authorities to expose students to the best art, the best theater, the best health programs
which can be made available to them. The judgment as to the
nature of the "best" determines the caliber of the authorities in
the judgment of onlookers. It seems reasonable that exposure to
the "best" in worship is no violation of the principle of freedom.
Indeed, education which is so secular that it refuses to recognize

worship as a fact of experience with which students should be acquainted seems to be, to that degree, both unrealistic and unfree.

Academic Freedom is far from an academic question in these days of critical decision about the kind of world we are trying to build. Late in 1950 John Foster Dulles told an assemblage in New York:

> There is no direct dispute of any consequence between the Soviet Union and the United States. Rather, the source of tension in the world today is the existence of two basic philosophies about world order. Whereas the United States and many other countries believe in a free world order tolerant of differences in political and religious beliefs, the Soviet Union believes in achieving uniformity by control of the media of communication, regimentation of all man's activities, and forcible liquidation of those who do not conform.[9]

If we are to achieve a "free world order" we must establish or maintain the condition of freedom at home and let our own land be a convincing demonstration of the desirability of a society free enough to tolerate differences of belief. It behooves proponents of such freedom to examine the fundamental presuppositions of freedom. This is a task for scholars, especially for those whose Christian conviction gives them security for a fearless search for truth.

[9] Quoted from an undated news release from the Federal Council of Churches.

PART IV

Correlations and Implications

Conclusions and implications

12

Religion and Democracy

GREGORY VLASTOS

A RESPONSIBLE discussion of this topic requires a definition of religion, on one hand, and of democracy, on the other. For any number of purposes—inspirational, polemical, or propagandist—it may be possible to leave these terms explicitly undefined, trusting that the substantive assertions that are made about them will implicitly define the meaning they carry in the speaker's mind. However permissible on other occasions, such indirection would be unworthy of this volume, whose authors are united not only by a common conviction of the valid place of religion in the academic community but also by a common loyalty to the disciplines of rational inquiry. Whatever recommendations we may make to our colleagues in the universities will be cogent only if they issue from an analysis of the facts that is as honest and as rigorous as we can possibly make it. A number of partisan bodies are now vociferously urging their claims to a share of the pie of the college curriculum. Our own contribution in this volume will be, we hope, neither to add one more voice to the cacophony of sectarian claims, nor yet to arrogate the role of judge and arbitrator for which we have as yet received no mandate from anybody. It will be rather to make our own independent inquiry, and advance conclusions whose claim to thoughtful consideration rests on nothing more than the thoughtfulness of the reflection by which we have reached them. To this end I submit this essay in definition.

I. DEMOCRACY

What do we mean by political democracy? We mean a state, and a certain kind of state. A state is an order of human relations, enforced by the supreme coercive power of a public authority. This is a necessity for any civilized society. Without it, no one, in the well-known phrase, could have a "calculable future"; no one could embark on any long-range course of action, secure against the upsetting of his plans by the arbitrary intervention of others. To meet this common need men must co-operate to maintain an authority which issues commands which all must obey; and the "must" here is not in the first instance a moral but a political "must," secured upon instruments of coercion sufficient to preserve the common order against the dissidence of any individual or group, whether it be willful or absent-minded, whether it be criminal evasion or conscientious objection. This coercive power of state-authority is the A B C of political theory, and any attempt to side-step it, however well-meaning, can only end in a sentimental muddle. It exists in all states, democratic or autocratic. What is more, it ought to exist, and this not because we like it, but because we cannot do without it.

But though we cannot do without some kind of state, there are many kinds of state that we can and should do without. This is the choice to which democracy is the answer. It is a moral choice, and a momentous one. For in committing ourselves to a certain kind of state, we find ourselves committed to a whole "way of life." However thoughtlessly or tendentiously this phrase may be used in current propaganda, it nevertheless affirms a profound truth sadly neglected in the era of *laissez-faire*. The state is not an impersonal mechanism, whose value can be reduced to cheap and frictionless efficiency. Everyone in his senses wants an

efficient state. But efficient for what? For war or peace? For freedom of thought and discussion or for stream-lined conformity to
certified dogmas? For the equalizing of opportunities or the protection of inequalities? These and a hundred other issues are at
stake in public policy. When we decide for or against a given
type of state we are deciding whether its supreme coercive power
will serve or flout our cherished values. In this respect the state
is not an instrumental but an intrinsic good (or evil). The
power of the state indeed is and ought to be a mere means. But
the *form* of the state is no mere means to anything else, but a
moral entity which is good or evil on its own account. It is a
moral entity not because it is anything over and above the people
who compose it, but precisely because it is just these people
themselves, deciding for or against things which they hold good
or evil. It is a tissue of human relations in which values are realized or forfeited, no mere piece of social plumbing, but a community which embodies or prevents, creates or destroys moral
values.

Now the basic decision in this matter concerns the locus of
political power. In any state there must be a sovereign power,
supreme over all its subjects, whether they be ditchdiggers, four-
star generals, or prelates of the church. Who is to have this
power? To whom does it belong? Democracy expresses the decision that this power belongs to the people and to all the people
equally. This, of course, is the literal meaning of the word: the
demos has the *kratos*; and the current term "people's democracies"
hides a linguistic redundancy which seems to be lost on both
those who uphold and those who despise this term. This is no
mere matter of etymology; etymology here is simply the faithful
record of a historic fact. Wherever democracy has arisen, in
classical antiquity or in modern times, it has come about as a
struggle for power, in which a ruling minority's monopoly of
state power has been successfully contested in the name of the
whole community's right to have and to hold this power. His-

torical states have been more or less democratic in the degree of their realization of this professed goal. We know whether a given state is or is not democratic, and just how democratic it is, when we look behind the constitutional front and determine just how many people have a share, and how effective a share, in the making of public policy. A state is democratic in the degree in which the people of that state can decide who is to govern them and to what end.

The moral values of such a state have been stated over and over again. I do not think we can improve on the classical triad, liberty, equality, fraternity. But I think that we can, and should, reverse the order of the triad. In most discussions, classical and contemporary, fraternity gets little more than a polite nod. It is nevertheless the rock-bottom foundation of the moral scheme. It means that the community of value and equality of personal consideration which is proper among brothers in the family is also proper to a fraternal association in the state. In the family there is a common good in which all share and to which each is required to subordinate his private goods. Brothers are personal equals, however unequal in specific abilities; each is cherished as a person, for what he is in himself, and the resources of the family are put at his disposal to meet his individual need and develop his peculiar capacities. Political fraternity is a like ordering of the resources of the political community for the sake of the needs of personal equals. The welfare of each, his dignity as a self-determining being, have an equal claim upon the resources of the state with that of everyone else. Nothing less than this fraternal conception of dignity can justify the equality of political and civil rights and the freedom of thought and expression which are basic to democracy. Men can claim equal rights to select their lawmakers and to benefit by their laws only because the sovereign power of the state is their common possession, shared in equally by all. Men can claim the right to think and speak freely their individual thoughts about the policies of the state only because these policies ought to be the expression of their common will, each having the fullest personal right to share in the shaping of the common will. The protection of minority rights rests on precisely the same foundation. A minority, however small, consists of persons each of whom shares in the sovereign power of the state and is entitled to its benefits in the same degree as the members of the majority.

Of the moral criticisms of democracy which are on record, the one which comes closest to the heart of the matter was first raised by Plato, and has been repeated in modern times by critics who differ as widely from Plato and one another as neo-Thomists and existentialists. Its butt is the doctrine of popular sovereignty. The charge is that this is tantamount to political amoralism. "Democracy," wrote Berdyaev, echoing Kierkegaard, "is indifferent to Truth . . . , for it is only on condition of ignoring or not believing in Truth that one accepts quantitative power [*sc.* as arbiter of Truth] and reveres the opinion of the crowd. . . . Power in the people's hands is not ordered toward any object, and good and evil are alike to Democracy."[1] The answer, it seems to me, can only be given in terms of each man's personal dignity, political and moral, which the members of a fraternal community are pledged to respect. To respect another's dignity is to recognize him as a self-determining being, whose life decisions must be the products of his own choice, and cannot be forced on him by any-one else, not even in the name of Truth and Morality. Unless these decisions are free, they would not be moral at all. When they are free, they may not be wise and sound. Men may, and sometimes do, decide against the good they know; more often they are misguided as to the nature of the good, and decide for evil believing it to be good. This risk is inherent in moral freedom. The Creator of traditional theology could find no way

[1] *The End of Our Time* (London: Sheed and Ward, 1923), pp. 174-75. Much the same criticism of democracy is made by Maritain in *Scholasticism and Politics* (New York, 1941), pp. 93 ff.

around the difficulty, and we cannot expect weak and fallible mortals to solve the problem that stumped the omniscient and omnipotent Godhead.

In politics the same logic justifies self-government and accepts the possibility of its misuse as a calculated risk. And it applies not because we resign ourselves to the doctrine of the moral man and the amoral society, but precisely because we do not. If political decisions involved merely questions of means, there would be no justification for democracy, on moral or any other grounds. Politics would then be a matter of pure technology and then could (and should) be handed over to the social engineer. It is just because questions of good and evil are at stake in public policy, that responsibility for its decisions must ultimately rest with those whose lives must embody the substance of these decisions. The ends of the state cannot be moral ends, unless they are the products of the choice of the people who must live by them. And in so far as decisions with respect to means are seldom mere questions of administrative efficiency but commonly entail decisions with respect to ends, open or disguised, they too must be subject to the review of the citizens themselves.

There is singular irony in the fact that the existentialists who have laid supreme stress on the self-determining, self-creative powers of the person, should have shown savage hostility to the theory of government which is pre-eminently a doctrine of personal freedom. There are good sociological reasons for this anomaly, which do not concern us here. The logic of their position is all that matters now. It turns on the assumption that self-determinism is the prerogative of the isolated individual, and is inapplicable to collective life. The group for Kierkegaard and many of his followers is always the "crowd." There is a patent sophism here, which begs the question at issue. For a "crowd" is just the sort of group in which people renounce their individual power of reflection and choice, and are swayed by mass emotion and mass prejudice.[2] If this were the only form of personal association, then certainly no collective decision could be responsible and free in the proper meaning of the words. But so far from being the only, it is not even, strictly speaking, a form of personal association at all, because in it persons sacrifice the very thing which is constitutive of personality, responsible self-determination. The question which Kierkegaard does not even raise is whether men can meet, act, and think together not in subpersonal, but personal terms, conscious of their interdependence and facing common problems as free, responsible beings. Here, as elsewhere, he is the victim of the individualist preconception that freedom and society, self-determination and interdependence are in principle antagonistic, rather than complementary, terms. The logical implications of this assumption are pure anarchism or pure despotism. They can be reconciled with democracy, as in Benthamism, only on the makeshift that all government being a sacrifice of personal freedom, democracy is the best (or rather, least bad) government because it is the least government. Whatever one may think of the logic of this position, it would founder on the facts. It has been pointed out that the machinery of British government never expanded more rapidly than in the heyday of liberalism, inspired by the Benthamite apostles of least government.

A theory of democracy which is logically self-consistent and in line with historic fact must recognize that men can, and must, be interdependently free; that the co-operative pursuit of common values need not be the negation, but the expression of their personal freedom; that decisions with respect to these common values can be moral decisions, and that they will be such only

[2] I pass over the correlative point that personal *irresponsibility* need not take a collective form but may find just as effective private channels. There are a thousand ways in which individuals "escape from freedom" in the privacy of their individuality, ranging all the way from indulgence in fantasy to indulgence in alcohol. Collective life is neither the necessary nor sufficient condition of evasion of personal freedom.

when made under conditions in which each recognizes the right of all to share freely and equally with the rest in making these decisions. That the infinite complexities of government will limit the degree and mode of individual participation in public policy is obvious. What matters here is the guiding principle of whatever technique of government may be devised for its implementation. And this is that the values of a state are the personal *and* common values of those who compose it. They are *common* values; they express their interdependence, and can only be achieved in co-operation. Yet they are *personal* values; the right and duty to choose them by themselves and for themselves is definitive of their personality, and they cannot surrender it to anyone without forfeiting their status as personal beings. This ultimate dignity of personality-in-community is the only basis I know for the moral justification of democracy.

When democracy is thus conceived in ethical terms it should be contrasted with its most instructive alternative which has claimed to be *the* "ethical state." Unlike positivist views of the state, for which all morality, individual or social, is ultimately a matter of nonrational sentiment and habit, and unlike individualist views, which recognize only individual morality, and look upon social ends as, at most, instrumental to individual ends, we find in Plato, Hegel, and in modern corporatism,[3] a doctrine of the state as a moral community whose common ends are genuinely and supremely ethical ends. Because they are ethical ends, this doctrine holds, they must be protected against the egoism and caprice of private individuals; they must be determined by those whose wisdom and disinterestedness qualify them for reliably moral decisions. This is the core of the theory when trimmed down to fundamentals. It denies every person's right to self-determination, and this for his own good, and the common good. In this fundamental respect (and in

[3] For an engaging and lucid exposition of Italian corporatism as the ethical state see J. S. Barnes, *Fascism* (London and New York, 1931).

others logically deducible from it) it is a nonequalitarian or hierarchic theory of political community, for it rejects the equal right of all to share in the determination of the ends of the common life. It is, therefore, an organic theory of community, in the strict meaning of that term. Just as in an individual organism, or in an organic society of bees or ants, many parts are harmoniously ordered for the good of the whole without any ability to understand or decide upon their common good, so, this doctrine assumes, the members of a state must serve common ends which many of them are quite unfit to judge for themselves and which must therefore be judged for them by their betters. This organic relation between superiors and inferiors in the political community is formally recognized by this theory, and the organic metaphor plays a great role in the major statements of the theory, implicitly in Plato, explicitly in Hegel and the corporatists.[4]

Another aspect of the same relation, less flattering to the theory, must also be recognized. If self-determination is definitive of personality, then to deny it to any one is to treat him not as a person, but as a thing. This is to exploit him, not in the vulgar sense of willful injury, but in its more profound sense, first defined by Kant. One may intend the highest good for another person and act with sincere solicitude for his welfare; but if one deprives him of the power to decide his own good for himself, one reduces him to a mere adjunct of one's will, and the effect is exploitation, however well-meaning. In ignoring his capacity of self-determination, one offends his dignity as a person, and no benevolence of intent or self-sacrifice in its execution can atone for this ultimate injury. The practical differences between the authoritarian state and the democratic state could be discussed at length. They need not concern us here. It is sufficient for our purposes to recognize the ethical abyss which separates the one

---

[4] For a further critique of the organic concept of society see the contribution of Walter G. Muelder above (chap. 5).

from the other. Both look upon the state as a community, and a moral community whose supreme coercive power must be used for the protection of moral ends. But each stands for different types of community: equalitarian in one case, hierarchic in the other; personal for the first, organic for the second.

Can one accept this pattern of human relations in the political field, but reject it in others? Of all the incongruities of our common life to bewilder the proverbial visitor from Mars, none would be more perplexing to his innocent eye than the spectacle of men zealously loyal to the democratic state who are no less zealous in defense of an economic order which, in principle, is flagrantly undemocratic. Political democracy holds that political power belongs to the community. *Laissez-faire* capitalism holds that economic power is the private property of its titular owners. For the meaning of private property we may remind ourselves of Blackstone's formula: "that sole and despotic dominion which one man claims over the external things of the world, in total exclusion of the right of any other individual in the universe."[5] Blackstone sweetens the pill by saying that this "sole and despotic dominion" is not over persons but over "the external things of the world." But power over things is directly or indirectly power over persons. For the things in question are not abstract fixtures in the landscape, but the means of livelihood of men and women, the necessities of their life, on which their human needs, material and spiritual, depend for their satisfaction. Economic no less than political power is a necessity of the common life which is secured by a vast nexus of co-operative action. But while democracy recognizes that the ends which collective power must serve are the ends of the men and women who maintain it, determined by their common choice, *laissez-faire* capitalism holds that the ends of economic power are the ends of its owners, determined by their own exclusive choice. The

[5] *Commentaries on the Laws of England* (11th ed., London, 1791), II, 2.

first vests authority for the use of power in the community; the second vests it in private owners, responsible to no one but themselves. The first recognizes the equal dignity of all persons, and safeguards their dignity by according them an equal right in the sovereign decisions of the state. The second denies the dignity of a large number of persons who enter the economic equation not as persons, but as things, their services being bought and sold, like commodities, on the open market, for whatever price the higgling of the market will fetch.

Laissez-faire is, of course, a very inaccurate description of our contemporary economic order. For its proper denotation one would have to turn back the pages of history by a century or more, and watch the operation of the free labor contract, to force men, women, and children to work for twelve or fourteen hours a day to earn the bare necessities of a miserable existence. Capitalism has since been tamed by innumerable regulations and restrictions, forced on it by the democratic state, in the interests of protecting the right of everyone to be an end, and no mere means, of the economic process. This has mainly taken the form of the principle of a minimum of social decency, guaranteeing that every person, employed or unemployed, will be assured of the basic needs of self-respecting life, by way of income, education, health, and housing, and this not as a matter of charity, private or public, but as a matter of civic right. The real issue before the civilized states of the West is no longer whether this principle is right, but how it will be implemented and how far. And there is also, of course, the further question which concerns not individual benefits from the economic process, but the authority which the community may justly claim over it, asserting such common sovereignty over the means of economic power as has already been asserted over the agencies of political power.

In other fields of human relations the democratic pattern is equally applicable in principle and has already been accepted to a far greater extent than we commonly stop to recognize. In those intimate relations whose common value lies directly in the free exchange of thoughts and feelings, the principle of equal dignity is axiomatic. When men and women seek each other's company not in order to "make friends and influence people," but simply to *be* friends, they meet as personal equals, with the sort of consideration and respect for each other that forms the delicate, but none the less essential, framework of friendly intercourse. In the family, the reign of the domestic autocrat is over in theory, if not often in practice. A pattern of personal equality between the partners of the marriage contract, and an ideal of parent-child relations which respects the dignity of the child and not only permits, but fosters, the child's self-determination within the full limits of its maturing powers, are now the guiding axioms of the enlightened family. In racial relations, the white man is now perhaps for the first time in history properly shamefaced about the arrogance of his claims to superiority and the immorality of the mores which continue to enforce it upon his victims. In the church the battle was fought as early as the fourteenth century and for the Protestant communions had largely been won by the seventeenth. The essential principle was defined by Marsiglio of Padua in 1324: that in the church, as in the state, authority rests with the community itself, and that no sacramental prerogatives confer on priest or bishop any right of church government which is not derived from the body of believers and held only as their trust.

II. Religion

This brings us to the second term in our discussion, religion. The question whether religion does, or does not, provide spiritual foundations for the democratic pattern of human relations is unanswerable so long as its first term is indeterminate. Before we can even try to answer it, we must first decide what kind of religion we are talking about or, indeed, whether we are talking about religion at all. As popularly practiced throughout history religion has been commonly alloyed with magic. Fused and confused in popular piety, mixed together in almost every conceivable proportion, these two ingredients are not only different but antithetical.[6] The essential thing about magic is its presumption of coercive control over the supernatural to insure the realization of human wishes. Man turns to magic in the face of the frustration of imperious desire. If he were able, or willing, to accept this frustration, there would be no magic. Magic arises when he turns to supernatural beings which he credits with power to achieve what his own natural powers obviously cannot. And magic flourishes because he credits himself with power to coerce these supernatural beings and make them do what he wants done. The astonishing variety of the arts and tricks by which he bends gods or spirits to his will is immaterial to the point at issue. It does not matter here whether he tries to get his way by coldly impersonal devices, by the more personal form of bribe or barter, or by the still more intimate appeal of direct supplication or entreaty. As every child knows, one can coerce the will of superior beings by whining or squealing when other ways fail. In this, as in all other forms of magic, the constant element remains the coercive grip of the practitioner or client of magic upon the supernatural object, whether this be conceived as a thing, or as a personal or quasi-personal god, or spirit.

It is just this element which is not only lacking in, but is positively incongruous with the only attitude which deserves the name of religion. Religion is the sense of reverence for, and commitment to, an object which is held to be good, and supremely good, on its own account. In religion one seeks communion with an object whose worth is so much greater and

[6] I am well aware of the fact that some anthropologists ignore or even reject the validity of this distinction. But see Malinowski's essay in *Science, Religion, and Reality* (New York, 1928) edited by Joseph Needham, and R. Firth's article on *Magic* in the 14th edition of the *Encyclopaedia Britannica.*

higher than one's own that one would willingly dedicate one's life to it and transform one's will to bring it into harmony with its demands. Whereas the magical object is instrumental to the human will, the religious object is sovereign over the human will. The typical prayer of magic is, "My will be done." The only truly religious prayer is, "Thy will be done." Yet these two prayers, antithetical in themselves, have been regularly combined in magical religion. All too commonly men have approached God in reverent humility, celebrating his sovereign goodness, and declaring their will to devote all their powers to his service, and then have proceeded to switch over to a wholly different attitude in which they lecture him with list in hand of all the things he should get busy to produce for their convenience and comfort.

This jumble of religion and magic is not peculiar to primitive societies. It survives the transition to the higher forms of ethical religion, and finds as much scope for its operations in the yearning for righteousness as it ever did in the more primitive anxieties over drought, disease, or death. The desire for goodness runs into frustration as often as any other. Time and again man finds himself in the grip of moral defeat, forced to confess: "The good that I would, that I do not; the evil which I would not, that I do." Magic brings a defense against this form of anxiety and despair. It offers, at a price, ways and means to guarantee moral victory or, at least, relieve the intolerable burden of guilt. The price may be as heavy as the sacrifice of one's first-born son or as cheap as the absolution pronounced gratis by a priest. Morally it is always cheap, since it guarantees a nonmoral short cut to the moral purity required by one's conscience and one's God. Yet it is also prohibitively expensive. In relieving man of personal responsibility for his own moral condition it subjects him to the priestly dispensers of certificates of moral health satisfactory to a righteous God. One cannot conceive a more formidable instrument of authoritarian subjection than a faith which puts a magical tollgate across the way to righteousness. It is at just this point that the relevance of religion, on one hand, and of magical religion, on the other hand, to the assumptions of democracy can best be examined. Since I am wholly incompetent to deal with any religion other than that of the Hebrew-Christian tradition, I must restrict my remarks to this one religious tradition.

In the prophets of Israel and in Jesus we find an ethical religion that renounces magical short cuts to morality, and turns with stubborn enmity against the piety which sponsors them. The prophets declare that God requires of man one thing and one thing only: justice, mercy, and love. Magical substitutes by way of the burnt offerings and all the other prerequisites of the ceremonial stink in God's nostrils.[7] In Hosea's powerful metaphor they are "as heaps of stone in a furrowed field": an irrelevance, and a nuisance. Jesus clashes with the religious leaders of his day on the central issue of the religious value of ceremonial purity. Absolution from sin cannot be bought at the price of tithes and washings, and it need not. No price whatever need be paid for it. God's forgiveness is free, and free to all. Here man is no longer the tributary of any priestly authority. Spiritually he is free, and responsibly free. To come to God he need not come to any man; he need only come to himself. He can meet God face to face whenever he chooses to leave the swine and return to his Father's house. And the only demand God will make of him is that he live as God's son and as brother to his fellow men. His response to that demand is his own; no one can make it for him, no other man, nor even God. God leaves the choice with him. "See, I have set before thee, good and evil, life and death; therefore, seek life, that thou and thy seed may live." "The Kingdom of God is at hand: repent ye."

[7] Neither here nor subsequently do I suggest an equation of ceremonial and magic. The ceremonial may be either magic or religion, depending upon the beliefs and attitudes it expresses. Whenever it becomes a substitute for ethical conduct it *is* magic, and the prophets condemn it as such.

Such a faith involves a declaration of independence from the authoritarian community of magical religion. The magical apparatus in religion is the jealously-guarded monopoly of those who claim privileged knowledge of its lore and exclusive competence in its rites. The religion of the prophets and of Jesus is the common possession of the people. The prophets assume that the knowledge of God and of God's will is a matter of common knowledge; they are grieved and shocked when it is lacking precisely because they assume that it ought to be universal: "The ox knoweth his owner, and the ass his master's crib; but Israel doth not know, my people doth not consider." They look forward confidently to the day when the whole earth "shall be full of the knowledge of the Lord as the waters cover the sea." New insight into God's law may come from time to time. But it is not restricted to a professional priesthood, is not induced by some magical rite, and need not be certified by ecclesiastical patent. There is no notion of a closed corporation that monopolizes the conduits of revelation and the means of salvation. There is not even a notion of a spiritual elite, whose higher religious attainments entitle them to special favor with God and authority over man. It is the salvation of the whole people, not the perfection of a class of religious virtuosi, that is the object of God's concern. The universal priesthood of believers, which had to be asserted as a formal dogma in the Reformation in the face of its dogmatic repudiation by the sacramental doctrine of the church, is taken for granted by the prophets and asserted not as a controversial doctrine but as an obvious truth: "Ye shall be unto me a kingdom of priests, a holy people."

The moral application of this concept of religion is never crystallized into a formal ethical and political system. Its precepts center about the teaching of justice and the commandment of love. In the prophets the stress falls upon the evil of the oppression of the masses by the arrogance and greed of the aristocracy. In Jesus the stress moves nearer to the inner springs of conduct; it falls on that complacent self-centeredness which makes the rich fool content to enjoy his harvest by himself and for himself and prompts the religious zealot to seek his own salvation, ignoring the need of the wounded man on the Jericho road. It would be futile to look here for proof texts in support of the institutions of political democracy which are foreign to the national tradition of the Jewish people. What we do find in the prophets and in Jesus is simply the general pattern of fraternal relations of which political democracy is a special case. Fraternal conduct is not only recognized as correct in itself, but is exalted as the supreme requirement of religion. In Jesus the law of love is the law of the kingdom of God; to prepare for the kingdom one must fulfill the law of love in one's immediate, personal relations. Current institutional relations are bracketed off by religious eschatology as spiritually and morally inconsequential. When God chooses to bring in his kingdom, he will wipe them off the map. Meanwhile one may put up with them, without excusing their moral perversities, and never permitting them to stand in the way of one's only important business, dedication to the kingdom of God. The pursuit of wealth, and the possession of great wealth, do stand in the way. One cannot serve God and mammon. As for Caesar, one may pay the shilling he demands without elevating this forced compliance to the armed will of the imperial robber to a moral principle of passive obedience. To "render unto Caesar the things that are Caesar's" is in itself lean comfort for Caesar, since whatever things are Caesar's will not be his very long and can never touch the dedication of the will to a pattern of human relations which is the very opposite of Caesar's, where the greatest is not he who lords it over others but he who serves. What Caesar needs most of all from the religious institution is the spiritual and moral approval of his power. This he could never get from the teacher of the kingdom of brotherhood and service. He did get it, and very soon after, from Paul the apostle.

The innumerable theologians and churchmen who have justified the most abject submission to autocratic governments have read the command to "render unto Caesar the things that are Caesar's" not in the context of the ethic of the gospels but in the light of the Pauline prescription: "Let every person be subject to the governing authorities. For there is no authority except from God, and those that exist have been instituted by God" (Romans 13:1).[8] If we want to understand this text, rather than excuse or explain it away, we must keep two things in mind: first, the justification Paul offers for the authoritarian community not only in the state, but also in the relations of wife to husband and slave to master; secondly, the religious faith that both prompts and qualifies the justification. Wives must submit to their husbands "as is fitting in the Lord" (Col. 3:18); slaves are enjoined to "be obedient to those who are your earthly masters, with fear and trembling, in singleness of heart, as to Christ" (Eph. 6:5). The demand for submission could not be more categorical. Husband is to wife, and master to slave, as the divine Head of the Church to its human body. This command is, of course, conditioned, as in the gospels, by eschatological expectation of the kingdom, whose arrival will level sexual, racial, political, and economic distinctions. Yet neither is the command itself a mere matter of interim ethics. In the family relation the inequality is rooted in the order of creation: "neither was man created for woman, but woman for man" (I Cor. 11:9). Not only in the home, but in the church, woman should recognize her inferiority, and "ought to have a veil [the sign of her subjection] on her head, because of the angels" (I Cor. 11:10). Her inequality is no mere accommodation to the arbitrary facts of the *status quo*, but is inherent in her created being.

But Paul does not thereby reject the personal equality of the gospel ethic. He affirms it with fervent sincerity: "There is

[8] The biblical quotations appearing on this and the following page are from *The Revised Standard Version of the New Testament*, copyright 1946 by the International Council of Religious Education.

neither Jew nor Greek, there is neither slave nor free, there is neither male nor female; for you are all one in Christ Jesus" (Gal. 3:28); and he might have added, "neither political superior nor political inferior." The essential principle of this affirmation is the initial term "in Christ." This is of the essence of Pauline mysticism. For Paul, Jesus is a cosmic power in whom "dwells the whole fullness of deity bodily" (Col. 2:9). In him "all things were created, in heaven and on earth, visible and invisible" (Col. 1:16). He, therefore, has the power to release man from his relation to the natural order, which Paul regards as abject bondage. The dualism of the two orders, natural and supernatural, is reflected in man's own dual being, as flesh and spirit. These are not only different, but antagonistic, "For the desires of the flesh are against the Spirit, and the desires of the Spirit are against the flesh" (Gal. 5:17). Man is helpless in this conflict. The only thing that can liberate him is Christ, whose power is supreme over "the weak and beggarly elemental spirits" (Gal. 4:9) of the natural order, and who has demonstrated his power by the fact that he "has been raised from the dead, the first fruits of those who have fallen asleep" (I Cor. 15:20). The promise of immortality which the magical ritual of the mystery religions offered to its initiates, is fulfilled for Paul by the mystery of Christ's resurrection which guarantees a similar resurrection to all who live "in him" and thus share his miraculous power. It is this metaphysical dualism which is at the bottom of Paul's ability to affirm both the unconditional equality of all persons *and* their unconditional inequality in the relations of marriage, slavery, and the state. Equal in spirit, they are unequal in the flesh.

If we look closely at this position we will find two ideas which permit, along quite different lines, Christian accommodation to undemocratic forms of personal relations: ethical dualism and ethical authoritarianism. Neither of them is a Christian innovation. Dualism is foreign to the main stem of the Hebraic tradition; one will search for it in vain either in the prophets or in the Synoptic Gospels. The metaphysical and ethical dualism of flesh and spirit goes back to Plato, though its political implications were drawn only later, notably by a pagan contemporary of St. Paul, the Stoic, Seneca.[9] Here we find in all essentials the doctrine which was absorbed by the fathers of the church, systematized by St. Augustine, and revived a thousand years later by Luther. It is the view that temporal inequalities are necessary evils, the consequence of sin, and remedies against it. One need only compare St. Augustine's justification of slavery with its classical Aristotelian model to see the crux of this position. For Aristotle slavery is natural, an integral part of the teleological order of the whole universe, wherein the less perfect form of existence finds its proper fulfillment as matter for the more perfect form immediately above it in the cosmic hierarchy. For Augustine, as for the Stoics, on the other hand, slavery is "contrary to nature." By nature men are equal and free. So they were in the state of innocence. It is the corruption of man's nature by sin that necessitates slavery as well as the patriarchal family and the authoritarian state. For all practical purposes this is a pretty effective justification. A master versed in Augustinian theology could tell his slave that his servitude "comes not to pass but by the direction of the highest, in whom is no injustice" and clinch his domestic sermon with the further reminder that, under the circumstances, this hurts the master more than it does the slave: For "as humility does benefit the servant, so does pride endamage the superior."[10] Nevertheless the slave does come off better in Augustine than in Aristotle. Both are benevolent in principle, and purport to envisage the slave's good. But while Aristotle seals slavery into a cosmic scheme, Augustine leaves the slave an irreducible spirit-

[9] See G. H. Sabine, *History of Political Theory* (New York, 1937), chap. X, "Seneca and the Fathers of the Church."

[10] Both citations from *City of God*, XIX, 15, tr. John Healey (London and Toronto: J. M. Dent, 1931).

ual dignity, absolutely equal to that of his master, and even leaves open the question whether some other way might not be found to deal with the consequences of Adam's sin, a way which, among other things, would be kinder to the master, since it would not expose him to the mortal sin of pride. This last would be a dangerous thought. It would imperil not merely the slave's docility, but the basic ethical dualism on which the Augustinian doctrine precariously rests. The vital question for all social ethics is whether political and economic relations can themselves be moralized; whether they can be conceived as the relations of free and equal spiritual beings to one another who in these, as in all other, relations must respect one another's freedom and equality. The Augustinian view forecloses this very question by subtracting this whole sphere of human action from the area of fully responsible moral conduct. The best it can do is to prescribe here a second-class morality, a morality of submission to inevitable fate, rather than of free choice in the shaping of destiny. Unkind as it may seem to say it, it is infected by the moral irresponsibility which is endemic to any system of moral dualism. To say that any set of social arrangements are a necessary evil is to withdraw them from the responsible choice of those who submit to them. It is to justify acquiescence in evil by calling the evil necessary.

The Lutheran version of this doctrine and its far-reaching effects on the social conscience of German Protestantism are only too well known. But one is apt to forget in this connection the secularized transposition of the doctrine which flourished in Anglo-Saxon communities to justify acquiescence to *laissez-faire* capitalism much as Lutheranism in Germany justified acquiescence to the autocratic state. It is the view that the economic order is a nonmoral "natural" order; nature being here conceived not in terms of Aristotelian teleology, but in terms of mechanistic materialism. Even John Stuart Mill's humane and liberal spirit could believe that "the laws and conditions of the production of wealth partake of the character of physical truths. There is nothing optional, or arbitrary, about them."[11] Mill at least held that the *distribution* of wealth is a matter of "human institution," and that for this reason man could and should be held responsible for the inequalities of wealth and poverty. The classical exponents of *laissez-faire* would not have countenanced this concession. Integral to their doctrine was the view that personal income derives from each man's place in production and is regulated by the natural automatism of the market. Here production *and* distribution both partake of "the character of physical truths" and "there is nothing optional" about either. Malthus was only developing a logical complement of the doctrine when he showed how not only the production of material wealth, but of human life itself, was caught in the economic juggernaut, and regulated by its immutable, impersonal laws. The frightful evils of the economic order could then be acknowledged by men of good conscience and acquiesced in with a clear conscience. The sphere of morality is the sphere of the optional. Morality can only begin where physical necessity leaves off.

Like ethical dualism, Christian authoritarianism has roots in Pauline teaching,[12] though its main rootstock is not Christian, but Greek. Its classical statement was given by a faithful Aristotelian, St. Thomas Aquinas. Against the dominant view, Stoic and Augustinian, of the natural equality of man, St. Thomas holds that even in the state of innocence natural inequalities would prevail: some men would be naturally masters, others naturally subjects.[13] He justifies this by appealing to natural inequalities in the angelic hierarchy and, still more broadly, to

[11] *Principles of Political Economy*, Bk. II, chap. 1 (p. 123 of the "People's Edition," London, 1871).

[12] Especially in Paul's conception of woman as the natural inferior of man, and his organic concept of the church as a whole of many members of unequal dignity.

[13] *Summa Theologica*, I, Q. 96, Art. 3 and 4.

the whole hierarchical order of the universe itself.[14] The very term "hierarchical order" is, strictly speaking, tautologous in this system. For St. Thomas order *means* hierarchical order; equalitarian order is never even considered.[15] "Suitable order," he writes, "consists in a proportionate descent from the highest to the lowest." And what is "proportionate descent"?—"This proportion consists in this, that just as the highest creatures are subject to God and governed by Him, so the lower creatures are subject to, and are governed by, the higher."[16] It would be grossly unfair to St. Thomas to assume that this subjection is servile. God governs men as free spirits, not slaves. The human ruler should similarly hold authority over "free subjects."[17] But just as God, ruling men for their own good, decides in his superior wisdom what is the good by which they must live, so the head of a human community, political or domestic, can and must decide its common good. When in the *Summa Theologica* St. Thomas raises the question, to whom does the making of law belong, he replies: "The making of a law belongs either to the whole people or to a public personage who has care of the whole people."[18] He poses here the fundamental alternatives between which any political theory must decide. He proceeds immediately to accept the second, and formally defines law as "a dictate of practical reason emanating from the ruler who governs a perfect community."[19] The power of the people them-

---

[14] *Summa Theologica*, I, Q. 96, Art. 4, and Q. 108, Art. 1; *Summa Contra Gentiles*, Bk. III, chaps. 79-81.

[15] *Summa Contra Gentiles*, Bk. II, chap. 45.

[16] *Ibid.*, Bk. III, chap. 78; Anton C. Pegis, *Basic Writings of St. Thomas Aquinas* (New York: Random House, 1945), II, 145.

[17] *Summa Theologica*, I, Q. 96, Art. 4.

[18] *Summa Theologica*, II-I, Q. 90, Art. 3; Pegis, *op. cit.*, II, 746; cf. II-II, Q. 57, Art. 2.

[19] *Ibid.*, Q. 91, Art. 1; Pegis, *op. cit.*, II, 748. The transition had already been made in the concluding Article of the preceding Question, where law was defined as "nothing else than an ordinance of reason for the common good, promulgated by him who has the care of the community" (*ibid.*, p. 747).

290 Liberal Learning and Religion

selves to make their own law is here dismissed in favor of the law-making power of the ruler, and this without argument, without justification of any kind. The justification is implicit in his hierarchical conception of all order and it is made explicit in his shorter treatise *On Kingship*, where he holds that the king is "in the kingdom what the soul is in the body, and what God is in the world."[20]

St. Thomas does not, of course, follow the logic of this position to its strict absolutistic conclusion. He clings to the medieval conception of the king as a representative of the people and to the classical preference for the "mixed constitution." These, and other factors, lead him to a doctrine of constitutional monarchy. But they do not, and could not, lead him to a doctrine of popular sovereignty, which would make nonsense of the concept of hierarchical order. In our own time not even so liberal a Thomist as Jacques Maritain, whose devotion to democracy is a matter of public record, can reconcile himself to the notion of popular sovereignty; he is forced to reject it as a matter of principle.[21] The democratic concept of community as an association of politically *and morally* self-determining beings is unacceptable to this position. Whatever concessions to personal freedom may be made in the political realm, none can be made in the moral realm. In matters of faith and morals the authority of the head of the religious community is absolute. Here the claim of men and women to choose for themselves

[20] *On Kingship*, II, I; Eng. tr. by I. T. Eschmann (Toronto: Pontifical Institute of Medieval Studies, 1949), p. 54.

[21] And herewith "the parliamentary system of the British type." *Scholasticism and Politics* (New York: Macmillan, 1940), p. 114. He leaves his readers in grave doubt of the propriety of stretching the word "democracy" to cover the system he proposes whose aim is "to render the State . . . independent of . . . political parties"(*ibid.*).

I have just read, as this goes to press, Maritain's new book, *Man and the State* (Chicago: University of Chicago Press, 1951). I find here an explicit acceptance of the principle of political self-government, which was missing in his earlier work. I welcome this new development, and regret that it is now too late to discuss it in this paper.

and by themselves the truth and values of their individual and collective life is denied as immoral. The infallible answers to all questions of spiritual truth and value are in the keeping of the church. In such decisions the head of the church has the *plenitudo potestatis*, the right to judge all men and himself be judged by no man.

III. CONCLUSIONS

The upshot of this survey of the main forms of our western religious tradition which are relevant to the democratic ordering of life is both negative and positive, and the implied negation is fully as important as the implied affirmation. When liberal Christians discuss the religious foundations of democracy they assume all too easily and all too commonly that the main, or even sole, opponent of their contention is the so-called secularist. This assumption is false to the facts. There are many forms of historical religion, including historical Christianity, which are essentially either indifferent to the democratic faith or subversive of it. Their opportunistic accommodation to democracy at certain times and places may be gratefully accepted. But neither can it be mistaken for a supposed foundation for democracy on the strength of isolated dogmas, like the belief in the infinite dignity of the human soul. One may believe in the infinite dignity of man's soul, with St. Paul, St. Augustine, St. Thomas, and Luther, yet sanctify the subjection of slave to master, of woman to man, of the people to autocratic rulers. One cannot excuse these sanctifications of undemocratic and antidemocratic forms of human relations as absent-minded lapses, one cannot explain them away as insincerities or inconsistencies. One must face the tragic fact that Christians of the highest stature, intellectual and moral, formidably clear-headed and intensely earnest, may still hold a faith which is alien or even hostile to the democratic faith. This fact has grave implications for the widespread assumption that religious instruction, in school or university, will reliably nourish the spiritual roots of the democratic way of life. Before any such policy can be honestly recommended as an asset to the democratic state, we should at least have to examine what kind of instruction would be offered and in what. The mere fact that the instructors would be devout exponents of the faith is no answer to this question. For it is possible, and in some cases probable, that what will be taught, confidently and sincerely, as *the* Christian faith, will be an amalgam of religion with magic, and that even the religious ingredient will be mainly of the dualist or authoritarian variety.

When one looks at the historical record and considers how often religion in general, and organized Christianity in particular, has been either ambiguous in its support of democracy or unambiguously on the side of undemocratic institutions, one is tempted to write off any connection between democracy and religion as a snare and ask democracy to stand henceforth on its own secular feet. Over the past three centuries an increasing number of humane and intelligent persons have been coming to this conclusion. But for all its high sponsorship this alternative is an oversimplification, plausible enough in the era of *laissez-faire* which regarded democracy as a public convenience, but powerless to meet the desperate need of our own time, when democracy must live, if it is to live, not as a utility, but as a faith. One may prize a utility, but one cannot accord it reverence, one cannot dedicate oneself to it and risk in its defense the totality of one's utilities and life itself thrown into the bargain. It would be nonsense to say, "Give me this utility, or give me death." But it is not nonsense to say, "Give me liberty, or give me death." It is a tragedy of our time that men should be asked to act upon a faith they lack. The Spanish peasant, Pillar, in Hemingway's *For Whom the Bell Tolls*, says to Robert Jordan, the American intellectual who is fighting for the Republic: "I believe in the Republic as religious people believe in the holy mysteries. Do you believe in it too?" "'Yes,' he replied, *hoping it was true."* It was in just this frame of mind that many men fought and died for democracy in the last war, and more of their kind live today. Their predicament is a far more serious menace to democracy than the lusty sneers of an H. L. Mencken or the bald disclaimer of a popular columnist of the day, "I am not interested in democracy. Where it isn't, I don't miss it." It is the Jordans, not the Menckens, who are in the vast majority today, in and out of our universities. They know that they are interested in democracy, and they know that they would miss it if it weren't, but they don't know whether they have, or can have, faith in it.

It is the essence of faith that it is demanding and exclusive. If it demands anything, it demands everything. We may believe a thousand things, but we can have only one faith; for we have only one life, and our faith, if it deserves the name, demands all of it. That is why faith in democracy has to be a religious faith in the sense in which religion has been here defined. If there is to be faith in democracy it has to be of a piece with our commitment to the Highest we know. The trouble with modern man is that he lacks faith not only in democracy but equally in everything else. He has no faith, and what he enters as his faith in public records is not faith, but only a profession of faith. This is a spiritual sickness and only religion can heal it. And the religion which must heal it, is the ancient faith of the prophets and of Jesus of Nazareth translated into the idiom of our own life and thought and purged of all magical accretions, so that we can embrace it with our whole mind, as well as our whole life, heart, and soul. It is a faith in God who *is* love, and who demands of us that all our ways, political, economic, domestic, cultural, and educational be ordered by the law of love, with brotherly solicitude for the welfare and freedom of all men, that of our fellows as much as our own. This faith can provide the religious foundations for democracy; and I know of no other that can.

Can such a faith be taught in the university? If it is a true faith, it can submit to the search for truth, which it is the university's function to pursue. It can invite the most merciless factual and logical examination of its claims. It can plead no dogmatic exemption from critical inquiry. It cannot, and need not, ask to be shielded either from honest doubt or from any rival faith, whether it be that of communism, or fascism, or anything else. To ask for any such privileged protection would be not only a confession of fear, alien to the spirit of faith, but would be a betrayal of its own professed faith. If one believes in freedom and equality for all human relations, one must affirm them in the university community. Here, as everywhere else, a fraternal community must treat its members as persons, that is to say, as intellectually and morally self-determining beings. It will not prejudge the result of free inquiry into the truth, and will not seek to influence the result by political intimidation or academic bribes. Men of all faiths and of no faith must be welcome in the community of seekers after truth. To bar anyone because he has the wrong faith, or no faith, is to countenance a means which destroys the end and mocks the spirit of a fraternal faith.

There are positive implications here for the university curriculum, on one hand, for the structure of its community life, on the other. The religious traditions of humanity are, on any theory, an integral part of its culture. To exclude their study from the university is indefensible on any grounds, intellectual or moral. But we can and should insist on both intellectual and moral grounds that in the classroom religion should be studied, not preached. Sectarian indoctrination can have no place in a course of study worthy of the name, for it subverts the unfettered examination of fact and analysis of truth which is the first concern of a university. Conversely, it would be sheer confusion to expect that intellectual examination and analysis is of itself sufficient to create faith. Faith is more than belief; it is dedication. The task of the teacher is not that of the preacher. The teacher can discharge his professional task whatever may be his faith, and even if he has no faith, if he can pursue the search for truth and lead others to pursue it. His faith, if he has one, he will declare in his personal capacity as a religious man. And he will succeed in communicating it to others in so far as it is something by which he lives and which lives in him. And what is true of the university teacher is equally true of the university as a whole. Not the content of its instruction but the quality of its community life is in the end the decisive witness to its faith. If it betrays equality of opportunity and freedom of inquiry in its policy of admissions, in the relations of students to faculty, of students to administration, of faculty to administration, and of administration to trustees, it declares its faith or lack of it more forcefully than by any number of courses in religion and ethics which it may have, or add, to its curriculum. The highest service it can possibly render to the Christian faith of democracy is to live by that faith.

13

Psychotherapy, Religion, and the Achievement of Selfhood

Rollo May

I. A Perspective on Emotional Illness and Health

WHAT shall be our attitude toward the pervasiveness and growing incidence of emotional disruption and mental illness in our society? What stand shall we take with regard to the fact that almost every sensitive person, on or off the campus, even though he may never experience mental illness diagnosed as such, has profound difficulty in arriving at sufficient emotional integration that he can love and accept love maturely, and create to a degree that has some relation to his potentialities? What meaning do we find in the fact that tension and apprehension have become the daily fare for many people in our "age of anxiety," and that "scientific" and "religious" books which promise reassurance and easy cure of emotional problems leap to the top of the best-seller list and are frantically grasped by people in the manner of starving persons seizing food? This frantic grasping occurs despite the fact that the proffered "food" often consists of superficial religious sentimentality which bears no relation to the profound understanding of man in the historical religions, and the "science" may consist of fantastic theories whose only relation to conscientious scientific work is the purloining of the name in order to capitalize on its authority.

There are several fallacious attitudes toward these phenomena which we cite at the outset in order to avoid. The first is the *sentimental* attitude: it consists of ostensibly admitting the degree of emotional illness among people in our society, but the cures it offers from the pulpit or in the counseling room are routine platitudes: "If one has confidence in God, one is freed from anxiety"; "Faith is the answer"; or "No person who has a good religion suffers a nervous breakdown." Such counsel varies from statements which are borrowed from some of the profound truths about the effective relation of religion to health (like the first), to statements which are pharisaic and untrue (like the last). What is significant, however, is that such counsel is offered without any real understanding of the conflicts causing the given person's emotional suffering, and hence the counsels in that immediate situation are cant and hypocrisy. People who are suffering psychologically often have a keener than usual insight into hypocrisy and ungenuineness, and consequently they often turn from religion and lose a source of profound help.[1]

Another fallacious attitude toward the prevalence of emotional ills in our society is that of *obscurantism*. This is the ostrich policy, the attitude of people who "pooh-pooh" these ailments as though they were something one automatically outgrows like adolescence, or in any case were not particularly im-

---

[1] It is no denial of the profound significance of religious attitudes for mental health to point out that it is a delusion to suggest that if a person's religion had been effective, he would not have had his problems. Such a statement is based on a misunderstanding both of religion and the nature of emotional problems. If religion in the form in which it existed in our culture in the nineteenth and early twentieth centuries had been able to solve or obviate these emotional problems, obviously they would not be so prevalent now. But it is not realistic to single out religion from the other aspects of a culture, and make that demand of it. As a psychoanalyst who has worked a good deal with theological students and religious persons, I can say that there is no reason whatever to think that the incidence of emotional problems is any less among religious people than in the rest of the population. And this statement (for reasons which will be clearer later in this chapter) is not at all to be taken as a basis for a simple criticism of their religion.

portant. Reading of the facts that more than half the beds in hospitals in the United States are now filled by mental patients, that at least one person out of twenty in our society will spend some of his life in a mental hospital, and that the states cannot keep pace with the increasing incidence, persons with this attitude console themselves by remarking, "The rising incidence is simply due to the increased facility of psychiatry in diagnosis." This consolation is only partially true in fact, but, more important, its psychological impact is, in the minds of the persons we are now discussing, to obscure and suppress the full implications of the problem of mental illness in our society. During the early stages of World War II, the *Christian Century,* commenting in an editorial (unfortunately later summarized in *Time*) on the fact that the largest incidence of rejectees for the army was for psychoneurotic reasons, suggested that these young men should be called "pampered children" rather than psychoneurotics. This ostrich attitude falls in the same category as the tendency a century ago to assume that persons who had tuberculosis were simply "lazy," since to the external and lay observer it was not apparent that they had a disease.

The attitude of obscurantism we have just mentioned does not occur simply out of ignorance. Often uneducated and simple human beings have an intuitive understanding of the reality of the emotional ills of others, like the broken heart, anxiety, grief, or loneliness. Rather, the attitude we are discussing gets its chief dynamic from the fact that it is a defense against the threat to deeply established emotional patterns in certain forms of American religious life. The pietistic, sectarian strains in American Protestantism have been historically (and still are) characterized by rationalistic, moralistic voluntarism, chiefly taking the form of the belief that a man should be able to think out consciously the solution to his problem and then by will power put that solution into action. The possibility that one's problems may be due to emotional conflicts which are unconscious, and over which therefore one does not have immediate control via "will power," is a profoundly threatening idea to such voluntaristic patterns; it literally shakes the foundations of the emotional defenses of many persons in the pietistic traditions.

This obscurantist attitude is a syndrome which generally involves also a contempt for other people and a need to dominate them—which is clear in the *Christian Century's* use of the term "pampered children." As though these psychoneurotics should simply be spanked and made to take their responsibility! We here emphasize the obscurantist attitude, together with its accompanying attitudes of contempt and domination, because it constitutes probably the major stumbling block in Protestant religion to the creative understanding of, and dealing with, emotional problems in our society.

A third fallacious attitude—related to the above moralism—is the assumption that emotional problems occur chiefly among the *"unfit,"* the *"inferior."* Persons with this attitude often hold that emotional illness is synonymous with "lack of adjustment," that it is the "unadjusted" student, for example, who is the problem, and that the goal of counseling and psychotherapy is to help persons to become better "adjusted." It is important here to emphasize that this whole adjustment category has a false basis. It generally implies socially that the person should "fit" his environment like a mechanical cog in the automatic running of society. And it generally implies individually that a person should develop such control over himself that he can treat himself as though he were a machine, on which he pulls a lever here or turns a dial there. The concept of adjustment as the goal, as used among religious thinkers in our society, is a bastard offspring, born of the union of the mechanical ideals of our culture with moralistic Protestantism, baptized at the altar of the lowest common denominator and dedicated to the achievement of mediocrity.

This concept of adjustment as the goal of personality development is erroneous on both clinical and theoretical grounds.[2] Anyone in clinical practice knows that often the person most gifted in endowments is the one who has the highest potential of emotional conflict, and often therefore is the one who may most need psychotherapy. It is not at all unusual on a college campus, for example, that the student who seems to be getting along the most successfully—the one who is talented, achieves office and honors and is popular—is the one who has serious problems underneath. In college counseling some years ago in which I was able to deal with fairly wide cross-sections of the student bodies on two different campuses, I found that, to be sure, the students who were failing in academic work and in social life came for help; but as prominent in needing help (though they were perhaps able to postpone specific therapy because their defenses were more effective) were the eminently successful students, whom the superficial observer would have voted supremely "well adjusted."[3]

The theoretical fallacies underlying this "adjustment" criterion are evident when we recognize that emotional difficulties, and neuroses, do not come from lack of "will power" or inferior potentiality. Rather, they have their source in *the presence in the individual of potentialities together with the presence in the environment (past or present) of authoritative suppressive forces which make the realization of these potentialities impossible.* In one sense a person is emotionally ill because he cannot be a slave —either a slave to rigid external mores or a slave to his own intro-

[2] I deal with the term here as it is used in nontechnical discussions. It has been used in psychology in the past two decades with a somewhat more tenable, but still inadequate, meaning, i.e., in the "psychology of adjustment." For excellent discussions in psychology and learning theory of the need to substitute the term "integrative" for "adjustive," see the papers of O. Hobart Mowrer, in *Learning Theory and Personality Dynamics* (New York: Ronald Press, 1950).

[3] This problem was brought home forcibly to me also by the fact that I have known, unprofessionally, two such very successful students—one a roommate in college—who later committed suicide.

jected mechanical requirements. Unless there is some unused potentiality there is no emotional conflict; one then could easily "fit" a fascist social system, be content in a cramping business situation and in the monotonous routine of suburbia, or follow unquestioningly parental laws and precepts without going through the struggle to find one's own. There is no emotional problem except when the human being needs to be free, or in other words when he needs to be a person and not a machine. Hermann Hesse is profoundly correct in this respect when he writes that the neurosis of our generation is "a sickness which attacks . . . precisely those who are strongest in spirit and richest in gifts."[4] Of course I do not mean to imply that persons who are gifted will always be "unadjusted" or that to be "unadjusted" is necessarily a sign of potentiality; I mean rather to say that the adjustment category is irrelevant to the profound meaning of human difficulties and of psychotherapy. The category comes into psychotherapy only in the incidental respect that a person should become free from the unconscious compulsions (generally hangovers from adolescence) to defy and rebel against his group. But the sound goals of becoming able to love one's fellows and live productively in community must be based on more profound criteria than adjustment.

It is clear that the attitudes of sentimentality (the "soft" approach with the easy solution) and obscurantism (the "hard-boiled" approach with the repressive solution), though they seem to be opposites, nevertheless have in common one central point: they do not take the problem of emotional illness in our society seriously. We do not need to labor to readers of this chapter the unsatisfactory quality of the sentimental attitude—whether that attitude takes a religious form or the form it assumes among devotees of psychoanalysis, namely, making a "fad" of the new psychological theories. But it cannot be em-

[4] Herman Hesse, *Steppenwolf*, tr. by Basil Creighton (New York: Holt, 1947), p. 28.

phasized too often that the obscurantist approach is self-defeating for the religious thinker. The new understanding of man which arose with Freud—the appearance for the first time in human history of techniques for the objective investigation of the vast realm of unconscious motivations in personality, so that understanding of the depths of character no longer depended simply on each man's intuition but could be communicated—this new understanding can be ignored by the religious thinker with no more impunity than would attend his overlooking the discoveries of Darwin in the nineteenth century and Einstein in the twentieth. Indeed, since the nature of man is so immediate and crucial an issue in every religious concept and practice, there is reason for believing that failure to take seriously the psychological and cultural revolution begun by Freud would be a greater loss to religious thinkers than the ignoring of the Copernican revolution and those in the biological sciences.

The attitude we propose, and which shall guide the discussion in this chapter, is one of trying to understand the nature and causes of emotional ills in our society sufficiently profoundly that we can discover the underlying meaning of these ills. This means asking ourselves not only what emotional problems mean to the individual who suffers them, but also asking what is revealed about our society as a whole that so many persons in it cannot find integration. Such an approach involves facing directly the fact of the widespread psychological breakdown in our day, recognizing the prevalence of anxiety and despair; and it involves being able to see these problems in ourselves as well as in other members of our society. For if we think that we as individuals are apart from the common emotional problems, we simply have not understood the problems.

The attitude we propose is that of endeavoring to go below the external phenomena of psychological and emotional ills to find the presuppositions of value in their causes, and thereby to be able to work toward clarifying the ultimate concerns (to use Tillich's term) involved in the solution of these problems. It is at these points that the discoveries of Freud and subsequent students of depth psychology are no substitute for religion and philosophy—and it has been a sound instinct on the part of religious persons not to subsume religious thinking under psychoanalytic. Whenever Freud or other analysts, psychiatrists, or psychologists have tried to deduce philosophical and religious attitudes solely from their scientific data, the results have generally been naïve and palpably untenable.[5] The techniques of psychoanalysis and other forms of therapy are based on certain presuppositions of value, and they point toward goals which also represent certain values; and to admit this in no way undermines our rigorous scientific attitude at the same time. Indeed, it is a demonstrable fact that the progress of psychoanalysis in the last two decades can be in part measured by the analysts' increasing recognition of the importance of value judgments, and by the admission of the facts that the analyst not only cannot escape dealing with values in his work but that it is illusory and self-defeating for him to try to do so.[6] Successful psychotherapy consists of the use of new and complex techniques by which an individual, working with a professional helper, is aided to overcome the unconscious patterns which have bolstered his false set of values, and to achieve the freedom and strength to discover and thereafter live on the basis of a more indigenous and sound set of values. These values, both as presuppositions and as goals, make religion and philosophy involved implicitly in psychotherapy at every turn.

II. Emotional Problems and the Loss of Selfhood

We shall now endeavor to summarize the basic sources of emotional problems in our day, the central causes of blockages which prevent contemporary people from attaining self-fulfill-

---

[5] See Freud's essays in this field, for example *The Future of an Illusion* and *Civilization and Its Discontents*.

[6] The writings of contemporary psychoanalysts demonstrating this point are legion: see the works of Fromm, Horney, the more progressive Freudians like Alexander and French, Kubie; psychologists like Mowrer, etc.

ment and integrity. The difficulty in arriving at such generalizations is obvious, and it should be clear that no specific case ever fits a generalization perfectly. But our endeavor to discover below the many diverse emotional problems of our day some essential common pattern should yield us the concrete, experiential data on the basis of which to inquire into the religious and philosophical meaning of these problems. The data I am using as a basis for this endeavor come partially from my clinical studies, but chiefly from my clinical work as a psychologist and as a psychoanalyst with many different kinds of people, perhaps half of them being persons from specifically religious backgrounds and with specifically religious interests, and also about half of them (only partially overlapping with the former group) being undergraduate and graduate students.[7]

In the time of Freud's early work before World War I, the most common occasions (and to an extent causes) of emotional problems were what Freud accurately described: namely, the conflict between Victorian morality and emotional promptings, the need of the person to repress emotions, especially of a sexual nature, and the consequent disunion of the personality, with hysterical symptoms often appearing as a result. Later, in the 1920's, Otto Rank described the prevalent neurotic type in our culture as being characterized by "feelings of inferiority and inadequacy, fear of responsibility and guilt feeling, in addition to a hyper-selfconsciousness."[8] By the middle 1930's when Horney offered her description in *The Neurotic Personality of Our Time*,[9] it was beginning to be recognized among many

[7] I regret at this point, as at other points in this chapter, that it is not possible for reasons of spatial limitation to present all the data on the basis of which I make certain statements. Much of the supporting data can be found, however, in my book, *The Meaning of Anxiety* (New York, 1950).

[8] Pearce Bailey, *Theory and Therapy; An Introduction to the Psychology of Dr. Otto Rank* (Paris, 1935).

[9] Karen Horney, *The Neurotic Personality of Our Time* (New York, 1937). We do not at all mean to imply that Rank and Horney are the only psychoanalysts who had made summaries of the basic sources of emotional problems; almost all leading writers in the field have done so, and the reader can investigate other summaries as he sees fit.

psychoanalysts that the problems that had appeared as conflicts between "reason" and "emotion" in nineteenth-century terms, were really contradictions between incompatible goals held on unconscious levels within the personality. The cultural changes, as well as the development of psychoanalytic and depth-psychological techniques, have resulted in the facts that neuroses of the original hysterical type have almost disappeared in the clinic. Most neuroses and allied emotional problems of the present day are the less dramatic but often more serious and more difficult to cure "character neuroses." This is a technical term meaning that the neurosis arises from basic patterns of behavior, including goals and defenses, which the individual has been forced to develop as an infant in order to survive psychologically in his interpersonal milieu.

In the present day the problems or symptoms which bring persons for professional psychotherapeutic help are of course varied: they cannot make marital or vocational decisions, for example, and are immobilized; or are victims of irrational compulsions to make unsatisfactory decisions over and over again.[10] Or the persons cannot love or accept love maturely but get into symbiotic and sadomasochistic love affairs; and as one expression of these conflicts they may exhibit sexual inversion symptoms. Or the individuals may complain of tensions and pervasive suffering which have no positive function but simply constrict and impoverish personality; or they may be seized by recurring attacks of anxiety or rage or experience continuous undercurrents of resentment and hostility which they know have no rational or conscious cause. To the extent that these latter emotions are repressed into unconsciousness, they tend to take the form of overt symptoms, psychosomatic and otherwise. One could, on the basis of these phenomenological descriptions,

---

[10] For example, divorce and remarriage and new divorce in our society often represent a repetitive pattern of jumping out of the frying pan into the fire, a "vicious circle" which the individual typically cannot escape from short of a clarification of unconscious patterns in psychotherapy.

conclude that these problems result from the different underlying emotional conflicts which Freud and others described.

But when we penetrate below these phenomena, we discover
a common element in practically all of these problems in our
day, namely, the individual is alienated from himself. We find
that behind his anxiety, or his clinging dependence or sadomasochistic sexual patterns, or what not, his more basic trouble
is that he *cannot experience himself as a self in his own right*.
That is to say, he cannot affirm himself as a being who has
powers and desires, who can decide and take responsibility and
move toward self-chosen goals. Rather, his desires are not his
own but are reflections of his bourgeois culture; his decisions
are reflections of parental precepts carried over as introjected
pressure and never understood or affirmed by himself. It is not
surprising, then, that so often the overt symptom he chooses
(for unconscious reasons) involves—as in most cases of sexual
inversion or vocational failure—a bitter rebellion against society and its expectations. The basic problem of these persons
is that their reason for living is to please someone else, generally
as an infant seeks to win approval—and permission for psychological survival—by pleasing all-powerful parents.

We are submitting, therefore, that the essence of human
emotional problems is that the human being has never become
a self, or, more accurately, has never learned to experience himself as a self. In normal development the birth of the self should
be occurring by the age of two or three, when the infant begins
to experience himself as an independent entity, no longer completely dependent on his parents but a being in his own right
who must relate in one form or another to his parents and other
significant persons in his environment. The emotional problems
we are discussing go back in various ways to the fact that this
birth of selfhood was more or less blocked, generally by exploitative, dominating or overanxious attitudes and behavior

on the part of parents or other important persons in the infant's world.

In philosophical terms, as Tillich phrases it, the person's problems are due to the fact that he has never been able to affirm his own being over against the nonbeing of the inorganic world and the other beings of the social world. Or, in Kierkegaard's words, he has never grown from the stage of innocence (before the "fall" in the biblical sense) to the stage of self-awareness, with its attendant responsibility and independence. He has never, as Kierkegaard continues, really "chosen himself." And when one has not moved through the "fall" in the mythological sense—that is, has not eaten of the tree of life and learned the difference between right and wrong, which of course implies being able to accept the anxiety and guilt and responsibility which such knowledge entails—one never moves on into becoming a person. Speaking of the lack in modern man of the "sense of the ontological—the sense of being," Gabriel Marcel writes, "Indeed I wonder if a psychoanalytic method, deeper and more discerning than any that has been evolved until now, would not reveal the morbid effects of the repression of this sense and of the ignoring of this need."[11] Such psychoanalytic methods have been evolving, perhaps without Marcel's being aware of the fact; some of the results can be seen in Fromm's penetrating discussions of the psychological meaning of selfhood.[12] Fromm holds, for example, that mental illness may be described as the lack of the "sense of I-ness." One can see the results of this lack of the capacity to affirm one's own self most clearly in its extreme form in schizophrenics, for whom the early environment was so disastrously exploitative or unloving that they must either isolate themselves entirely to find some semblance of self experience, or in extreme forms must assume

[11] Gabriel Marcel, *The Philosophy of Existence* (New York: The Philosophical Library, 1949), p. 1.

[12] Erich Fromm, *Man for Himself, An Inquiry into the Psychology of Ethics* (New York: Rinehart, 1947).

some other form of identity, for example in calling themselves by some other name.

This lack of the capacity to experience one's self as a being in one's own right is the basic source of emotional problems shown on very many—in my experience, the large majority— of Rorschach tests of contemporary persons who come for psychoanalytic help. The Rorschach likewise typically shows in such cases that the individual feels empty, weak, powerless, and without strength in his own right.

The person himself, of course, is rarely able to see that his problem is that he has not become a self. If the therapist should say, "Your problem is that you are not free; nothing you feel is really your own desire or indigenous experience; you have no real self-esteem; your potentialities, being unused, turn inward and fester in resentment; what you do experience is limited to feelings of emptiness and meaninglessness on one hand or feelings of being a slave on the other; and your symptoms arise from the fact that, unconsciously, you know all this, hate it, and do your best through the symptoms to rebel against it,"—if a therapist, in our experiment, should say this, the person would generally not at all comprehend what it means.[13] He perhaps would politely indicate that he thinks the therapist is talking in unscientific platitudes. The unconscious presupposition that he is not a self but rather an extension of parents, a faithful servant who gives the professor what he wants, gets A's, makes college teams, receives honors, and in other ways does things which redound to his parents' credit and make him a useful investment—his presupposition about himself being such, he of course has no vantage point from which to experience what a self might be. The fact that a person can have no inner comprehension in his own deepest feelings of what being a self means is one of the clearest indications that he has never been a self in his own right.

---

[13] I do not mean that a therapist would actually say all this in one speech to someone coming for help (heaven forbid!); this is a generalized statement.

In therapy we must, of course, start with the person where he is. What he does experience is that he wants someone—now the therapist—to tell him what to do, to be his "substitute" self; and he often feels considerable anxiety (and a feeling of being gypped) if the therapist gently but firmly refuses to do this. What he does experience is generally profound feelings of emptiness and weakness; often also self-contempt; guilt feeling when he tends to go against others' expectations, but likewise guilt feeling when he does not live up to his own insights; dependence on others, but a need to fight this dependence; and open or covert methods of rebelling against and defying the forces which keep him from being himself. If a human being could really stay in the stage of innocence, could remain merely dependent, life— and psychotherapy—would be a different matter. We discover, however, that a person can remain in an undeveloped state psychologically with no more impunity and no less morbidity than as if he were to remain in the cradle physically, and never learn to use his legs. We find that underneath the person's symptoms of weakness, guilt, and anxiety, he is still fighting his parents; his previous defeats, his loss of freedom, and his enslavement still smolder; the compromises which he has been forced to adopt succeed at the price of impoverishment and constriction; he is unfulfilled as a self, and the unused capacities turn inward and cause morbidity.

Often the person has to develop slowly through months of psychoanalytic work until some birth begins to occur, until some real capacity for indigenous experience, some inner feelings of strength, some experience of "I-ness," begin to appear. Then he can begin to experience, often with profound joy, what it means to be a person; he can begin to affirm himself (if I may put it in philosophical terms which obviously never come up as such in the consulting room) against the whole world of nonbeing or other selves, which is probably the most profoundly gratifying experience to which the human being is heir. It is certainly true that a lack of community, a lack of the capacity to love or be loved, is a central aspect of emotional problems in our day. But the experience of being a self must be gone through before love becomes possible or meaningful; for unless one is a person in his own right, unless one loves as something more than a mirror of the other person, love is dependent symbiosis and is bound to be frustrating and ultimately self-defeating.[14]

One can find a description of this disease of modern man—the failure to become a self—expertly given in the novels of Kafka, such as *The Trial*, and in the poetry of W. H. Auden as well as in almost every other area of modern literature. One sees its sociopolitical end results in fascism, which may be defined psychologically as the mass symptom of groups of people—in this case the middle and lower middle classes in western culture—developed in the desperate endeavor to find a substitute source of strength and meaning to save them from the anxiety and torture of continual feelings of inner emptiness. It is by no means an accident, speaking psychologically, that people who have lost the center of values (economic, psychological, and spiritual) on which their own feeling of selfhood was based, should embrace an authoritarian, sadomasochistic system like fascism, or, in some similar respects, like communism.[15]

The alienation of the individual from himself is intimately related to certain historical developments which have come to a head in the form of the profound cultural upheavals and changes which mark the middle decades of the twentieth century. Some of these historical factors are: the preoccupation in modern times with the mechanical and mathematical methods of interpreting human experience; the dehumanization of man which,

[14] Ideally speaking, of course, the self is born in the family in relationships of love; the capacities to love and be loved, and to be a self, go together. We emphasize the latter because that is generally where the emphasis must be placed in the later overcoming of emotional problems.

[15] For an excellent discussion of this point, see the chapters having to do with authoritarianism and fascism in Erich Fromm's *Escape from Freedom* (New York: Rinehart, 1941).

as Marx pointed out, characterizes the monopoly capitalism stage of modern industrialism; the diminution of efficacy in the nineteenth and twentieth centuries of the humanistic and Christian ethical and religious traditions; and the general tendencies toward compartmentalization of life in the nineteenth century.[16]

It should be obvious, from a theoretical point of view, that the capacity of an individual to affirm his own being in self-awareness is the unique characteristic which differentiates man from animals and the rest of nature. It is this capacity which enables man to see himself both as subject and object, to distinguish the subjective and objective in the world about him, to reason, and to use language and symbols as forms of interpersonal communication. Furthermore, it is this capacity which makes man a historical creature, in that he possesses self-awareness of his history as animals and machines do not.

Now, we should like to raise the question of the relation between this capacity for affirming one's own being and the historical and psychological meaning of the term "soul." As I understand it, the concept of man's soul has meant through history that center of the human being's self-awareness in which inhered his capacity for self-direction, ultimate choices, and responsibility; the center in which his decisions transcended time and space in that they dealt with his ultimate concerns; that center of self-awareness which distinguished the human beings from animals and the rest of nature. To the extent that the term "soul" has been used in the sense of a reified object—such as in the phrase "man *has* a soul"—it is not surprising that the whole concept was avoided by academic psychology. When "soul" was

[16] I have endeavored to summarize these historical developments in some detail in *The Meaning of Anxiety*, and the reader who wishes to pursue the interrelation of these points with psychological developments may find that discussion helpful. For an excellent summary of the cultural situation bearing on these points, see Paul Tillich's chapter in *The Christian Answer*, entitled "The World Situation." For a likewise excellent discussion of these problems from the more exclusively philosophical angle, see Ernst Cassirer, *An Essay on Man* (New Haven: Yale University Press, 1944).

used in the Cartesian sense of an entity residing in the pineal gland, and serving as a convenient escape from facing the most difficult problems of the relation of mind and body by the simple expedient of saying they were connected in this soul in the pineal gland, it is understandable that science, and specifically psychology, should have contemptuously disregarded the concept as a source of intellectual laziness and dishonesty. To be sure, scientific psychology, in its marriage to the constrictive forms of mathematical and atomistic research, has handicapped itself in understanding the more basic functioning of the human being, and it has not been a simple journey to arrive in psychology at some workable concept of the human self. But could we not, both as psychological and religious thinkers, assume that there must be some classical, operational truth embodied in the concept of "soul" for it to have persisted so long in history? Perhaps Freud and the European psychoanalysts are not so far from the truth when they use the term "psyche" literally. We wish here to suggest that it might be a very rewarding investigation in the area of the interrelationship of psychology and religion to try to discover how far the classical meaning of the term "soul" is parallel to what is meant in this discussion by man's capacity for self-conscious affirmation of his own being.[17]

III. Issues in the Achieving of Selfhood

Achieving selfhood does not mean arriving at a state of complete unity of personality in which conflict and contradiction are completely obviated. Such an ideal is foreign to the human situation. But it does mean overcoming the artificial blockages, the

[17] See Fromm's discussion of the "Psychoanalyst as Physician of the Soul," in his recently published Terry Lectures *Religion and Psychoanalysis* (New Haven: Yale University Press, 1950). I read Dr. Fromm's book after this chapter was completed, and I can only add that his discussion, though from a nontheistic viewpoint, bears most importantly and fruitfully on the discussion in this chapter. The Terry Lectures given by Paul Tillich, entitled *The Courage To Be* (New Haven: Yale University Press, 1951), should also be of great importance for our discussion.

self-defeating forms of tension, and the sources of suffering which only impoverish one's own personality and issue in envy and bitterness toward one's fellow men. It means achieving a dynamic unity which is manifested chiefly in the expanding use of one's own creative potentialities in productive work and the expanding meaningfulness of one's relations with one's fellow men in love and community. There are and always will be conflicts and contradictions in one's feelings and decisions; the crucial question is whether these conflicts are used creatively. Achieving selfhood means being able to live not on a basis of repression of the unconscious levels of personality, but rather achieving a dynamic uniting of unconscious depths with conscious choices and direction. What we are unconsciously—for example, what we are in our dreams—will then not be foreign to what we are consciously and in our waking moments. It means living from within; at this point the concept and practice of the "inner light," as it has appeared in its varied forms from Platonism through Augustine down to modern Quakerism, is of great importance psychotherapeutically. Achieving selfhood means arriving at the psychological and spiritual integrity which is characterized by the capacity—and practice—of judging one's actions by one's own, inner criteria rather than by the vain and narcissistic standards of public (and parental) acceptance and applause.

We shall now consider several issues involved in the achieving of selfhood, issues which are not meant to cover the topic systematically but which do point up some important aspects of it.

1. *Selfhood in relation to the body.* Creative selfhood means that the body (including the instincts like sex and the bodily aspects of emotion) will be experienced as part of the self. It involves not treating the body as an entity apart from the self— either as an enemy, as in dualism and Puritanism, or as the chief vehicle of freedom, as in the gospels of "release of inhibition"

in early and oversimplified interpretations of Freud and in the present-day theories of Wilhelm Reich.

Since the conflicts underlying contemporary emotional problems are on one side related to the repression of bodily functions in nineteenth-century voluntarism, it is obvious that we need to arrive at a new acceptance of the body based on the attitude and experience of psychophysical unity. This will not be achieved merely by adding up more and more discoveries of the interrelations of psyche and soma as produced by modern psychosomatic investigations. These investigations and discoveries are of great importance, to be sure, as are the advances in other phases of modern medicine. But since medicine and its affiliated disciplines in their modern form are themselves a product of a cultural situation in which there was a dichotomy of mind and body, an increased emphasis on one side or the other or on both sides of the dichotomy will never overcome it. It is no depreciation of medicine itself to point out that one of the problems in our culture is that an irrational authority is granted to, and an unconditional faith placed in, medicine. This is one practical application of the irrational authority placed in all the physical sciences in our culture since the Renaissance. One serious form in which this irrational authority appears is the tendency on the part of many people in our society to assume that emotional problems are medical because they happen to be mediated by the neurological and physiological bodily systems. Emotional problems, rather, are due to disturbed forms of an individual's relatedness to himself and to his world. Such problems by their very nature involve the "whole" person acting and reacting in his environment, not the bodily part of the person; and thus such problems, I believe, have more centrally to do with the social sciences, ethics, and religion than they do with medicine as such.[18]

To overcome the dichotomy of mind and body new presupposi-

[18] It is the treatment of the psychoses and the specifically psychosomatic symptoms that falls in the area of medicine as such.

tions are needed. It is interesting to me to note that the thinkers in the modern period who were able to overcome this dichotomy are often those who—like Spinoza and Kierkegaard—had a religious as well as a philosophical and psychological attitude toward human experience. Spinoza was able to overcome the Cartesian split between mind and body by basing his ontology on a concept of reality which underlay both body and mind, and of which body and mind were two aspects. Professor Tillich holds that the crucial issue with respect to overcoming this dichotomy in the modern period is an ontological issue— namely, having an ontology (a concept of being) which under- cuts the dichotomy and embraces both mind and body. He holds, for example, that the mystic Jacob Boehme was particularly able to overcome this dichotomy by his dynamic, vitalistic ontology.[19] However this important ontological problem may be worked out —and we leave it at this point to Dr. Tillich and the philoso- phers—it is certain that an attitude and way of experiencing life, a dedication to the proposition of "seeing life steadily and seeing it whole," is more crucial for the overcoming of this dichotomy than is the mere piling up of new discoveries in the physical sciences. Kierkegaard rightly held that we need more than a union of psyche and soma; we need an "intermediate determinant," which he termed the "pneumatic." This is vari- ously spoken of by him as "spirit," "the possible," "the self," but however it is defined, it is closely parallel to what we mean in this chapter by the function of self-awareness. In other words, the important point is not the union of psyche and soma, but how the self relates itself both to psyche and soma.

On the existential level the dichotomy between mind and body can be actively overcome by the person through treating one's body as an aspect of one's self. This means *experiencing* one's body—one's physical feelings, such as the pleasure of eat- ing and resting or the exhilaration of the use of toned-up muscles,

---

[19] In personal conversation.

the sexual impulses and the pleasure of their gratification, and so forth—as parts of the self. It is not the attitude of "my *body* feels" (which is what most people mean when they speak of feeling good or bad), but "*I* feel"; it is not "my sexual needs require something," but "*I* desire to relate sexually with so-and-so." The attitude and behavior we are here describing are opposite to those customary in our culture, by which a man drives himself in work for weeks until he breaks down with the flu or something worse, as though his body were an object to be driven like a truck until it runs out of gas. It is, rather, a learning to "listen to the body" in deciding when to work and when to rest—a lesson of great importance in overcoming chronic diseases, like tuberculosis. The emphasis here made places the self in the center of the picture of bodily health; it is "I" who am sick or well. It removes the concept of health from the passive framework which generally characterizes it in our culture ("I *got* sick, and penicillin got me over it") to the active voice: it is "I" who grow sick or achieve health. It is, again, no depreciation of the great value of the new medical drugs to emphasize that we shall make lasting progress in health only to the extent that we go beyond the discovery of means of killing germs and bacilli and external organisms which invade the body, and discover means of helping people so to affirm their own beings that they will not need to be sick.

With regard to sex, the attitude we are proposing holds sex to be a part of the self, specifically one form of relatedness of the self to other persons. Separating sex from the rest of the self, as has been the tendency in past decades in our culture, is no more tenable than it would be to isolate one's larynx and speak of "my vocal cords wanting to talk with my friend." Experiencing the body as part of the self implies that standards of behavior in sex, or other aspects of bodily function, are not matters of physical function as such, but rather are matters of will and attitude. Evil and good, to speak in ethical terms, are not to be found in the body as such, but in how the self relates itself to bodily functions, and how it relates itself to others *via* these functions. As many readers will already have seen, this discussion brings out the psychotherapeutic parallel to the ethical and religious insights which are central in the Hebrew-Christian tradition, and specifically, for example, in Jesus' many statements which carry the implication that evil does not lie in sex itself or other bodily functions. "Out of the heart are the issues of life."

2. *Selfhood in relation to authority, autonomy, and responsibility.* One qualification running through the minds of many readers during our discussion of the basic need for the affirming of one's own being will be roughly as follows: "But man is contingent and finite; his knowledge and capacity to will rightly are limited; and does not affirmation of himself result in egocentricity, selfishness, and pride, and an assertion of his own limited will over the wills of others?"

We are aware that the contemporary emphasis on man's contingency and finiteness has been of great importance in overcoming the superficial view of human nature which characterized the "liberalistic" tradition of two decades ago. On one hand, the new emphases on human contingency spring from a wider concept of the dignity of man and God, in that they treat the problems of human life with greater seriousness. On the other hand, however, the emphases on the weakness of man, the authority of God and the evil of pride, are sometimes used for the purpose of rationalizing neurotic and harmful attitudes. Hence it is of the greatest importance that clear distinctions be made between neurotic forms of authority and pride, and the normal and potentially creative forms of autonomy and self-esteem.

In the first place, the affirmation of the self which we are proposing is not only not synonymous with egocentricity, but is the opposite to it. Clinically it can be very clearly demonstrated that the person who is egocentrically preoccupied with himself is the one who is still fighting the childhood battles of vanity and prestige. He is the one who has never become a person with sufficient confidence in his own adult strength that he does not always need to prove it by flexing his muscles or challenging the next person. It also can be clearly demonstrated clinically that in the great bulk of day-to-day actions, a person's attitudes toward other persons will be parallel to his attitudes toward himself; if he cannot really esteem himself, if he treats himself as though he were a freight car to be pushed and hauled this way and that to fit a rigid schedule, then he will not be able to esteem others and will likewise manipulate them as objects. In this respect Fromm makes an exceedingly important point when he holds that self-love and selfishness are *opposites*.[20] Likewise Kierkegaard saw that unless the individual has a basic self-love, the succeeding problems and steps in relatedness to others have no meaning or foundation. Self-love in this context means self-esteem; it is the psychotherapeutic form of the classical Hebrew-Christian doctrine of the infinite value of the person, and means the affirmation of oneself as created in the image of God as one is adjured to recognize and affirm this in others.

We are aware of the issue of the partiality of one's own insights, of the existential dichotomy between the individual and the group that was recognized at least as far back as Anaximander's piercing statement of it in Greek archaic times, "The part does penance for its separation from the whole." A recognition of the finiteness of man, the contingency of human life and the certainty of death, should go hand in hand with a recognition of the dignity and courage needed in human life, and should make for attitudes of charity and acceptance toward one's neighbors, who share this contingency.

But what is pathetic is to find, as we often do in clinical work, that theological students and other literate religious persons use the emphasis on finiteness as a rationalization for their own

[20] See chapter "Selfishness and Self-Love" in *Man for Himself* (New York: Rinehart, 1947).

emptiness, and as a kind of last attempt to grasp some vestige of personal dignity. Often such persons who, on the basis of their Rorschachs as well as other partially objective data, are as empty of self-strength and capacity to affirm their own beings as though they were psychological and spiritual vacuums, use the contemporary attacks on man's belief in himself as a verbalization of their own repressed contempt for themselves and for their fellow men, and use the emphasis on man's powerlessness and the assertion that one can do nothing without God's help as a rationalization for their own weakness and for the fact that they can do nothing without God's help or teacher's help or parent's help. These rationalizations not only reinforce the neurosis but they make for a very subtle pride in themselves: "At least," such a person can say to himself, "I am the way I ought to be—without pride, without any belief in myself, a contemptible worm in fact."

It is important in distinguishing between the normal and neurotic forms of these religious and psychological attitudes to see that, regardless of the fact that human beings possess much in common as generic Man, they also are different in given human situations and cultures. It is my observation in religious and historical studies from Luther and Calvin to the present day, that the theologians and philosophers who emphasize most the attack on the pride of man and the need of man to question his belief in himself, are individuals who are very strong in their own right.[21] They are persons who do have a confidence in their own viewpoints which give them tendencies to assert their own wills and their beliefs with finality and absoluteness; who are often quite prepared to force their wills upon others (*vide* Luther's affirmation of the suppression of the peasants and the

---

[21] This may be a compensatory strength in many of these cases, serving to cover up the person's unconscious and repressed feelings of weakness. That is a well-known psychological mechanism in the dogmatic and authoritarian individual; but we shall not endeavor to go into this point in this brief discussion.

Calvinistic attitudes toward nonbelievers). For such persons, pride in the sense of arrogance may well be a real problem, and their tendencies to run roughshod over other persons may indeed need to be curbed by any means whatever.[22] What these leaders apparently do not see is, as Gabriel Marcel states, that "pride is in no way incompatible with self-hate."[23] And, we should add, self-hate is very compatible with hatred of others.

One needs to ask whether the group with which one is working—let us say on this or that university or college campus—is predominantly of the above psychological type or not. I have had considerable experience with students of several theological seminaries, and I submit that it certainly is doubtful that the widespread interest among seminary students in self-condemnation (along with certain pietistic and liturgical compensations) is a creative, courageous realization of the finitude and contingency of man, arising out of a constructive humanity as one realizes one's own relation to the ground of being, and issuing in renewed charity and forgiveness toward one's neighbor. Rather, these attitudes are very frequently rationalizations for the powerless state in which most such individuals, in the middle twentieth century, find themselves, and therefore are a product of defeatism, not courage. We do not wish to imply that there is not plenty of ground for feeling powerless with regard to the world situation in our day; but is it not obvious that the "world situ-

[22] In contemporary society we get this type of person chiefly in the business and industrial world (or, sometimes, in an executive or academic administrator who seeks to deal with others as though he were a captain of industry running a factory). For industrialism and capitalism have had powerful and central formative influences on modern social concepts of the self. Ideally, it should be, therefore, that the churches whose congregations are composed of the economically and culturally "successful" people should rightly preach against pride and arrogant belief in one's own power. Unfortunately, however, it is just in such churches that one often finds just the opposite—sermons consisting of psychological pabulum and optimistic religious reassurances of perpetual social and financial success if one continues in the same pride and does not fail to vote the conservative ticket.

[23] *Op. cit.*, p. 20.

ation" is often used as a way of shifting one's own problems to the outside, a way of escaping fighting through one's own issues of achieving selfhood?

In distinguishing between normal and neurotic attitudes toward authority, it is helpful to phrase the problem in the positive form, namely, as the problem of *responsibility*. Neurotic dependence on authority, together with neurotic depreciation of one's own powers, is generally connected with endeavors to avoid taking responsibility for one's own life. It is typically the expression of needs to stay on a childlike level of dependence on external power—needs which may be quite unconscious, and the product of early childhood situations in which the child was actually powerless. In clinical psychoanalytic work it is easy enough to distinguish between a genuine humility and respect for authority, whether it be named in the form of "truth" or "God" or however, and the spurious subservience to outside power for the purpose of avoiding having to take responsibility for oneself. For in the latter kind, the person tries to give himself over to the therapist just as he does toward God (and originally did toward his parents), and tries to demand the same unconditional care from the therapist. In fact, such persons not infrequently have dreams in which they identify God, parents, and analyst. And it is easy enough to demonstrate that the analyst is not God.

In working through this difficult problem of authority and responsibility which is crucial for the interrelation of psychotherapy and religion, it is necessary for one to have a sufficiently profound belief in the value of the other person—a sufficiently profound belief in his capacities as created in the image of God— to believe in his freedom, and to operate on the realization that in the last analysis the other person's destiny can only be worked out, decided, and affirmed by himself. The final act of immorality, from this viewpoint, is that in which one takes from another person his basic freedom to find and affirm himself. The present writer has great admiration for T. S. Eliot as poet and dramatist, and for the excellence of the poetry and drama in his latest play, *The Cocktail Party*. But in this play Eliot has his symbol of authority, namely, the psychiatrist, manipulate the three persons involved, all the way from having accomplices entice them into his office to making final decisions for them about their destiny. From the view of human nature we are here discussing, Eliot's play is therefore definitely immoral.

The achievement of selfhood involves the humility of the person who realizes that he did not create the world, that he affirms himself, as Kierkegaard put it, on the ground of meaning which is God. It is an attitude of respect and reverence for the "given," the created; but it does not permit this to serve as release from one's own responsibility to choose oneself. That one has complete and ultimate responsibility for oneself, but that one still lives and moves on the basis of the ground of meaning which is given—this indeed sounds paradoxical; and it is a paradox which can only be solved in the active, affirmative day-to-day living of the responsible human being.

3. *Selfhood in relation to decisiveness.* It was the great contribution of Freud and his colleagues to show the far-reaching effectiveness of unconscious dynamics in individual motivation, and to demonstrate the actual ineffectiveness of the concept of an isolated "will power" used against the rest of the personality. But many psychoanalytic emphases have tended to throw out the baby with the bath water in underemphasizing the deciding functions of the self. When Groddeck says "We are lived by our unconscious," and when Jung speaks of "the autonomy of the unconscious," the emphasis is, to be sure, an important one for corrective purposes; but it is unhealthy in its omission of the point that, no matter how far-reaching the influences of unconscious factors and no matter how deterministic past historical factors, it is still the self which must decide as best it can in the immediate situation. It is a false view of psychotherapy that implies a giving over of oneself to impulse; therapy should result in a capacity to will, to choose, on the basis of expanded self-aware-

ness, and is certainly aimed toward an increase of effective self-direction. The distinction between neurotic forms of "will power" and decisiveness of selfhood is that the latter does not consist of willing *against* unconscious levels in the personality. It is a willing based on awareness so far as possible of the deeper levels in oneself. It implies willing that works *with* the innumerable creative tendencies, insights, intuitions, and so forth, which exist on various levels of one's consciousness or unconsciousness. This kind of decisiveness does not thwart dynamic creative power, as for example in the arts, but is a way of marshaling this power.

We do not mean to imply that this kind of decisiveness is easy or does not involve tension and at times conflict. In most ways it is infinitely more difficult than striving to follow external rules. To be sensitive to one's insights and intuitions as an inner guidance for decisions takes constant vigilance; and at times decisiveness, especially at periods of marked growing, requires struggling through great conflict. In this respect, those who imply, as does W. H. Auden in *The Double Man*, that psychotherapy is designed to reduce suffering, are inaccurate; it is designed to overcome self-defeating suffering and conflicts, but it makes unavoidable existential conflicts, and the conflict involved in attaining the courage to create, even clearer. Any psychoanalyst, or anyone who has participated in analysis thoroughly, knows that the biblical stories of man wrestling with the devil (or, in the case of Jacob, with the angel of God) are experiences not at all foreign to the human situation. And if a person turns a deaf ear to his deepest insights, the inner promptings he receives today, or funks his decisions on them, he does not receive clear insights on the morrow. We must will and decide before we can see new truth. In this sense, though the achieving of selfhood means affirming our being at every moment in the immediate situation, it is at the same time an "eternal becoming." A lifetime is not too long to meet this challenge of achieving selfhood, of creating our self in our day-to-day decisions.

14

The National Council on Religion
in Higher Education[1]

Patrick Murphy Malin

HOWEVER loosely organized it has been, and still is, the National Council on Religion in Higher Education is an organization—that is, it is a group of persons working together to achieve a purpose. Its board, its donors, its staff, and its Fellows (the last-named figuring increasingly in the first three categories

[The National Council on Religion in Higher Education in the twenty-five years of its existence has been continuously involved in the issues with which the present volume is concerned. During the last two years it has undertaken a careful study of the changing aspects of the problems involved. This has meant a review of the whole field of religion in higher education during the last quarter century and a consideration of present responsibilities and opportunities in this diverse field. How the Council sees its own role in the immediate past and its own special tasks in the new circumstances of today will assuredly have its significance for all those interested in the wider topic. No apology is necessary, therefore, for the somewhat special or "intramural" character of the present chapter. As the Council is here overheard, canvassing its own tasks, dilemmas, and challenges, those cognizant of the situation will welcome this candid picture of one of the chief agencies in the field and will find their own tasks illuminated. It is in line with this intention that the author of the present concluding chapter has been asked to retain here the direct and informal style of presentation used by him in addressing his colleagues in the Council.—Ed.]

[1] In the preparation of this statement, the present Executive Director and all past Executive Directors were consulted. For a more detailed record of the Council's first twenty years, readers are referred to *Two Decades*, published by the Council in 1942.

also) put time and money—which purchases other people's time —into its various activities. That time and money might conceivably be put to better uses. Therefore, an appraisal—it should be a continuous reappraisal—of the Council as an organization involves asking the following four questions: (1) What is its purpose? (2) What activities does it engage in? (3) What are its values (including its distinctiveness), and what are its defects; could time and money now put into it be better invested in other organized or unorganized ways? (4) Should the Council, taking it as it is, expand in one way or another—using more time and money, obtained from those now interested or from others who might become interested?

I. Purpose

In dealing with the first question, purpose, I must grasp the nettle and define the Council's subject matter, religion. We have sometimes said, half-apologetically and half-defiantly, that our name should be "The National Council on Religions in Higher Education"; that the many conventional affiliations which we represent (Jewish, Roman Catholic, Protestant; Episcopalian, Presbyterian, Quaker, etc.) are only the beginning of our diversity, which extends to the point of there being almost as many individual religions among us as there are board members, donors, staff, and Fellows! Well, I object to that only because of the half-apology; I think we should proclaim it in full defiance! The Council has deliberately, from its inception in Charles Foster Kent's mind, defined religion in such a way that all those individual religions are included. For us, at the narrowest, religion must be what the *Concise Oxford Dictionary* says it is, "human recognition of super-human controlling power." Or it may be defined in words like those which I use in my own thinking—as the self-consciousness of the macrocosm in one of its microcosmic forms; as a person's concern about the relationship between himself and everything else that exists, especially other human beings; or as the conscious search for all that can be known about the nature of things and the duty of man, and the conscious embodiment in life of what is held to have been discovered in that search. The central fact is that the Council, within the limits of human frailty, is dedicated to a religion of search and truth—comprehensive and endless, individual and free. There is nothing mysterious about the meaning of truth, in this sense: it means that every one of us, for himself, is engaged in the most accurate possible observation, description, analysis, and generalization concerning all that exists in the heavens above, in the earth beneath, and in the waters under the earth; it means that every one of us, for himself, is engaged in fashioning ends for life which seem consistent with that observation, description, analysis, and generalization; and it means that every one of us, for himself, is engaged in selecting means which seem appropriate to those ends.

This subject matter, in the Council's specialized function, is to be promoted in the field of higher education. Now education in general is the development of powers, the use of experience to bring latent abilities into action. It is ultimately individual; a man must, in the last analysis, develop his own powers, within the framework of his own choices as to ends and means, by using all the experience which he can command. Formal education is one means by which a man gains help in that ultimately individual development; it represents an attempt at systematic help in the use of experience—a man's own experience, and the experience of other people, near at hand or far away in time or space. The Council is dedicated to aiding in the provision of the best possible systematic help, in that stage of formal education called higher education, in the use of religious experience—a man's own, and that of other people near at hand or far away in time or space. Toward that end, we have made propaganda—mild but persistent—for the inclusion of religious experience as a proper subject in the curricula of our colleges and universities, and we have sought for ways of making its treatment intellectually respectable in the highest degree. That was what Charles Foster Kent was about when he launched his original crusade for schools of religion adjacent to the campuses of state universities; that is what we have all been about in the development of our enterprise to include, in all sorts of institutions of higher education, the teaching of subjects normally considered "religious," and the teaching of other subjects with a sense of religion. And that "teaching," Charles Foster Kent said, and we have said after him, is not to be confined to the classroom; the teaching of religion in higher education demands teachers as whole persons dealing with students as whole persons.

That's all we are trying to do, in its prosaic simplicity; that's *all*(!) we are trying to do, in its frightening ambitiousness. My only justification for reminding myself and you of it is that, in the humdrum round of our daily occupations, we lose the glory of the purpose which brought us together and keeps us together —a glory, which, if recovered from time to time, may invest our daily chores with incandescent light.

II. Activities

Turning to the second question, activities, I am forced again to remind myself and you of the obvious: the Council, in an era of mass movements and multiple operations, has chosen to be small and single-minded. I need only three headings under which to describe our activities: (a) the discovery, training, placement, and encouragement of our Fellows as teachers; (b) the maintenance of the Society of Fellows; and (c) the inevitable miscellany.

The discovery of persons best qualified to achieve the Council's purpose means looking for them in the ranks of those who have already decided on the career of religion in higher education; in the ranks of those who are considering such a career, but who are undecided; and in the ranks of those who have not yet considered the possibility. It means the discussion of that career, and of the means of forwarding it to be found in association with the Council. It means the selection as Fellows, with or without stipend, of a few of those who are interested in becoming candidates. Once they are discovered and selected, their training means financial help (usually), advice on graduate courses, and gradual induction into the Society of Fellows—of which more later. It means urging the completion of the doctorate in the Fellow's special subject, an acquaintance with religious thought and educational methodology whatever the Fellow's special subject may be, and some preparation for extracurricular contact with students. Once graduate training is ended, the placement of Fellows—and their later re-placement—means learning of opportunities (easier and easier as the Council has become well and favorably known, and institutions take the initiative in inquiring of its office about suitable personnel), and conscientious matching of man and job. Encouragement, from the moment of selection onward, is provided in the form of the Society of Fellows; but, before talking about it, I want to insert a vital parenthesis— about the basis of selection.

What we say we are looking for in the selection of a new Fellow is this: religious interest, and interest in students; ability in his chosen field, and desire to relate that field to the whole of life; attractive personality, and emotional stability; open-mindedness, and the art of co-operation with other people. We want Fellows of both sexes, any race, various denominational affiliations and individual beliefs, many geographical locations and fields of specialization. We used to take most of our new Fellows from the ranks of college seniors or recent graduates; lately we have been taking a much larger proportion from among those well along in their graduate training, or already in the midst of careers. We exact no promise from a Fellow about anything, merely asking that at the moment of election he genuinely intend to pursue a career aimed to promote the cause of religion in higher education, and to participate fully in the life of the Society of Fellows and shoulder his share of responsibility for the continuation and development of the Council.

A number of our Fellows are now doing jobs different from those which they intended to do, but continue to give effect to their intention of participating in the Society of Fellows and in Council responsibility. That is one revealing bit of evidence on the worth of the Society of Fellows, which is the instrumentality devised by the Council for the encouragement of the growth of Fellows as teachers. Our Society of Fellows is indeed a "fellowship of kindred minds," and the hackneyed sound of that phrase should not deafen us to an understanding of the transcendent importance of such a comradeship, which age cannot wither nor custom stale. Thornton Merriam put its fine excitement into a letter he wrote me about the Council's usefulness; he said he had always been able to draw on this fellowship for an "inner security" in his work, because it so conclusively demonstrates "the idea made flesh." Even people like us, who must be among the luckiest people in the world in the matter of mental and spiritual self-sufficiency, might become starved and lonely if left to our own private devices. The Council has with rare wisdom not left us to our own devices, but has put a great deal of attention into keeping the Society of Fellows in a state of lively health.

The annual Week of Work, as you all know, is the principal means employed. It is a cross between a learned society meeting and a class reunion, and—unlike most hybrids—it is anything but sterile! New life and accelerated growth emerge from it precisely because it is both scholarly and merry. The new life and accelerated growth take the forms of those qualifications which we look for in new Fellows, especially open-mindedness and the art of co-operation. Cross-fertilization is one keyword we have used in explaining how it happens; continuity and intimacy are other keywords. Fellows do not come to the Week of Work to get away from home; they bring their wives, or husbands, and children with them, and thus put into practice in their association with one another the principle we have enunciated for their association with students on their respective campuses—they are whole persons dealing with other whole persons. In the atmosphere of that kind of gathering, it is natural that we do what our beloved Counselor, Richard H. Edwards, long ago characterized as "talking closer to the edge of our information than we do anywhere else"! It is not in the consolidated urban area of their thought that people grow most, but out on the unsubdued frontier of doubt and venture; that is why the Council has had such success in the encouragement of growth in its Fellows as teachers, by means of its Society of Fellows and its Week of Work.

With that growing edge, it is not to be wondered at that the Council, however small in size and single-minded in activity, should have found occasion to do a few miscellaneous jobs. It has provided many colleges and universities with expert consultants (from among its own Fellows, and others as well) on various phases of the problem of presenting religion in the field of higher education. It has arranged for visiting professorships. It has sponsored, or shared in sponsoring, conferences—on the theme of student counseling, for example. It has undertaken research jobs every once in a while, and issued some publications— or prompted a group of Fellows to publish a book, in the case of *The Vitality of the Christian Tradition*.[2] It had, for several years when the issue was specially in the foreground, a committee on academic freedom. It has maintained cordial working relations with other organizations dealing with religion in higher education, and with individuals at work in that field—notably with many unsuccessful candidates for election as Fellows.

[2] New York, 1944.

III. Assets and Liabilities

There is our purpose, and there are our activities. How do I go about justly assessing our worth and our faults? I can begin this way: "Religion" and "education" are the two most inclusive words in the vocabulary, and the endeavors they denote are never-ending; the only question is whether a particular set of purposes and activities, seeking to bind religion and education together, are justified—by comparison with whatever else could be done with the same time and money. The cause of religion in higher education seems to be in much better shape in recent years than it was in the middle twenties; for documentation, take a look at Merrimon Cuninggim's *The College Seeks Religion*,[3] and Albert Outler's *Colleges, Faculties and Religion*.[4] But they are at pains to point out, also, that there will probably be plenty to be done for some time to come! We have only to note what Victor Butterfield has to say about the "meaninglessness" of much graduate study and much teaching;[5] what Gregory Vlastos writes about democracy's dependence on religious loyalty to the cause of expanding "fraternity";[6] and what Howard McClusky writes about the terrifying task that confronts us in trying to make "free and creative individuals in an era of collective interdependence, private and public."[7]

The tasks we work at through the Council all receive, fortunately, organized and unorganized attention beyond the amount we give them; and they would doubtless receive a good deal of attention from us ourselves even if we were not banded together in the Council for that purpose. The question, to repeat, is

[3] New Haven, 1947.
[4] Subtitle: "An Appraisal of the Program of Faculty Consultations on Religion in Higher Education, 1945-1948." The Hazen Foundation, 400 Prospect St., New Haven 11, Conn. Also published in *The Educational Record*, January, 1949.
[5] See chap. 6 above.
[6] See chap. 12 above.
[7] See chap. 10 above.

whether our being so organized represents the best possible use of the time and money we now put into it, the best possible contribution toward the quantity and quality of religious instruction in our colleges and universities. I hardly need tell you that I have no conclusive statistical answer to that question, but I suggest that there are two rough-and-ready answers which are constantly being given to it: the number of requests for help of many sorts, particularly in the matter of teaching personnel, which come to our office from educational institutions; and the importance of the positions which the Fellows increasingly hold. Frank Aydelotte, formerly president of Swarthmore and later director of the Institute for Advanced Studies, and American Secretary to the Rhodes Trustees, has said that our selection of Fellows has panned out better than any comparable process he knows about. He likes us, and he is an enthusiast; but who are we to say that he is wrong! At any rate, I will risk saying that the Council, despite its small size and concentration of activity— *because* of them!—comes reasonably close to deserving the adjectives "unique" and "indispensable."

But, much as it pains me to admit it, we are not perfect! Our name sounds to the uninitiated as if we did far more than we actually do, and—attached to our exclusive membership—makes for some bitterness or amusement in the mind of the outsider looking in. It is too late to do anything about the name, and we are not going to do anything much about the number of Fellows; so, we must turn our attention to doing something about remediable faults. Those seem to me to be as follows: (a) We have recently been placing too little emphasis on the job of discovering likely teachers among those who are undecided about their careers, and among those who have not yet considered the possibility of a career dealing with religion in higher education. (b) We have recently been veering too far away from taking risks on college seniors or younger graduate students. (c) We have slackened in the urgency which we once felt about finding and cultivating in our Fellows an intense interest, not only in specialized subject matter, but in students as people. (d) We do not have enough natural scientists in our fold. (e) We have drifted a little too much, at Weeks of Work, into reading highly intellectual papers at one another, and have come to neglect exercises in the creative arts. (f) We have failed to hold our Roman Catholic Fellows in active participation in the Society of Fellows and in responsibility for the Council in general; and we have failed to a lesser degree in regard to our Jewish Fellows. (I can guess at some of the basic difficulties which Fellows of those two groups experience, but I shall not rest content until I have done all I can to remove any difficulties which are not basic; I need what the Fellows of those two groups have to contribute to our common enterprise, and I want them to get what the rest of us have to contribute; I want more candidates from those two groups to apply for election as new Fellows.) (g) Finally, we engage in too little corporate service to the cause of religion in higher education; from those who experience such encouragement in association as we do, something more can rightly be expected—not necessarily from all our members in one body, but at least from *ad hoc* groups functioning under the stimulus and blessing of the whole body. (Let no one be under any illusion about what more corporate service requires, however; it means, in practice, the diversion of some time of some Fellows from other tasks which now consume their so-called "leisure," and the investment of some more money from some source.)

IV. The Problem of Expansion

Should we, therefore, expand—even as we try to get rid of those faults which can be remedied and which do not require expansion for their remedy? I say yes, but not much. I think we should go on adding Fellows, but at not much more than the present rate—partly because we are not likely to be suddenly rolling in wealth, and more because we cannot really incorporate

a much larger annual increment of Fellows into the intimate comradeship which is one of our brightest distinctions. We should
develop the Society of Fellows regionally, with special emphasis
on that 8 per cent of our membership which resides on the Pacific
Coast. We should multiply our contacts with other cognate organizations, not arrogantly assuming their "co-ordination," in
forgetfulness of our small size and its inevitable concomitant of
exclusiveness, but in more active co-operation. We should expand our "corporate service"—in, for example, studies looking
toward the development of a religious philosophy of education,
programs for departments of religion, analysis of the place of
ethics in the social sciences, and pilot experiments in the presentation of religion in state universities.

Just as changing circumstances during the last quarter century
have elicited new initiatives whose character and fruitfulness
could not earlier have been foreseen, so with the future. New
needs in our area are constantly emerging; old resistances are
breaking down. We have now a matured and ever-renewed corps
of workers. The faith and imagination requisite for the new
tasks will not be lacking.

Our purpose is one in which we may take the highest pride.
Our activities go to the very root of the matter. Our defects,
though serious, are not fatal to our values, which are truly unique
and indispensable. Our expansion should occur "as way opens"
—a good old Quaker idiom which means as our own energetic
and careful thought shows us what to do and how to do it.

INDEX

The Index confines itself to names of persons, titles of books, and certain other capitalized terms. Quotations are indicated by bold-faced type.

335